IRELAND'S WILD ATLANTIC WAY

A Guide to its His

For Cúan

Neil Jackman

IRELAND'S WILD ATLANTIC WAY

A Guide to its Historic Treasures

The Collins Press

FIRST PUBLISHED IN 2018 by
The Collins Press
West Link Park
Doughcloyne
Wilton
Cork
T12 N5EF
Ireland

A CIP record for this book is available from the British Library.

Paperback ISBN: 978-1-84889-336-8

Print origination by Liz White Designs

Typeset in Chaparral Pro

Printed in Poland by Białostockie Zakłady Graficzne SA

Photograph on p. i: Slieve League, Co. Donegal
Photograph on pp. ii–iii: Teampall Bhéanain, Inis Mór, Co. Galway
Photograph on p. vi: Skellig Michael, Co. Kerry

VISITING THESE MONUMENTS

Although a monument may be in the care or ownership of the State, some are not easily accessible. Some of the sites featured in this guidebook are perched on cliffs or exposed coasts, others lie in the middle of agricultural fields, or on the summit of mountains, without a public pathway that provides easy access. In such cases, it is recommended that you ask permission from the landowners to cross their land. This often brings benefits, as they can tell you exactly where the monument is located. Take particular care when crossing fields with livestock and heed any warning notices. Please do not climb on walls or on top of the monuments: despite their robust appearance, many are in a very fragile condition. As many of these sites are coastal, please take particular care of weather and tidal conditions, and heed all recommendations and warnings issued by Met Éireann.

Readers should note that this is an information guide and does not act as an invitation to enter any of the properties or sites listed. No responsibility is accepted by the author or publisher for any loss, injury or inconvenience sustained by anyone as a result of using this book.

CONTENTS

ACKNOWLEDGMENTS

I must begin by thanking my family, most especially my wife, Róisín. This book has necessitated a lot of time on the road this year, so I am incredibly fortunate to have shared the journey with someone who shares my love for Irish archaeology and heritage. My love of history comes from my parents, Roy and Mary, and my grandfather Bill, who was always up for adventure and exploration. I am very grateful to Róisín's parents, Philomena and Bartley, and Róisín's grandmother Kathleen. Not only are they a constant source of support and encouragement, they are the world's best dog sitters and take great care of Peig when we are out on our travels.

I am grateful to Dr Conor Ryan of Abarta for his fantastic maps and help with research. As ever I am grateful to all the team at The Collins Press for their forbearance and support. Due to a combination of lousy weather and worse timing I missed my opportunity to revisit the island of Inishbofin to collect photographs for this book, so I wish to thank Terry O'Hagan for generously sharing his fantastic images.

I am also especially grateful to the various landowners, private and state, who allowed me access to these incredible places. Particular mention must be given to the support and professionalism of the Office of Public Works staff and guides. I am also deeply grateful to the staff of the National Monuments Service and the National Museum of Ireland, the guardians of our heritage, in ensuring the ongoing protection of our monuments. I am also thankful to Fáilte Ireland for their support and the Heritage Council and all the various heritage officers, for all of their vital work with communities around the country to ensure the appreciation and understanding of our heritage.

As I found when writing *Ireland's Ancient East*, compiling a guidebook such as this, which is focused on Ireland's archaeological and historical sites, is only made possible through the work of archaeologists, historians, academics, authors, geographers, scientists, storytellers, *seanchaithe*, researchers and guides who compiled the information that has been so vital to this publication. I am eternally grateful for all of your work, and any errors or omissions in this work are entirely my own doing.

Producing a guidebook such as this is a true privilege. The process of exploring the Wild Atlantic Way steadily reinforced my unshakeable belief that Ireland is the most beautiful country on earth. Our natural and built heritage is our national treasure, and like any treasure it needs to be protected and passed on intact to future generations.

Cahergal Stone Fort, County Kerry

INTRODUCTION

Stretching from west Cork to the very northernmost tip of County Donegal, the Wild Atlantic Way (*Slí an Atlantaigh Fhiáin*) is fast becoming one of the world's favourite long-distance touring routes. After spending much of 2017 visiting every nook, cranny and cove of Ireland's rugged western coast, it is easy for me to see why it has captured so many people's imagination. The untamed beauty of the green Irish landscape that ends in soaring cliffs often provides a seemingly endless view over the deep blue Atlantic Ocean. This is a journey that seeps into your bones, enriches your blood and quickens your soul.

This is a landscape that has inspired countless painters and artists, writers and musicians. To travel the route and breathe in the fresh Atlantic air is nothing less than a balm for the spirit. Ireland's western coast can be a warm and comforting companion, or a capricious and terrifying master. You can find yourself blanketed in Achill's white ethereal mist, as soft as a kiss, or you can find yourself on top of a Kerry mountain, scoured and buffeted by gnawing western winds, feeling as though you have lost layers of worries and concerns along with your skin, and with a sense that you have become renewed and rededicated to the land of living, with your only ambition a pint of stout by the pub's fire and a comforting bowl of chowder.

The Wild Atlantic Way is rightly renowned for its stunning scenery, but along with incredible views, Ireland's western coast has a deep and rich cultural heritage, full of stories of mythology, romance, violence, intrigue and tragedy. This guidebook will lead you to some of the places where you can experience these tales. With this guide you will visit megalithic tombs, sacred Neolithic landscapes and Bronze Age stone circles. The book will lead you to an ancient fort high on a Kerry Mountain, and bring you on a voyage to early monasteries on remote islands. You will witness medieval castles still locked in a gruelling siege with the relentless foe of the Atlantic Ocean, and you will explore elegant stately homes and vibrant towns where the past is ever present.

This guidebook leads you to 100 of my personal favourite places along the route. Our journey begins in the lovely town of Kinsale

Notice on gate to Kealkill Stone Circle, west Cork

in County Cork, and we will work our way steadily westward along Kerry's famous Rings of Kerry and Dingle, around the mouth of the River Shannon, along the jaw-dropping Cliffs of Moher and the grey stony landscape of the Burren. We will explore a number of amazing places in Galway and Connemara, then travel up along the lesser visited (but equally spectacular) coast of Sligo and south Donegal, before finishing in the Inishowen Peninsula and at Malin Head, Ireland's most northerly point.

As I found when writing my guidebook to Ireland's Ancient East, and again in compiling this guidebook, the greatest challenge in writing a book such as this is not what sites to include, but what sites to leave out. Up until the time of publication it has been a tremendously difficult process, gradually to choose one and not another, when both are equally worthy, spectacular and fascinating. The sites were chosen on the visitor experience, their accessibility, suitability and safety and their location. The Wild Atlantic Way concept does have rules, guidelines and boundaries issued by Fáilte Ireland (Ireland's national tourism development authority, which developed the Wild Atlantic Way concept). These rules stipulate that, naturally enough, any sites or attractions for the Wild Atlantic Way should be in proximity to the coast. That makes the selection of sites somewhat more straightforward, but it does mean some truly incredible places like Poulnabrone Dolmen in the Burren, or the Carrowkeel passage tomb cemetery on the Bricklieve Mountains in County Sligo are ineligible for inclusion within this guidebook, but are certainly well worth a detour.

As all of the sites are within a coastal landscape, certain site types and themes are relatively prevalent, and reflect the nature of their location and geography. You will encounter a number of megalithic tombs overlooking the sea. As well as being repositories for the dead perhaps these great tombs served as territorial boundaries millennia ago, a clear symbol of ownership and boundary on the landscape for anyone travelling by the ocean – the highway of the day. You will visit remote ancient monasteries that reflect the tradition of seeking out isolated places for devoted worship; you will see great stone forts and later medieval castles that show the desire to protect and command safe harbours on this unforgiving coast; and you will see numerous Martello towers, coastal batteries, signal towers and other defensive installations from the nineteenth century, when the British sought to fortify the coast to prevent Napoleon's armies from gaining a foothold in Ireland.

However, despite similarity in some individual cases, each region of the Wild Atlantic Way route offers a different story, a different vista and a different feeling. I have subdivided the route into sections in an attempt to make it easier to plan a day out, or a weekend trip. Each entry has a table with coordinates and directions to help you navigate. The sites are a mix of the well-known and well-visited stops, mixed with hidden gems where you can soak in the atmosphere and enjoy it all to yourself.

Many of these sites are vulnerable, battered by elements and countless years. Please tread softly, and follow the good general life advice so eloquently given by this sign I encountered in Kealkill in west Cork: 'Leave Gates As Found. Leave Only Footprints. Beware of Livestock.'

I truly hope that you enjoy your journey and explorations. There are few places on earth that are as beautiful, or as full of stories, as Ireland's Wild Atlantic Way!

WEST CORK

Occasionally, there is an almost dreamlike quality to the scenery of west Cork. The coast is full of inlets and tiny coves, with some of the most beautiful beaches in the world.

A number of historic gardens are bounteous with subtropical plants that thrive here thanks to the warming effect of the Gulf Stream. It is like a world apart, one with its own personal climate.

Glengarriff Harbour

West Cork has become renowned for the quality of the food and its hospitality, and there are many wonderful towns and villages in which to enjoy both. Kinsale, Bantry, Baltimore, Clonakilty, Skibbereen, Rosscarbery, Castletownsend and Schull are all to be explored and enjoyed. However, along with its charms, west Cork is also a place steeped in history, where on every headland you can discover mysterious prehistoric monuments, stone circles and mighty medieval fortresses. Tales of seafarers abound here, from the medieval lords who became rich on the wine trade to the tragedy of an entire village that was stolen away by corsairs from the Barbary Coast.

The landscape becomes ever more rugged and wild as you travel westward along the coast. We will venture down the Mizen Head Peninsula to explore remote castles, and explore Bantry Bay to find prehistoric monuments, early medieval art and stately homes. From the aptly named Roaringwater Bay to the enchanting Beara Peninsula, there is a wealth of heritage to be discovered and a story around every corner.

1 | KINSALE

Kinsale has long been a place of strategic importance. The origins of this charming and vibrant town are thought to date to the foundation of a monastery here in the sixth century by Saint Multose. The site of the early monastery has never been conclusively proven, but it is generally believed to have been located where the parish church stands today. It is also thought that Kinsale was a Viking port. The town is now popular with visitors from all over the world, who come to enjoy its fun atmosphere, winding and colourful streets and superb seafood.

One of the many colourful narrow and winding medieval streets in Kinsale

The history of the town is perhaps best experienced at the atmospheric church of **Saint Multose**, one of the few parish churches in Ireland to have been in continuous use from the medieval period to the present day. Traditionally, the foundation of the church was ascribed to the Anglo-Norman, Milo de Cogan, and the majority of the early features are certainly of thirteenth-century date; however, there may be hints of an earlier church building in the fragments of sandstone that have been reused in the north doorway of the tower, which bear worn Romanesque-style decoration. These fragments possibly provide a clue that there was a church here in the middle of the twelfth century. There are no visible traces earlier than that, however, despite the suggestion that this was originally the location of an early monastery.

By the end of the medieval period, Kinsale had become one of the most significant ports on the southern coast. This is reflected on the north side of Cork Street where you can find the three-storey urban tower house known as **Desmond Castle**. The tower house dates to around 1500, and it was built for the powerful FitzGerald Earls of Desmond. Like **Lynch's Castle** in **Galway city** (see Site 48) the arms of the FitzGeralds can be seen on the exterior of the building, along with the arms of King

Desmond Castle

Henry VII of England. As well as being a secure base for the FitzGeralds, the castle has had many roles throughout its history. It served as an arsenal for Don Juan Aguilla during the Spanish occupation of Kinsale in the run-up to the Battle of Kinsale in 1601. Other uses for the building include its use as a customs house, and it became locally known as 'The French Prison' as it was converted into a gaol for prisoners of war in the eighteenth century. Conditions for the prisoners were said to have been very poor, with overcrowding combined with a lack of good food and sanitation causing frequent outbreaks of disease. A fire in 1747 is said to have killed 54 inmates. Today, Desmond Castle is a Wine Museum that reflects Kinsale's important role as a wine port in the medieval period. It also commemorates the 'Wine Geese', the Irishmen who fled Ireland after the Battle of Kinsale to go on to become successful in the international wine trade.

The Battle of Kinsale was one of the most influential moments in Irish history. In 1601, Spanish forces in Kinsale took the strategically vital points at Castle Park (where James Fort was later established) and Ringcurran. This prevented the English fleet from using the harbour. The ensuing Battle of Kinsale ended the Nine Years' War, and led to the Flight of the Earls. The defeat of the Irish Earls and their Spanish allies allowed the policy of plantation to continue, and the English tightened their control over Ireland.

In the decades following the siege of Kinsale, English forces began to fortify the headlands and promontories to deter any further attempts to capture the strategically vital port. In around 1677, the Earl of Orrery, who was charged with the defence of Munster, ordered the construction of a new fort to command Ringcurran Point on the eastern side of Kinsale Harbour. It was to be built in the most modern design of the time, as a pentagonal bastion fort that offered a seriously daunting obstacle for any enemy ships. The fort was named **Charles Fort** in honour of

Charles Fort

King Charles II, who was on the English throne at the time of its construction. It has a series of pointed bastions with two levels of batteries giving overwhelming firepower in all seaward directions. It was designed by noted architect William Robinson, who designed other key public buildings like the Royal Hospital in Kilmainham.

The military engineer Thomas Phillips, who inspected Charles Fort in 1685, was impressed by the quality of workmanship and the fort's bristling seaward defences, but pointed out that the fort was vulnerable to land-based attack as it was overlooked by higher ground. His fears were proven all too accurate when Charles Fort found itself under siege for the first and only time in its history in 1690. King James II had landed in Kinsale the year before at the head of an army of Catholic supporters and French allies in order to retake the English throne, which he had been denied by the English Parliament following the Glorious Revolution in 1688. Parliament, wary of James's attempts to return England to Catholicism and fearful of another civil war like the one that wreaked havoc across England and Ireland just a generation before, deposed James and offered the crown to William of Orange. James and his army marched north from Kinsale to meet the Williamite forces. The two armies clashed at the Battle of the Boyne in 1690 and, after the Williamites won, James fled the battlefield and eventually Ireland. The war continued in his absence, and the Williamites marched south to take Kinsale.

Charles Fort was defended by forces loyal to King James, but after his defeat at the Battle of the Boyne, the Williamite army swept southwards and arrived at Kinsale soon afterwards. The Williamites established cannon batteries on the high ground above Charles Fort, and dug trenches to protect the assault troops. After a thirteen-day siege, which included five days of continuous cannon fire, a breach was made in the mighty walls. Fearing a massacre, the defenders had no choice but to surrender, and Charles Fort fell. In the years that followed, Cork Harbour overtook Kinsale as the key strategic southern port, and Charles Fort reverted to becoming an English militia depot. The fort remained in use until 1921, when the British garrison withdrew, following the establishment of the

Irish Free State. Shortly after, anti-Treaty forces destroyed the barracks and burned the buildings. Charles Fort was listed as a National Monument in 1973, and today it is under the auspices of the Office of Public Works (OPW).

There are a number of other places of interest close to Kinsale. **James Fort** stands directly across the water on the western shore of the harbour. Like Charles Fort, it was constructed in the aftermath of the Battle of Kinsale. In 1611 a stone citadel was added to the fort, but despite the formidable defences of James Fort it was captured without a struggle by Cromwellian forces in 1649. The fort was attacked and seized at the same time as Charles Fort in 1690 by a Williamite force led by the Duke of Wurttemberg and John Churchill, who later became the first Duke of Marlborough. The inner stone citadel was said to have been captured when an accidental explosion blew out the gate. Following its capture in 1690, James Fort was never garrisoned again.

James Fort

Farther out, the dramatic scenery of the headland, the **Old Head of Kinsale**, is known for its popular golf course built on the site of a de Courcy castle, and the scenic lighthouse. This is also the nearest land to the site where the RMS *Lusitania* sank with the loss of 1,198 people in 1915, after being struck by a German torpedo. The tragic story of the *Lusitania* is told in the Old Head Signal Tower (entry fees apply), and its memorial garden with a striking bronze sculpture that commemorates those who lost their lives. The signal tower was originally constructed in the nineteenth century as part of the coastal defence against the threat of invasion by Napoleon's forces. The upper level of the tower offers stunning views over Old Head and the coast.

The Old Head of Kinsale

 MAP 3

Coordinates:

Charles Fort: Lat. 51.697816, Long. -8.499019

James Fort: Lat. 51.698579, Long. -8.512749

Desmond Castle and Wine Museum: Lat. 51.707185, Long. -8.524723

Saint Multose Church: Lat. 51.705710, Long. -8.525605

Lusitania Museum and Old Head Signal Tower: Lat. 51.620199, Long. -8.542278

Irish Grid Reference: W 65547 49392

Opening hours/entry fees:

For Charles Fort, visit: www.heritageireland.ie/en/south-west/charlesfort/

For Desmond Castle, visit: www.heritageireland.ie/en/south-west/desmondcastlekinsale/

For Saint Multose Church, visit: www.kinsale.cork.anglican.org

For Lusitania Museum & Old Head Signal Tower, visit: www.oldheadofkinsale.com

For general information about Kinsale, visit: www.kinsale.ie

Directions: For locations of the main points of interest in Kinsale please see Map 3.

To get to Charles Fort, head east from Kinsale on the R600 for approximately 1.5km and turn right onto Ardbrack Heights (signposted for Charles Fort). The fort is 2.4km up this road.

The Old Head of Kinsale is approximately 25 minutes' drive from Kinsale. Head south-west from the town on the R600 and after 10.7km bear left onto the R604. Follow the R604 south for 4km to the Old Head.

Nearest town: In Kinsale. Cork city (28 km).

Timoleague Friary

The origins of the Franciscan friary at Timoleague are somewhat uncertain, but it is traditionally believed to have been founded as early as 1240 by Donal Glas McCarthy, though it may have been established on an earlier foundation and later taken over by the Franciscans. The name Timoleague may hint at an older, perhaps early medieval, monastery, as it derives from *Tigh Molaga*, meaning 'Saint Molaga's Church', though no trace remains of such an early foundation. However, there are certainly architectural clues of an earlier building in the choir, in the blocked 'giant order' arches and closed-up windows that suggest a different architectural style and function that may be late twelfth or early thirteenth century, suggesting that the Franciscans were granted an existing monastery that they then adapted to suit their own needs.

Whatever the exact origins of the site, it is easy to see why this location was seen as an important place to establish a religious house, as it was certainly constructed in a strategic place, being positioned on the banks of the estuary of the River Argideen and overlooking Courtmacsherry Bay. By the middle of the thirteenth century, this area had a burgeoning and bustling market port. In the fifteenth

A view through the window at Timoleague

century, there was another phase of expansion and renovation, and the Franciscan Bishop of Ross, Edmund de Courcy, added the tall tower, along with a library and a new dormitory and infirmary. Like all monastic foundations, Timoleague was officially dissolved during the Dissolution of the Monasteries enacted by King Henry VIII in the middle of the sixteenth century, but friars were still in possession of Timoleague up until it was attacked by the English in the 1630s.

TIMOLEAGUE FRIARY MAP 2

Coordinates: Lat. 51.643125, Long. -8.764004

Irish Grid Reference: W 47205 43607

Opening hours/entry fees: No entry fees or opening hours applied at the time of visit.

Directions: Timoleague is approximately 35 minutes' drive west of Kinsale. From Kinsale head west on the R600 for 24.5km, and you will see the friary on your left as you cross the bridge into the village.

Nearest towns: Clonakilty (11.5km), Kinsale (25km).

3 | BOHONAGH STONE CIRCLE

Bohonagh Stone Circle

This wonderful stone circle is certainly worth the effort to find. It consists of thirteen stones (only nine of which still stand), with two tall portal stones on an east–west axis to the recumbent stone. An interesting boulder burial lies close to the east, less than 10m away from the stone circle. The large capstone has a number of cup marks on its surface. This monument is also thought to date to the Early Bronze Age period. The burial and stone circle were excavated in 1959. A shallow pit containing a few fragments of cremated bone was found in the middle of the stone circle, and a similar token cremation burial was found in a shallow pit underneath the large covering stone of the boulder burial. No other artefacts were recovered, though the foundations of a rectangular hut structure were found suggesting that people perhaps lived in the immediate vicinity of these monuments, though as none of the monuments were radiocarbon dated we cannot say with certainty as to whether the hut was contemporary with the stone circle.

BOHONAGH STONE CIRCLE   MAP 2

Coordinates: Lat. 51.580851, Long. -8.999944

Irish Grid Reference: W 30754 36851

Opening hours/entry fees: No entry fees or opening hours applied at the time of visit, but please seek permission if possible.

Directions: You'll find this lovely stone circle just five minutes' drive from Rosscarbery. From Rosscarbery, head eastwards on the N71 for 3.3km. Then turn left (signposted Reenascreena). You will reach a Y-Junction after 240m. Bear right and continue for another 140m. You will reach two gates opposite each other. Try to park unobtrusively and go through the gate on your right (always be sure to close the gate behind you) and follow the track uphill to the stone circle. Cattle are likely to be present so please do not bring dogs. This is private farmland, so please seek permission if possible.

Nearest town: Rosscarbery (3.3km).

---

4 | COPPINGER'S COURT

Coppinger's Court near Rosscarbery in Cork, is one of Ireland's finest examples of a late medieval fortified house. This style of building appeared during the early seventeenth century, a period that bridged the end of the medieval era and the dawn of the modern age. Fortified houses combined elements of the defensive castles or tower houses with the more practical, palatial and grand country houses that had become fashionable during the Elizabethan era.

Coppinger's Court (also known as Ballyvirine Castle) was built by Sir Walter Coppinger some time around 1616. Sir Walter was a wealthy merchant in Cork and built his fine house to stand some four storeys high over the basement. The house is rectangular in plan, with two square towers flanking the central structure. Notable features include a series of projections that protrude

Coppinger's Court

from the top of the outside walls, similar to machicolations in earlier castles though at Coppinger's Court they appear to serve a decorative rather than defensive function. However, a number of gun loops are positioned at strategic points at ground level, indicating that, however palatial, the house would still be a tough proposition for any attacking force. Local folklore states that the wealthy Sir Walter had the house constructed with a chimney for every month, a door for every week and a window for every day in the year.

From historical records, Sir Walter appears to have been something of a difficult character. He was regularly involved in intractable legal disputes with Thomas Crooke over Crooke's new plantation at **Baltimore**. Sir Walter had also made himself unpopular in the region by his harsh and avaricious practice as a moneylender. He acquired large tracts of land from people who defaulted on the mortgages he provided, and even unto this day he is not looked on with much sympathy in local history. His fine house did not survive long after his death in 1639. It was attacked and burned during the Confederacy Rebellion of 1641. The house was never restored, and gradually the fire-damaged building fell into greater disrepair, to become the atmospheric ruin you see today.

COPPINGER'S COURT   MAP 2

Coordinates: Lat. 51.571325, Long. -9.066984

Irish Grid Reference: W 26091 35925

Opening hours/entry fees: No entry fees or opening hours applied at the time of visit.

Directions: Coppinger's Court is just five minutes' drive from Rosscarbery. From Rosscarbery head south-west on the R597 road for 1.6km. Then turn left and follow this smaller road for a further 700m until you come to a T-Junction. At the junction turn right and Coppinger's Court will be on your right-hand side after approximately 650m. Park your car as unobtrusively as possible in a disused gateway on the right, and walk alongside the hedge through the field to the site. Livestock may be present so please do not bring dogs.

Nearest town: Rosscarbery (3.3km).

---

5 | DROMBEG STONE CIRCLE

Drombeg is one of the finest of Ireland's stone circles and certainly the most popular, attracting large numbers of tourists due to its picturesque and timeless setting. Like most of Ireland's stone circles, the construction of Drombeg is thought to date to the middle and later period of the Bronze Age, approximately 3,000 years ago.

Stone circles are often considered to be places of ritual and ceremony. Drombeg is aligned with the setting sun of the midwinter solstice (21 December), an important time in the ancient calendar as it marked the shortest day and longest night of the year, a time of rebirth and renewal because from that point on the days begin to grow. Drombeg's celestial alignment was first noted by Boyle Somerville in 1923, who saw that when observed

Drombeg Stone Circle

from the entrance to the circle, the sun is aligned with the position of the large recumbent (horizontal) stone.

The site has long been imbued with folklore and mythology, with the large recumbent stone being called 'The Druid's Altar'. The site was excavated in 1957. The archaeologists discovered that there was a compact gravelly surface within the circle, with a central pit containing the cremated remains of an adolescent and a broken pot dating to 1124–794 BC.

Nearby the stone circle you can discover the stone foundations of Bronze Age huts and a well-preserved fulacht fiadh. These features are a relatively common discovery across the country. A fulacht fiadh generally consisted of a stone-lined pit or trough, that was filled with water. Stones were heated on a fire, and when the stones were red hot they were dropped into the water, eventually causing the water to boil. Their function has been long debated in archaeology, from the traditional view of cooking places, to dyeing clothes, bathing pools, sweathouses or saunas or possibly to brew ales or beer. Drombeg is a truly lovely site to visit, and on a bright sunny day there are few better places to be in the world than west Cork.

Drombeg Stone Circle, facing east

DROMBEG STONE CIRCLE MAP 2

Coordinates: Lat. 51.564561, Long. -9.086998

Irish Grid Reference: W 24672 35160

Opening hours/entry fees: No entry fees or opening hours applied at the time of visit.

Directions: You'll find the site less than ten minutes' drive from Rosscarbery. From Rosscarbery head south-west on the R597 road toward Glandore for 4.2km. Then turn left (just after you enter the village of Drombeg), following the sign for the stone circle. Continue on this road for almost 1km until you reach the car park of the site. In peak tourism months I recommend you visit early in the morning or after 4 p.m. to have the opportunity to have this wonderfully evocative site to yourself.

Nearest town: Rosscarbery (5.5km).

Drishane House

The temperate climate of west Cork, maintained by the North Atlantic Drift, has allowed the creation of a number of beautiful and historic gardens in the region, many of which are on the **West Cork Garden Trail**. You can find a charming historic house and garden at Drishane House. The house itself was constructed for Thomas Somerville in the late eighteenth century, though each generation of the family has left its own mark and personality on this lovely building. Drishane House is famous for its literary heritage as it was formerly the home of Edith Somerville. Her cousin Violet Martin, who wrote under the name Martin Ross, was a regular visitor. They are best known as Somerville and Ross and for their collaborations *The Experiences of an Irish R.M* and *The Real Charlotte*. You can discover more in the small museum, which has further information about Edith's life and work.

DRISHANE HOUSE

Drishane House and its gardens are open to the public during certain summer months, and it offers a wonderful and fascinating experience for visitors. The house is near Castletownshend, one of the most beautiful small villages in Ireland, which is certainly worth exploring. Take the time to see the Harry Clarke stained-glass windows in the church. Close by to Drishane you can find the remarkable **Gurranes Stone Row and Knockdrum Fort** (see Site 7).

> **DRISHANE HOUSE** MAP 2
>
> Coordinates: Lat. 51.526316, Long. -9.181188
>
> Irish Grid Reference: W 18077 30987
>
> Opening hours/entry fees: visit: www.drishane.com.
>
> Directions: Drishane House is situated at the western end of Main Street in Castletownshend
>
> Nearest town: In Castletownshend.

7 | GURRANES STONE ROW AND KNOCKDRUM FORT

There are few sites that evoke such an immediate sense of the wholly different belief system of our remote prehistoric past as the tall, almost skeletal fingers of **Gurranes Stone Row**. This was originally an alignment of five stones. Three stones still stand tall, one lies fallen and another was said to have been taken away in the nineteenth century. From the appearance of the stones that still stand, when all five would have been present it would have looked like the outstretched fingers and thumb of a giant hand. Seeing this site in the flesh really is an awe-inspiring experience. The tallest of these slender stones is a whopping 4.3m (14 feet) high! Stone alignments and rows, such as this one at Gurranes, are believed to date to the Bronze Age, around the same time as the stone circles like the wonderful nearby example at **Drombeg** (Site 5).

I recommend you visit this stone row in conjunction with a trip to **Knockdrum Fort** as they are in very close proximity. To get to the fort, carefully cross back over the road and go through the opposite gate and follow the track for approximately 400m to the fort.

Knockdrum, a fine example of a stone cashel, dates to the early medieval period, and measures some 22m (72 feet) in diameter. The fort was restored in the nineteenth century. Unusually for a stone fort, a large slab with Bronze Age cup marks lies just outside the fort, another is in the interior and an early medieval

The sun beginning to set at Gurranes Stone Row

cross-inscribed slab is positioned next to the entrance to the fort. These may have been brought to Knockdrum for safekeeping by the antiquarian enthusiast Boyle Somerville (of **Drishane House** Site 6). It was Somerville who excavated the fort in the 1930s.

Gurranes Stone Row

Knockdrum Fort

He discovered the foundations of a rectangular house in the centre of the fort and he excavated the souterrain. He found the souterrain was cut through both earth and rock, and it contained three chambers. These tunnel-like features are often found in association with early medieval settlement. Traditionally they were viewed as being refuges in case of raids, though it is believed that they acted as cold storage as they maintain a constant cool temperature, in a similar fashion to our refrigerators today. As cattle were the principle economy of early medieval Ireland, the reliable storage of dairy produce, such as milk and cheese, would have been of the utmost importance. You can enjoy truly lovely views over the coast from Knockdrum, it is certainly worth the walk.

GURRANES STONE ROW

MAP 2

Coordinates:

Parking: Lat. 51.529080, Long. -9.189157
Stone Row: Lat. 51.530800, Long. -9.190450

Irish Grid Reference: W 17438 31522

Opening hours/entry fees: No opening times or entry fees applied at the time of visit.

Directions: The stone row is located just two minutes' drive (1.3km) from Castletownshend, or ten minutes from Skibbereen and it is almost opposite Knockdrum Fort. Head south-west from Skibbereen on the R595 and take the first exit (turning left) at the roundabout onto the R596 (signposted for Castletownshend). After approximately 5.8km you will pass the Castletownsend National School on your left, continue on for another 700m and the gate leading to the site will be on your left. Park opposite in the entrance for another gate (that leads to Knockdrum Stone Fort), which has a sign for Skibbereen 8km and Unionhall 9km in front of it. Try to pull in your car as unobtrusively as possible, carefully cross the road, go through the gate and walk up the hill to the stone row.

Nearest towns: Skibbereen (9.8km), Castletownshend (1.3km).

KNOCKDRUM FORT

MAP 2

Coordinates:

Parking: Lat. 51.529080, Long. -9.189157
Fort: Lat. 51.526536, Long. -9.193583

Irish Grid Reference: W 17241 31042

Opening hours/entry fees: No opening times or entry fees applied at the time of visit.

Directions: Follow the directions above for Gurranes Stone Row, which the gate on your left leads to. The gate on the right, which has a sign for Skibbereen 8km and Unionhall 9km in front of it, leads to Knockdrum fort. Try to pull in your car as unobtrusively as possible and follow the track up about 400m to the fort.

Nearest towns: Skibbereen (9.8km), Castletownshend (1.3km).

8 | BALTIMORE AND SHERKIN ISLAND

Surrounded by beautiful scenery, Baltimore is a popular place for visitors, with opportunities for whale and dolphin watching, sailing and kayaking. It is home to a truly welcoming community and it is a lovely place to spend a few days.

The story of the charming west Cork village of Baltimore is bound with the story of the sea and those who sail upon it. The first fortification at the town is thought to have been a ringfort, before a motte and bailey were constructed in c. 1215 by the Anglo-Norman Robert FitzStephen. These were destroyed in an attack by the MacCarthys. Later, the O'Driscolls created a new fortification here known as *Dún na Séad* ('the fort of the jewels'). Today, a seventeenth-century fortified house stands on the site, presumably constructed by Thomas Crooke. In 1605 Crooke purchased a 21-year lease on the town and set about establishing an English colony. It is said that he used Baltimore as a base for piracy. A contemporary account from Venice states that Baltimore was one of the 'two chief nests of English pirates'. Following the death of Crooke, the colony became increasingly impoverished and largely relied on fishing.

In the early hours of 17 June 1631, two pirate ships from Algeria under the command of Murat Reis, a Dutch adventurer turned Islamic pirate, moored in Eastern Hole Bay to the east of the entrance of Baltimore Harbour. Under guidance of a captured fisherman from Dungarvan, over 200 corsairs with muffled oars silently rowed across the calm waters of the bay before running their boats up onto the shingle. The sleeping villagers in the lower part of the town were blissfully unaware of the danger, until suddenly their doors were splintered open and dozens of men, armed to the teeth with muskets and curved swords, poured into the houses, screaming and bellowing at the bewildered and increasingly panic-stricken villagers. The victims were herded outside, blinking in the smoke from their burning homes and their captors' torches. Some tried to resist. John Davis and Timothy Curlew were two such brave souls, though they were no

Baltimore Castle

match for the experienced pirates who hacked them down. The raiders were halted by quick-thinking people in the upper part of the town who had awoken at the sound of struggle in the streets below. One of the residents, William Harris, repeatedly fired musket shots to convince the raiders that a militia was on the way to confront them. Happy with the spoils they already had, the raiders returned to the boats with over 100 captive men, women and children. The raid was an enormous success for the pirates, who, with swiftness and professional efficiency and at no loss to themselves, captured a large number of slaves and killed two others. The unfortunate captives were taken to the slave markets of Algiers. Many of the men faced a hard life of dangerous toil, or the worse fate of being chained to the oars of a galley. Women and children faced domestic servitude and, in some cases, worse. Despite the protestations of the survivors, the London authorities were indifferent and refused to pay the ransoms or to launch a punitive raid to recapture the lost villagers. The raid cast a dark shadow over Baltimore. Terrified of further raids, the surviving population moved upriver towards Skibbereen. Very few of those who were taken would ever see Ireland again. The story of the Sack

Baltimore Beacon

of Baltimore is echoed in the village to this day, in the names of pubs like The Algiers Inn.

You can discover the story of Baltimore at the castle, where you can visit the great hall that contains artefacts and information about the story of the castle and the village, and offers fine views over the harbour from the battlements.

Just outside the village you can find the **Baltimore Beacon**, an iconic local landmark. The Beacon was erected following the 1798 Rebellion as part of a refortification and renewal of the coastal signal stations and defences. It offers a great view over **Sherkin Island**. This small island off the coast of Baltimore is a scenic and charming place to visit. It has a population of just over 100 people, but it can be a bustling place in the height of the summer as it is a popular place for those who want to get away from it all.

On the eastern side of the island you can find a small **Franciscan friary**, known as *Mainistir Inis Arcain*, which is thought to have been founded by Fineen O'Driscoll in the middle of the fifteenth century. The present ruins consist of a church with a nave and chancel that are separated by a low tower. The church also has a transept to the south, with two side chapels. A cloister and range of domestic buildings are positioned to the north of the church, some of which show different phases of construction and alteration.

Sherkin Friary

The friary was burned in 1537 by men from Waterford in retaliation for the O'Driscoll capture of a ship with its valuable cargo of wine. Unfortunately, the friary is often kept locked, but the island is still well worth exploring. Near to the friary, the squat O'Driscoll castle known as Dún na Long ('the fort of the ships') is situated just north of the pier. It may possibly be on the site of an earlier promontory fort, or perhaps a Viking ship camp, as the name may derive from *Longphort*, the Hiberno-Norse term for such a camp.

9 | ALTAR WEDGE TOMB

This fine wedge tomb was excavated in 1989 by William O'Brien, who discovered a pit containing deposits of seashells and fish bones in the eastern end of the chamber, and a small spread of cremated human bone at the western end. Flint tools were also found outside the tomb, and deliberately deposited whale or porpoise bone was discovered in a context relating to the construction of the tomb. The evidence discovered by the archaeologists demonstrated that the tomb had a long period of use, from the end of the Neolithic period up to the Iron Age.

The tomb may be aligned towards Mizen Peak, the hill shaped like a broad arrowhead or pyramid, which was the setting for the mythological story as the place where the god Lugh killed the

Altar Wedge Tomb

tyrant Balor. The sun sets directly behind this hill in late October and early November, around the time of the ancient festival of Samhain. A local tradition suggests that this tomb was used as a Mass altar for Catholic services during the time of the harsh Penal Laws. This series of laws and acts severely curtailed the freedom and power of the Catholic population. From 1607 Catholics were barred from holding public office or serving in the Irish army, but things became far more restrictive and punitive following the rebellions and wars of the mid-seventeenth century. After the Act of Settlement was enforced in 1652 following Cromwell's campaign, Catholics were barred from membership in the Irish Parliament, and the major Catholic landholders had most of their lands confiscated and redistributed to those faithful to the English Parliament. Catholic clergy were expelled from the country and were liable to instant execution when found. This led to Masses being conducted in hidden places in the countryside, like this wedge tomb. The prominent politician and moral philosopher Edmund Burke (1729–1797) described the Penal Laws as: 'a machine of wise and elaborate contrivance, as well fitted for the oppression, impoverishment and degradation of a people, and the debasement in them of human nature itself, as ever proceeded from the perverted ingenuity of man'. He stridently campaigned for a more compassionate system of governance, but it was not until Catholic Emancipation, led by Daniel O'Connell, (for more, see **Derrynane House**, Site 18) that true reform was achieved. The Government of Ireland Act in 1920 finally did away with the unfair system of laws.

ALTAR WEDGE TOMB   MAP 2

Coordinates: Lat. 51.514010, Long. -9.643888

Irish Grid Reference: V 85916 30228

Opening hours/entry fees: No opening times or entry fees applied at the time of visit.

Directions: Altar wedge tomb is close the town of Schull (approximately seven minutes' drive away). To get to there, head south-west from Schull for 7.2km on the R592 and the site will be on your left just after a fairly steep bend. There is a small area to park and to enjoy the view.

Nearest town: Schull (7.2km).

---

10 | DUNLOUGH CASTLE AND MIZEN HEAD

On the westernmost point of the Mizen Peninsula and on the southern side of Three Castle Head you can discover **Dunlough Castle**, undoubtedly one of Ireland's true hidden gems. On first glimpse, the castle is like something from an epic fantasy saga, with three tall towers joined by a long curtain wall that runs from the edge of a cold lake to high cliffs. A possible early reference to the castle can be found in Mac Carthaigh's Book, a collection of annals compiled from earlier accounts by Fínghin Mac Carthaigh Mór, an Irish nobleman and scholar who was imprisoned in London for many years. His account notes that in 1206: 'The castle of Dún Lóich was built by the Galls.' Though despite this possible reference to the castle being constructed in the thirteenth century, by appearance the visible ruins are perhaps fifteenth or even early sixteenth century in date.

The first view of Dunlough Castle

The three towers of the castle inspired the name of the headland, but the strategic nature of this site had long been noted. A promontory fort, perhaps dating to the Late Bronze Age or Iron Age, has been recorded on the site, with traces of earlier banks and ditches running in roughly the same direction in front of the later curtain wall. The curtain wall survives to a maximum height of around 6m (almost 20 feet). The westernmost tower is a brooding presence, and much broader and squatter than the two slender mural towers that are positioned one after another near the lakeshore. This tower was the key fortification and dwelling of the castle. Stone walling around the eastern shore of the lake may have formed part of the original defences of the castle, as it dammed the water and prevented it from pouring down into Dunmanus Bay far below.

The castle overlooks Dun Lough

The castle is believed to have belonged to the O'Mahony family. They had been gradually pushed back from their landholdings, which once stretched as far as east Cork, first by the MacCarthys and then by the Normans, led by the experienced warrior Milo de Cogan. The nineteenth-century antiquarian John Windele recorded that the icy waters of the lake are said to be the home of a supernatural creature, with the body of a serpent and a head like a giant horse, which is said to swallow unwary travellers. Local folklore warns of an enchanted woman who haunts the castle and the shore of the lake. To see her is an omen of imminent death.

Centuries of harsh weather along this exposed coastal promontory have taken their toll, but despite the depredations by the weather it still remains one of the most beautiful and fantastical historical sites in the country.

Nearby you can visit **Mizen Head**. For countless seafarers, Mizen Head was the last sight of Europe before crossing the Atlantic. It was also a significant location in the story of transatlantic communication as Guglielmo Marconi established a signal station here. The station now houses a museum that tells the story of Mizen Head's role in shipping and communications.

A view from Mizen Head

Three Castle Head is on the western side of the Mizen Peninsula, not too far from the lovely town of Schull (approximately 35 minutes' drive away). The drive down the Mizen Peninsula is one of the highlights of the Wild Atlantic Way: the scenery around Barley Cove and all the way down to the tip of Mizen Head really is special and I would recommend spending a whole day (or more if you can) in this gorgeous region.

DUNLOUGH CASTLE AND MIZEN HEAD

MAP 2

Coordinates: Lat. 51.482384, Long. -9.829132

Irish Grid Reference: V 72980 27076

Opening hours/entry fees: No opening times applied at the time of visit. A small donation is requested. For more information, visit www.threecastlehead.ie

Directions: To get to the castle, head south-west from Schull for 8.5km on the R592 (passing Altar Wedge Tomb). Keep left to merge onto the R591 (signposted for Goleen, Mizen Head and Crookhaven). Stay on this road for 6.7km and turn right for Barley Cove and Mizen Head. After 350m when you reach Rockview, go straight through the crossroads and continue on this road for 8km (continue straight on this road even when you see signs for Mizen Head pointing left). After the 8km you will come to a Y-Junction with another minor road. Bear left and park at the end of the road and walk up the track to the farm on your right. Follow the signs to the castle across the fields and over the hills. Good boots are recommended as the fields can be quite waterlogged in parts.

Nearest towns: Schull (24.5km), Bantry (42km).

The Kilnaruane Pillar Stone

An early monastery called *Cill Ruáin* once stood on this site, overlooking Bantry Bay. The most significant reminder of this ancient ecclesiastical centre is the wonderful Kilnaruane Stone. The stone may once have been the shaft of a high cross and is likely to date to the ninth or early tenth century. It stands a little over 2m (6½ feet) tall, and bears depictions on the upper parts of the stone. The stone is known locally as Saint Brendan's Stone, for the depiction on the north-eastern face of a boat, similar to a currach, being rowed through a sea of crosses by four men on oars, with a man steering the boat at the helm. This may be a depiction of a scene of Saint Brendan's voyage. Above it are four animals. The top of the south-west face is decorated with interlace, below which is a praying figure, and below that is an elaborately carved cross. The panel below depicts Saints Paul and Anthony breaking bread in the desert.

A possible depiction of Saint Brendan's voyage on the north-eastern face of the stone (highlighted below)

Four grooved stones near the base of the shaft may be fragments of the broken head of a high cross, or pieces of a stone tomb shrine or similar structure, and other evidence of the early monastery can be seen in the bullaun stone close by.

KILNARUANE STONE

MAP 2

Coordinates: Lat. 51.671296, Long. -9.467901

Irish Grid Reference: V 98497 47480

Opening hours/entry fees: No opening times or entry fees applied at the time of visit.

Directions: The stone is just a five-minute drive from Bantry. From Bantry, head west on the N71 and turn left at the Westlodge Hotel. You will see the signpost for the stone after approximately 500m. The stone is in a field to your right. Leave the car parked as unobtrusively as possible and walk up through the field to the stone. Good boots are recommended as the field can be quite mucky.

Nearest town: Bantry (2.7km).

A view of Bantry House from the top of the hundred steps above the Italianate garden

This elegant stately home was originally built in around 1710 in the Queen Anne style by the Hutchison family, and it has been considerably added to over the years, particularly during the middle of the nineteenth century under Richard White, the 2nd Earl of Bantry. The house enjoys stunning views over Whiddy Island and the Caha Mountains. The interior of the house has a number of important period details, such as Italian plasterwork and Venetian glass, which give an insight into the taste and wealth of the Earls of Bantry. The striking Aubusson tapestries were made for Marie Antoinette, and were acquired in the turbulent days of the French Revolution.

The White family rose to prominence in the late eighteenth century, and earned a fortune through fishing and the timber trade. In 1796, a fleet of French ships with over 16,000 men sailed from Brest to land in Ireland to support the United Irishmen in their rebellion against English rule. However, the fleet was struck by ferocious storms, and only sixteen of the fleet arrived to rendezvous in Bantry Bay. There they waited for the other ships in vain; unable to land the soldiers because of the wind, they had to abandon their plans and return to France, to the great disappointment of Theobald Wolfe Tone who was on board one of the ships. He noted his frustration in his diary: 'we were close enough to toss a biscuit ashore.' The Rebellion would finally break out fully in 1798, though it would end in disaster for the United Irishmen. It was Richard White who raised the alarm and organised local defences, placing Bantry House at the disposal of the Royal Navy. For his efforts, loyalty and zeal he was raised to the rank of Baron Bantry, and he was later made a Viscount. Shortly after the Napoleonic Wars in 1816, he was raised to the rank of Earl of Bantry and Viscount Berehaven. The title is now extinct and Bantry House has descended through the female line to the present owners. Like the house, the beautiful gardens also reflect the style of Richard White. They were influenced by the fashionable Italianate style, with handsome terraces that help to complement the stunning vista.

BANTRY HOUSE AND GARDEN   MAP 2

Coordinates: Lat. 51.677480, Long. -9.464613

Irish Grid Reference: V 98682 48144

Opening hours/entry fees: Visit: www.bantryhouse.com.

Directions: Bantry House is located just 1km west of the town on the N71.

Nearest town: Bantry (1km).

13 | KEALKILL STONE CIRCLE AND CARRIGANASS CASTLE

This important complex of prehistoric monuments, consisting of a pair of standing stones, a small stone circle and a stone cairn, is set high on boggy ground on the north-western slope at the western end of the Maughanaclea Hills, with splendid views overlooking Bantry Bay and Kealkill village. The site was excavated in 1938, and it was found that the stones were not sunk deeply into pits, but instead were kept upright by packing with small stones. The monuments at Kealkill appear to be part of a wider prehistoric landscape, as a number of other similar features can be found on the Maughanaclea Hills.

Kealkill Stone Circle

Nearby to the stone circle on the outskirts of the village of Kealkill you can find the ruin of **Carriganass Castle**.

This was an ancestral home of the powerful O'Sullivan Beare family, and it was thought to have been constructed in *c.* 1541 on the banks of the Ouvane River. One of the more famous residents was Donal Cam O'Sullivan Beare, who commanded the Munster army at the Battle of Kinsale in 1601. A grisly tale from local folklore tells that Donal flung the English commander, St Ledger, to his death from the castle tower in retaliation after Donal's wife was murdered at Gougane Barra by English soldiers.

It is well worth diverting off the Wild Atlantic Way here and travelling the short distance inland through the mountain pass to

Carriganass Castle on the banks of the Ouvane River

the wonderfully peaceful Gougane Barra. If you have the time you can walk the route along the *Slí Bharra* (Saint Finbarr's Way). This 15km route crosses over the high Conigear Ridge and so should only be undertaken in good weather conditions with suitable boots. It takes approximately five hours to walk.

The wonderfully tranquil Gougane Barra

Coordinates:

Kealkill Stone Circle: Lat. 51.745068, Long. -9.370758
Carriganass Castle: Lat. 51.754162, Long. -9.378792

Irish Grid Reference: W 05385 55586

Opening hours/entry fees: No opening times or entry fees applied at the time of visit.

Directions: This stone circle is situated less than twenty minutes' drive from Bantry, just outside the village of Kealkill. From Bantry head north on the N71 for 5.5km, then at the crossroads at Ballylickey turn right onto the R584 (signposted Macroom and Gougane Barra). Continue on the R584 for 4.8km and bear right onto the R585 in Kealkill village, then turn right again and immediately right again, almost as though you are doubling back on yourself on a parallel road. After 200m turn left up a narrow road that ends in a T-Junction. At the junction turn right, then after 130m turn left (signposted for Kealkill Stone Circle). Continue on this road for 650m and turn left (just immediately before a Y-Junction). Continue on this road for 300m to the site. The fields can often be quite waterlogged so waterproof boots are advised.

Nearest towns: Bantry (12.7km), Glengarriff (20km).

14 | ILNACULLIN (GARINISH ISLAND)

Situated in the sheltered harbour of Glengarriff in Bantry Bay, Ilnacullin Island (also known as Garinish Island) is a small island perhaps best known for its wonderful gardens. The gardens were created in the early decades of the twentieth century, after 1910, when the businessman John Annan Bryce and his wife, Violet, purchased the island from the War Office. They had the acclaimed architect and garden designer Harold Peto plan and develop a series of beautiful gardens, and for three years over 100 people worked to reshape the landscape of the island, by blasting rocks, shifting countless tonnes of soil, planting trees, laying paths, constructing the walled garden and clock tower and more. The island is ideally situated for the creation of such gardens, as it is bathed in the warm waters of the North Atlantic Drift, which, combined with the sheltered aspect of the island, creates a microclimate that allows a wide variety of plants from around the world to flourish in this temperate spot. Perhaps the most beautiful feature is the stunning Italian-style garden, with its fine pavilion, pool and casita. The work on the gardens was continued by the Scottish gardener Murdo Mackenzie, who worked to establish banks of Scots and Monterey pine to take the brunt of the Atlantic wind and storms, creating even more shelter for the exotic and delicate plants to thrive.

The Italianate Garden of Garinish

The gardens reveal different and equally stunning aspects throughout the year as the seasons change. In late spring and early summer the island is a riot of colour from the azaleas and rhododendrons, and the climbing plants and herbaceous perennials dominate in the later summer months. The Bryce family donated the island to the state in 1953. Visitors can explore the gardens and the newly restored Bryce House with a guided tour. The house has had many famous visitors throughout its history, including Agatha Christie, George Bernard Shaw and

The Martello tower at the highest point of Garinish

Douglas Hyde. At the highest point of the island you can also see one of the first Martello towers, constructed as part of the fortifications against Napoleon's forces in *c.* 1805.

Access to the island is by ferry. Please note there is a separate admission charge to the island. The ferry journey itself is a wonderful experience: if you are fortunate you may encounter some of the resident colony of harbour seals, or if you are even luckier you might catch a glimpse of the white-tailed sea eagles that nest on the island. After your trip to the island, I highly recommend a walk in the lovely Glengarriff Woods.

Some of the resident harbour seals

ILNACULLIN   MAP 2

Coordinates: Glengarriff Pier: Lat. 51.750546, Long. -9.542337

Irish Grid Reference: V 93308 54897

Opening hours/entry fees: Visit: www.garnishisland.ie

Directions: There are two ferry services running to Ilnacullin (both depart from Glengarriff Pier):

Harbour Queen Ferry: www.harbourqueenferry.com

Blue Pool Ferry: www.bluepoolferry.com

Nearest town: Glengarriff.

15 | THE BEARA PENINSULA

Whether wreathed in mist and cloud, or almost glowing under the sun, the landscape of the Beara Peninsula is an unforgettable place. The peninsula abounds with archaeological monuments, and it is particularly rich in prehistoric archaeology with numerous stone circles, megalithic tombs and standing stones. In the medieval period, it became the territory of the O'Sullivan Beare Gaelic lordship, who used to control the waters around Beara with armed galleys until the last O'Sullivan Beare was expelled following the Battle of Kinsale. During the seventeenth, eighteenth and nineteenth centuries, it became a place of plantation and later a focus for British military might as they sought to fortify and protect the strategic harbours of the area.

As you travel southward along the peninsula from Glengarriff you will encounter a large number of heritage sites. Begin your journey by taking the ferry from Castletownbere to **Bere Island**.

The story of Bere Island is shaped by the waters that surround it. Following the attempted landing at Bantry Bay by French forces in support of the Rebellion of 1798 (see Site 12), the British began to invest in fortifying the entire bay, particularly around the valuable anchorage at Berehaven. During 1805, four Martello towers, artillery batteries, an officers' barracks and a signal tower were constructed on Bere Island, and the island continued to be fortified at great expense throughout the first decade of the nineteenth century. However, following the final defeat of Napoleon at the Battle of Waterloo in 1815, the necessity to continue the costly defensive development began to wane, and by 1828 the batteries were described as being dismantled and in a state of dilapidation. By the late nineteenth century, the defences had largely been abandoned and allowed to fall into complete disrepair, though a new phase of defensive development began by 1900, with the establishment of a series of new defences that would protect shipping in the deep waters of Berehaven, including **Lonehort Battery**, the largest artillery battery on the island. This fort developed to have a series of watchtowers, gun emplacements, ammunition stores and barrack accommodation, all surrounded by a deep moat.

The name Lonehort may derive from the Viking term *longphort*, meaning 'a ship enclosure'; these were often temporary fortified camps. Further evidence of the Vikings can be seen just below the

Derreenataggart Stone Circle

battery, in the form of a boat-naust. This was a secure place where Viking ships could be pulled up onto the beach for repair or storage.

Berehaven became a key station for the Royal Navy during the First World War, and it continued as a British naval port following the War of Independence, becoming one of the 'Treaty Ports'. These ports, including Lonehort and the defences of Bere Island, were formally handed over to the Irish state in 1938. The Beara Way Walking Trail will lead you around Bere Island to give you a closer look at the formidable defences. At present there is no access into the battery, but the local community is working hard to preserve the site and hope to open it to the public in the future.

After returning to the mainland, it is well worth visiting the stone circle **Derreenataggart**. Bear right at the south-western end of Castletownbere following the road onto West End Park and then the Rock. Turn left after 1km (signposted for the stone circle) and the site will be on your right after 500m with a small parking area opposite.

Lonehort Battery on Bere Island

Positioned on level ground on the south-eastern slope of Miskish Mountain, the stone circle at Derreenataggart is another interesting example of the Bronze Age ritual landscape of Ireland's south-west. The circle appears to be incomplete: it is believed to have originally consisted of fifteen stones, of which only twelve survive and three of those now lie flat. One of the portal stones measures some 2.5m (approximately 8 feet) tall, but the other is broken. The other stones of the circle reduce in height from the portal stones, gradually getting smaller until they get to the recumbent stone at the back. The circle affords a lovely view over the landscape towards **Bere Island**. **Teernahillane Ring Fort** is further along the road to the north-west.

After visiting the stone circle, head back to the R572 and continue southwards through the stunning landscape all the way to the very tip of the peninsula (coordinates Lat. 51.609920, Long. -10.154708). Here you can enjoy the unique experience of a ride in Ireland's only cable car as you take a trip to **Dursey Island**. This is a quiet and scenic oasis, a haven for many seabirds, such as choughs and gannets, while the surrounding waters are frequented by whales, dolphins and basking sharks. The island has a long history and is believed that it was once used as a Viking trading base, and a small medieval monastery was founded on the island perhaps in the early sixteenth century. An O'Sullivan castle was built on the small neighbouring island of *Oileán Beag*, but it was destroyed and the garrison massacred in 1602. You can also find the ruins of a signal tower built during the Napoleonic Wars.

Following your visit to **Dursey Island**, head back north along the R575 and stop to see a fine example of a wedge tomb at **Killaugh** (at coordinates Lat. 51.612898, Long. -10.066384), before continuing on to discover the story of the peninsula's industrial history at **Allihies**. The south-west of Ireland has produced some of the oldest copper mines in Europe, with sites dating back to the earliest phase of the Bronze Age. Industrial copper mining in this area began in around 1812, when a landlord, John Puxley, noticed the bright malachite colouration on the promontory at Dooneen. Over time, six productive mines were established in the Allihies region. The first attempts at extraction were with an adit, or tunnel, driven deep into the quartz lode from the pebble beach below. Later, in 1821, two shafts were sunk to get to the copper. To defeat the constant threat of flooding, Cornish steam engines were erected on site to pump water away from the works, and machinery was installed to crush the quartz rock to separate out the copper ore.

Allihies Copper Mine Museum

At their peak, the mines provided work for more than 1,500 people. Accommodation was cramped and unsanitary; occasionally more than 25 men would be packed into one small hovel. With such close conditions, disease was a constant threat and in 1832 a number died from a cholera outbreak. Mining itself was a treacherous job, with the risk of tunnel collapse and floods, and death was a constant companion to the workers. With such dangerous conditions and with low pay, it is no surprise that a number of strikes are recorded in the history of the mines.

The ruins of an engine house emerge from the mist

The mines were sold to the Berehaven Mining Company, who invested considerable sums and a new steam engine in 1872; however, their endeavour soon came to an end due to the failing ore, and by 1884 the Berehaven Mining Company was wound up. As a result of the worsening conditions and with little pay, many of the miners emigrated from Ireland to work in mines in the USA, notably at the famous copper mines of Butte, Montana.

The story of the mines is excellently told in the **Copper Mine Museum**, housed in the nineteenth-century Methodist church that once served the Cornish miners. It tells the story of copper mining at Allihies from the Bronze Age right up to the 1960s, with interesting exhibitions and artefacts. You can also venture along one of the numerous Copper Trails from the museum to see the ruins of the engine houses and mine workings.

Continue further north along the R575 (merging onto the R571) you will come to the village of **Ardgroom**.

You can find a fine stone circle just outside the village to the north-east (at around coordinates Lat. 51.737297, Long. -9.872286). Follow the R572 (Main Street) west and bear right when it turns

Ardgroom Stone Circle

into a Y-Junction. Follow this road up for just over 1km and turn left (signposted for the stone circle). The site will be on your right after 500m. There is a small area to park before the site. Cross the waterlogged and muddy fields to reach the circle that stands proudly on the ridge above you. This circle once consisted of eleven stones, though one stone is now missing and one fallen. A tall standing stone is positioned just outside the circle. This site is one of around

The roads of the Beara Peninsula

100 stone circles in Ireland, and it dates to the Bronze Age. With its position at the foot of Coomacloghare Mountain and beautiful views over the landscape, it is easy to imagine why this was deemed to be a sacred place over 3,000 years ago. You can discover more evidence of Bronze Age ritual landscapes at **Cashelkeelty**, just a ten-minute drive or so from Ardgroom. Park (at Lat. 51.759861, Long. -9.803632) before the sign and stile that leads to the trail. The monuments are quite a walk (perhaps 30 minutes or so) through woods and then up a pretty steep slope to find the site. Here you will discover a small stone circle and standing stones, with a fantastic vista over the landscape.

BEARA PENINSULA   MAP 4

Coordinates: Castletownbere Harbour: Lat. 51.652019, Long. -9.908624

Irish Grid Reference: V 69225 44063

Opening hours/entry fees: visit: www.bereisland.net

Directions: There are two ferry services running to Bere Island.

– Murphy's Ferry sails between Rerrin Village, East End, Bere Island and the Pontoon. See: www.murphysferry.com

– Bere Island Ferries sails between Oileán na gCaorach, West End Bere Island and Castletownbere. See: www.bereislandferries.com

---

DERREENATAGGART STONE CIRCLE   MAP 4

Coordinates: Parking: Lat. 51.653339, Long. -9.928552

Irish Grid Reference: V 66581 46237

Opening hours/entry fees: No entry fees or opening times applied at the time of visit.

Directions: The site is easy to find from Castletownbere.

Nearest town: Castletownbere (2km).

DURSEY ISLAND   MAP 4

Coordinates: (Parking for the cable car) Lat. 51.609920, Long. -10.154708

Irish Grid Reference: V 50789 41845

Opening hours/entry fees: visit: www.durseyisland.ie

Directions: Follow the R572 all the way south along the peninsula and you will see signs for Dursey Island.

Nearest town: Castletownbere (2km).

ALLIHIES COPPER MINE MUSEUM MAP 4

Coordinates: Lat. 51.639139, Long. -10.045791

Irish Grid Reference: V 58424 44879

Opening hours/entry fees: visit: www.acmm.ie

Directions: Allihies Copper Mine Museum is situated on the R575. From Castletownbere, head south-west on the R572 for 15km. At the Y-Junction (just after Killaugh Wedge Tomb – certainly worth a quick pit stop), bear right onto the R575 (signposted for Allihies and Eyeries). Continue on this road for around 4km and you will reach the museum.

Nearest town: Castletownbere (19km).

ARDGROOM MAP 4

Coordinates: Lat. 51.737297, Long. -9.872286

Irish Grid Reference: V 70714 55477

Opening hours/entry fees: No opening times or entry fees applied at the time of visit.

Directions: Ardgroom Stone Circle is located just outside the village of Ardgroom. From Ardgroom head north-east on the R571 for 2km, then take a sharp right up a narrow road and bear left at the Y-Junction. Continue on for approximately 300m and the stone circle should be on your right.

Nearest town: Ardgroom (on the outskirts).

CASHELKEELTY MAP 4

Coordinates: Lat. 51.759861, Long. -9.803632

Irish Grid Reference: V 75519 57867

Opening hours/entry fees: No opening times or entry fees applied at the time of visit.

Directions: From Ardgroom head north on the R571 towards Kenmare and park at Lat. 51.759861, Long. -9.803632 before the signpost and stile that lead to the site. The monuments are approximately 30–40 minutes' walk through a forest and then up a trail.

Nearest town: Kenmare (26.6km).

THE IVERAGH PENINSULA – THE RING OF KERRY

The majestic Iveragh Peninsula is the largest of the five peninsulas that push out into the Atlantic in the south-west of Ireland. The scenery of the peninsula offers a perfect blend of mountain and sea, and visitors have been drawn here for centuries to marvel at the beautiful landscape.

The towns and villages of the peninsula, such as Kenmare, Sneem, Waterville and Cahersiveen, have been welcoming countless visitors for generations and they abound with charm and great places to eat and drink.

From the picturesque heritage town of Kenmare with its fine stone circle, we will travel ever westwards to see mighty stone forts and ancient monasteries. You will see evidence of the very first inhabitant of Ireland from at least 350 million years ago in the beautiful setting of Valentia Island, and we will venture to the iconic World Heritage Site of Skellig Michael.

The road from Kildreelig

16 | KENMARE STONE CIRCLE

Kenmare Stone Circle

Kenmare Stone Circle is the largest example of the many stone circles in the south-west of Ireland, such as those on the nearby **Beara Peninsula** (Site 15). Stone circles like this one generally date to the Bronze Age, and are believed to have been places of ceremony and ritual. Kenmare Stone Circle was established on a plateau that would once have offered good views across the landscape, though today it is a little divorced from its original vistas by careful landscaping and conifer trees. It consists of fifteen stones (with two now prostrate), forming an oval shape with an approximate diameter of 17m (55 feet). A burial was centrally positioned inside the circle, set within in a small chamber formed by a covering boulder that rests upon three supports. A small cup mark can be seen on the boulder.

The site is located just a short walk south west from the centre of Kenmare town, and it is well signposted.

KENMARE STONE CIRCLE   MAP 5

Coordinates: Lat. 51.878468, Long. -9.588311

Irish Grid Reference: V 90707 70767

Opening hours/entry fees: No opening times applied at the time of visit, though there was a collection point for donations from visitors.

Directions: Kenmare Stone Circle is located just off Market Street in the town.

Nearest town: In Kenmare.

Staigue Fort

The walls of Staigue stand up to 6m (19 feet) high and 4m (13 feet) thick, and form an enclosure nearly 30m (98 feet) in diameter. The walls are constructed of a rubble core with fine drystone masonry facings, displaying the considerable skill of the stonemason. Several flights of steps on the interior of the walls allow access to the top, providing extensive views to the south-west, over the river valley to the sea at Kenmare Bay. There was some reconstruction of the walls in the nineteenth century, but they have blended nearly seamlessly into the original fabric. The fort was further protected by an exterior defensive ditch and bank, today much reduced from its original height. The fort is likely to have been the seat of a powerful chieftain or noble, and protected his family, homestead and outbuildings.

According to local folklore, the fairies of Staigue had a rivalry with those of **Cahergal** (Site 24) and played ferocious games of Gaelic football against each other on moonlit nights. A local man, Coneen Dannihy, once joined in the game and scored two goals to help the fairies of Cahergal to victory. When his mother prevented him from taking part in the next game, he was cursed by the fairies and remained prostrate in bed for nine months.

The entrance into Staigue Fort

STAIGUE FORT MAP 5

Coordinates: Lat. 51.804932, Long. -10.016933

Irish Grid Reference: V 60920 63230

Opening hours/entry fees: No opening times applied at the time of visit, though there was a collection point for donations from visitors.

Directions: Staigue Stone Fort is just north of the Ring of Kerry (N70). From Sneem, head west on the N70 for 14.8km then turn right (signposted Staigue Fort). Follow this road for just over 500m and bear left (following the sign again for Staigue Fort). Continue on this road for approximately 3km and you will reach the small parking area for the fort.

Nearest town: Sneem (19km).

STAIGUE FORT

Derrynane House

Derrynane was a special place for Daniel O'Connell. Born near Cahersiveen in 1775, Daniel O'Connell was a lawyer, statesman and politician who became a key figure in the movement for Irish Independence. His campaigning secured the Catholic Emancipation Act of 1829, which allowed Catholics to take seats in Parliament. He inherited Derrynane House in 1825, and today the house has become a fine museum dedicated to the memory of this key figure in Irish history. Most of the demesne landscape is encompassed within the Derrynane National Historic Park, with charming gardens replete with hidden fairy doors and a Gothic Revival summerhouse, over 1.5km (1 mile) of coastline and a number of archaeological and historical sites including an ogham stone, cashel, souterrain and the ruins of **Ahamore Abbey**.

The house itself was originally constructed in around 1720, and it has been extensively renovated and altered, particularly during the time of Daniel O'Connell. A number of fascinating artefacts from the life of the Liberator are on display within the house, including the pistols he used to fight a duel, and perhaps most poignantly, his deathbed. The bed once stood in a room in the Hotel Feder, Genoa, where he passed away on 15 May 1847.

Ahamore Abbey is situated a little further along the coast on Abbey Island, accessible on foot at low tide. The ruined medieval church once belonged to an Augustinian abbey, but today the site has become a significant burial place, with a number of notable historic graves, including that of Mary O'Connell, wife of Daniel O'Connell, along with other members of his family. The grave of the eighteenth-century Gaelic poet Tomás Rua Ó Suilleabháin can also be seen. Derrynane is a lovely and evocative place to contemplate the life and legacy of one of the key figures in the story of Ireland.

Ahamore Abbey

A view from Ahamore Abbey

DERRYNANE

MAP 5

Coordinates: Lat. 51.763282, Long. -10.128559

Irish Grid Reference: V 52990 58776

Opening hours/entry fees: visit: www.derrynanehouse.ie

Directions: Derrynane House is located just off the Ring of Kerry (N70). From Waterville head south on the N70 for 10km then turn right (signposted for Derrynane House). Follow this road for 2.5km. The house is well signposted.

Nearest town: Waterville (12.5km).

The path to Loher Fort

Loher Stone Fort is beautifully situated, with wonderful views over Ballinskelligs Bay. Like the other stone forts of **Staigue**, **Cahergal** and **Leacanbuaile**, Loher is another early medieval stone fort. It was the fortified home of a local chieftain or noble and probably dates to some time from the ninth to the eleventh century. The reconstructed circular drystone wall that surrounds the fort stands around 2m (6.5 feet) high with steps that lead to a wide rampart. In the interior of the enclosure you can find the foundations of two structures, one rectangular and one circular, which were presumably houses. When the site was excavated it was discovered that these stone buildings were later replacements for earlier wooden houses. Within the circular structure archaeologists discovered the remains of a souterrain. These underground passageways typically date to the tenth or eleventh century, and there are a number of theories about what they were used for. Often people believe that they were used as refuges during raids, with the narrow passageway being difficult to assault and forcing any attackers to advance one at a time; alternatively they have been interpreted as an early form of refrigerator or cellar, as they would maintain a constant cool temperature, ideal for keeping the all-important dairy products fresh.

Near to the fort is a stone enclosure with a notice that informs you that this enclosure once served as the local animal pound. During the nineteenth century, wandering livestock, dogs or cats were impounded here and anyone wishing to get their animals back had to pay a fine and a maintenance charge. During our visit a local cat sat somewhat haughtily on top of the wall of the pound; I'm sure she was aware of the heritage and chose to show her disdain as only a cat can.

The walls of Loher Fort

LOHER

MAP 5

Coordinates: Lat. 51.78605509 Long. -10.165658

Irish Grid Reference: V 50612 61462

Opening hours/entry fees: No opening times or entry fees applied at the time of visit.

Directions: Loher Fort is quite easy to find, it is just off the Ring of Kerry, approximately fifteen minutes' drive from the village of Waterville. Follow the Ring of Kerry road N70 south of Waterville for about five minutes (3.7km) and you will see the fort signposted to the right. Take the turn onto a narrow road that winds on for around 2.5km; stick with it and you'll see a good car park on your right and a path leading to the fort below you.

Nearest town: Cahersiveen (23km).

Ballinskelligs Priory

It is thought that in the twelfth century, the monastic community on **Skellig Michael** abandoned the increasingly inhospitable island to establish a new monastery here at Ballinskelligs. However, most of the visible remains on the site date to after 1210, when the site became an Augustinian priory, dedicated to Saint Michael. The priory survived until 1585, when Queen Elizabeth I ensured that the Dissolution of the Monasteries was being enforced across Ireland.

The priory has suffered much from coastal erosion over the centuries. The main visible remains consist of the ruins of a church with a nave and a surviving portion of the chancel, and a building known as The Prior's House, connected at a slight angle to the nave. The grounds around the priory have been an important place of burial over the centuries. The priory also offers a fine view of Ballinskelligs Castle. The castle is a late medieval tower house believed to have been constructed for the MacCarthy family. Unfortunately, like the priory, the castle too has suffered much from coastal erosion and is now in a precarious condition.

A view of Ballinskelligs Castle from the priory

BALLINSKELLIGS PRIORY

MAP 5

Coordinates: Lat. 51.815752, Long. -10.272284.

Irish Grid Reference: V 43392 64973

Opening hours/entry fees: No opening times or entry fees applied at the time of visit.

Directions: Ballinskelligs Abbey is on the outskirts of Ballinskelligs, just over a 20-minute (17km) drive from Cahersiveen. Head south from Cahersiveen on the N70 (Ring of Kerry) for 7km. Turn right onto the R566, signposted Baile an Sceilg. Continue on the R566 for 10km, passing straight through Ballinskelligs village. When you reach the crossroads signposted Ballinskelligs Pier, continue straight for 600m. Turn left onto the minor road; the abbey is 200m down the end of this road.

Nearest towns: Ballinskelligs (on the outskirts), Cahersiveen (17km).

21 | KILDREELIG MONASTIC SITE

The remains of an enclosure at Kildreelig

For a combination of breathtaking scenery and fascinating archaeology, there are few places that can compare to Kildreelig, where you can find the remains of a small early Christian monastery, perched high on the south-eastern slope of Bolus Head. With such stunning views over Ballinskelligs Bay and the Atlantic Ocean all the way to the Beara Peninsula, it is easy to imagine why it was chosen as a place of spirituality and contemplation.

Upon first impression, the site can be a little difficult to decipher as it appears as a rough jumble of stones. However, on closer inspection you can make out an enclosure wall that surrounds the remains of a small oratory, a circular hut, three rectangular buildings, cross slabs (one in particular is very distinctively decorated) and a souterrain. Souterrains are covered tunnel-like passageways that some believed were used as a refuge during raids, but are also likely to have been used to store food, as the cool dark of the passage kept goods such as dairy products at a low and constant temperature. A holy well is located down the steep slope to the south-west, where a small stream issues from a pool. A pattern, or pilgrimage, used to be practised here until the early twentieth century. Kildreelig was used as a burial ground for unbaptised children until the nineteenth century. It truly is an atmospheric and evocative place, undoubtedly one of the most beautifully situated sites I have ever encountered.

Above: The souterrain

Opposite page: Cross-inscribed slab at Kildreelig

KILDREELIG

MAP 5

Coordinates: Lat. 51.796593, Long. -10.311064.

Irish Grid Reference: V 40616 62942

Opening hours/entry fees: No opening times or entry fees applied at the time of visit.

Directions: The narrow road up to Kildreelig can be a little nerve-wracking! To find the site from Ballinskelligs, head south-west on the R566 and turn right at the crossroads onto the road called *Ceol na hAbhann* (signposted Portmagee). Turn left at the next crossroads (signposted Skellig Ring) and take the first turn left. Continue on this road as it heads south for 750m and bear right at the Y-Junction. Follow this narrow road all the way for around 3km past the Cill Rialaig artists' retreat village and continue up the hill until you see the site on your left-hand side; try to pull the car in off the road as far as possible in a gateway (I recommend leaving a note with your phone number on it in case a farmer needs to use the gate). It is very easy to miss the site as there is no entrance as such into the field. Just drive very slowly and look out for the jumble of stone and the cross slabs sticking up. Enter the field via the stone blocks that form a sort of rudimentary stile. To turn the car I recommend continuing up the road and turning in a gate entrance farther along, unless you have a very small car or are particularly skilled at three-point turns: it is a very narrow road!

Nearest town: Ballinskelligs (4.7km).

KILDREELIG MONASTIC SITE

Skellig Michael viewed from Little Skellig

One of the world's most iconic places, the island of Skellig Michael lies some 12km (8 miles) off the coast of Bolus Head in County Kerry. When you first sight the island on the horizon, it appears almost like a rugged pyramid. The famous jagged rock that rises some 218m (715 feet) over the Atlantic waves is actually the tip of a submerged mountain, formed of the same 400 million-year-old Old Devonian Sandstone that runs all the way to the MacGillycuddy's Reeks. Skellig Michael appears in the eleventh-century *Lebor Gabála Érenn* (the Book of Invasions) in the story of the legendary king of the Milesians, who lost two sons to shipwrecks on the Skelligs during their ancient invasion to wrest control of Ireland from the mythological Tuatha de Danann.

After landing on the island, you are faced with a climb up hundreds of steep stone steps that lead you ever upwards until you reach the enclosure of the monastery. The siting of the monastery on a terrace just below the northern peak ensured that it had a south-facing aspect and that it was largely sheltered from the prevailing winds: as comfortable a place as you could possibly get on this exposed island. The monastery is thought to have been in existence at least from the seventh century, and it continued in use up

The famous steps of Skellig Michael

until at least the twelfth century, when the monks left the island to a new foundation at **Ballinskelligs** (Site 20). The monastery is traditionally believed to have been founded by Saint Fíonán; however, by the eleventh century the island and its monastery had been rededicated to Saint Michael. The monastery was founded as part of the eremitical practice of the early Irish Church, to withdraw to isolated places to worship God, unencumbered by daily life, society or politics. Despite the isolation of the island, the Vikings raided Skellig Michael, most notably in 824, when the Annals of Ulster record that the Vikings kidnapped the abbot Éitgal, who died of hunger and thirst during his captivity.

The drystone walls of the enclosure protect six beehive cells known as clocháns, two oratories (similar in some respects to **Gallarus**, Site 30), and a small church, along with outdoor altars (*leachta*) and a small platform known as the Monks' Graveyard, which contains a number of early grave slabs. Daily life in the monastery must have been difficult, as there are no freshwater wells or streams on the island; instead, the monks carved the rock to channel rainwater into cisterns. Despite the presence of a small area known as the Monks' Garden, which may have been used for cultivation, and the presence of seabirds whose eggs and meat would have undoubtedly have been exploited by the monks, much of the food and necessities of daily life would have had to be brought out onto the island, perhaps leaving the monks facing severe hunger and hardship during prolonged stormy spells.

If life in the monastery was not already harsh enough, a hermitage was established high on the island's southern peak, though it is difficult (and dangerous) to access today. Even after the monks had withdrawn, the monastery and hermitage became an important place of pilgrimage in later centuries. The monastery's appearance today is due to a programme of restoration and reconstruction.

There is nowhere else on earth like Skellig Michael. It has been perhaps best described by the writer George Bernard Shaw: 'An incredible, impossible, mad place ... I tell you the thing does not belong to any world that you and I have lived and worked in: it is part of our dream world.' Throughout its history, Skellig Michael has inspired pilgrims, though today they are joined by devotees of *Star Wars*, who climb the steps on their own intergalactic pilgrimage. Today, due to the wear from increasing numbers of visitors, and the unavoidable effect of the Atlantic weather, Skellig

A view of Little Skellig from the monastery

Michael has become a delicate place, deserving of the utmost respect and care. Conservation works by the OPW are often ongoing, but visitors should take every precaution to ensure the safety of both themselves and this wondrous, magical place.

Skellig Michael is a truly special, but also a truly fragile place. It has a necessarily short season, not only due to the weather but also to help to protect the island's wildlife, particularly its colonies of puffins, black-backed gulls and herring gulls, Manx shearwaters and stormy petrels. A small number of boats are granted a licence to bring people to the island from May until October. The OPW have staff present at that time, and to visit out of season is not permitted as it is a hazardous site. Unfortunately, in recent years, people have lost their lives falling from the steep steps, and the site is not suitable for young children or anyone who suffers from a strong fear of heights. Due to the many steps, it is also a difficult (and occasionally dizzying!) climb unless you are fit and healthy.

Clochán on Skellig Michael

SKELLIG MICHAEL MAP 5

Coordinates: The monastery: Lat. 51.771974, Long. -10.538517. Boat trips available from Portmagee or Ballinskelligs.

Irish Grid Reference: V 24726 60650

Opening hours/entry fees: Visit: www.heritageireland.ie/en/south-west/ skelligmichael/

A number of boat companies provide a service to Skellig Michael from either Portmagee or Ballinskelligs. The Heritage Ireland website has a list of licensed operators.

Directions: You can get a boat from Portmagee or Ballinskelligs. However, due to increased demand it is advisable to book your trip as early as possible to avoid disappointment. The trip is very weather dependent. A friend has made several attempts to visit and only landed once. I was incredibly lucky with my trip that there were calm, dry conditions and the ocean was like a millpond as that is the exception rather than the rule. Please wear sensible footwear and be advised that it is quite a long climb to the monastery.

Nearest towns: Portmagee, Ballinskelligs.

The lighthouse of Valentia Island

As you cross the bridge onto Valentia Island, you pass the **Skellig Experience**, an interpretive centre that tells the story of Skellig Michael. The beautiful landscape of Valentia Island abounds with fascinating places, including megalithic tombs, Cromwellian forts, slate quarries, the transatlantic cable station and, of course, the beautifully situated lighthouse, but my personal favourite feature of Valentia Island is undoubtedly the unique **Tetrapod Trackway**. Around 350 million years ago, a metre-long

The Tetrapod Trackway

amphibious creature ventured out of a cool pool to make its way ponderously across the sticky mud to bask in the warming sun. It is doubtful that the creature was blessed with good looks – it may have resembled a giant salamander – but it is an ancestor of all four-legged vertebrate animals that we know today. Before this creature and its kin, the only vertebrate animals were primitive fish. Over millennia, some species of fish had begun to specialise in feeding in the shallow waters at the edge of pools and rivers. Gradually, these fish gained the ability to breathe out of water, and fins began to evolve into primitive legs. It was just such a creature that left its footprints and occasional drag marks from its tail that, incredibly, you can still see in the north of Valentia Island. These tracks represent the oldest reliably dated evidence in the world of four-legged vertebrates walking on land. The transition of life from water to land was undoubtedly one of the most important moments in the story of evolution on earth. Therefore, these tracks are of immense international importance.

When you visit to see these humble, shallow depressions in the rock, it is hard not to imagine the world as it was all those millions of years ago. Much of the surface of the planet was covered by Panthalassa, the great World Ocean. The planet was warm, and there was a lot of tectonic movement of the plates, undoubtedly causing enormous earthquakes as many of the world's mountain ranges were formed at this time. Ireland was part of a large land mass, and Munster was on an enormous coastal plain, with great rivers cutting through distant mountains and depositing countless tonnes of sand and sediments, forming the rock that you see so clearly along the coast of Kerry. When the rivers were in flood, they deposited thick layers of silt on the coastal plains, and it was onto this silt that the creature slithered and crawled its way from a pool. Over the enormous expanse of time and pressure, the silt turned to stone and forever trapped the tracks of the tetrapod, as a visual echo from the unimaginably distant past.

VALENTIA ISLAND   MAP 5

Coordinates: Tetrapod Trackway: Lat. 51.929545, Long. -10.345785

Irish Grid Reference: V 38698 77809

Opening hours/entry fees: No entry fees or opening hours applied at the time of visit.

Directions: You can find the Tetrapod Trackway in the north-east of the island. From Portmagee head north-west on the R565 and cross the bridge onto Valentia Island. Continue following this road as it now heads north-east for around 3km and turn left (signposted Geokaun Mountain). Follow this road for a further 2km and at the T-Junction turn left (signposted for Slate Quarry and Grotto) then turn immediately right (signposted DHILLA). Continue on this road for a further 1.5km and the car park for the Tetrapod Trackway will be on your right. The footprints are a short walk down a pretty steep slope. Late afternoon is a particularly good time to visit as the light shows the tracks in better relief.

Nearest town: Portmagee (7.3km).

24 | CAHERGAL AND LEACANABUAILE STONE FORTS

The area around Kimego West is home to a series of three spectacular stone forts, two of which (Cahergal and Leacanabuaile) are accessible to visitors. A small parking area leads to a path where you can enjoy a very pleasant walk to see **Cahergal**. Similar in many respects to the larger **Staigue Fort** (Site 17), Cahergal is constructed on the crest of a rocky ridge with extensive views over the landscape. Its formidable circular stone rampart encloses an area with a diameter of over 26m (85 feet). Within the enclosure you can see the remains of a circular drystone house. When it was excavated in the early 1990s, archaeologists discovered domestic artefacts like quern stones for grinding grain, along with evidence of metal working on site. It is uncertain when precisely the fort was constructed, but it is generally believed to date to the early medieval period and may have been the home of an important family such as the *Ua Fáilbe* (Falvey) family, one of the key dynastic lineages in this area during that time.

Cahergal Stone Fort

The stone fort of Leacanabuaile

The fort of **Leacanabuaile** is located around a ten-minute walk from Cahergal. The fort was excavated in the 1940s, following which some of the visible remains were partially reconstructed. The fort is slightly larger than Cahergal, with a diameter of approximately 30m (98 feet). Like Cahergal, Leacanabuaile is also thought to have been the seat of a high-ranking family in early medieval Ireland, presumably around the ninth or tenth century. The 3m (9 feet) thick stone walls enclose the foundations of four stone structures, representing domestic houses and ancillary buildings, along with a souterrain. The concentration of structures gives the impression of Leacanabuaile being more crowded than Cahergal despite its comparatively larger size. Leacanabuaile also enjoys stunning views over the landscape, and a visit to these fantastic stone forts is always a worthwhile experience.

Coordinates: Lat. 51.955469, Long. -10.261422

Irish Grid Reference: V 44854 80537

Opening hours/entry fees: No entry fees or opening hours applied at the time of visit.

Directions: You can find these wonderful stone forts just over a five-minute (3.3km) drive from Cahersiveen. From the town, head north on Bridge Street. About 700m after crossing the bridge, turn left at the crossroads, signposted White Strand. Continue on this road for 2km and the parking area for both Cahergal and Leacanabuaile stone forts will be on your right. Cahergal is a 200m walk east of the car park.

Nearest town: Cahersiveen (3.3km).

25 | KILLAGHA PRIORY

It is believed that a monastery was first founded on this site by Saint Colman in the sixth century, though the visible remains belong to an Augustinan priory that was founded by the Norman Lord Geoffrey de Marisco in around 1216. The priory became very wealthy and influential, and once controlled a large and prosperous estate. The Papal Taxation List of 1302 shows that Killagha paid the third-highest tax in the entire Diocese of Ardfert. Archaeological excavations carried out nearby to the priory uncovered imported French pottery, hinting at the high status and relatively luxurious life of the monks.

The priory was eventually suppressed by 1576 and it was granted to Captain Thomas Spring, who turned it into a domestic residence. However, the site was badly damaged by Parliamentary forces in 1649, when the domestic buildings and cloisters were destroyed. It was then granted to the Cromwellian soldier Major

Killagha Priory

John Godfrey. Today the priory church is all that remains of this once-powerful foundation. The red sandstone windows and doors date to the thirteenth century, while the elegant east window is likely to be fifteenth century in date.

The interior of Killagha Priory; note the elegant tracery of the eastern window

KILLAGHA PRIORY

MAP 6

Coordinates: Lat. 52.149305, Long. -9.730785

Irish Grid Reference: Q 81579 01074

Opening hours/entry fees: No entry fees or opening hours applied at the time of visit.

Directions: Killagh Priory is around a 25 minute (20km) drive from Tralee. Head south from Tralee on the N22 and continue onto the N70 heading south, through the village of Castlemaine and Milltown. After Milltown turn right onto the L12231 (signposted Abbeylands) and follow this road through a crossroads to the site.

Nearest town: Tralee (20km).

DINGLE PENINSULA

There are few places on earth that can boast as dense a concentration of historic monuments as the Dingle Peninsula. Slea Head in particular has an almost bewildering array of fascinating places, so much so that I could have easily filled a hundred entries there alone.

The wonderful Músaem Chorca Dhuibhne (West Kerry Museum) is the perfect place to get your bearings and to gain a sense of the incredible archaeological heritage and history of this area from the curator of the museum, archaeologist Isabel Bennett.

The famous Conor Pass

Like the Iveragh Peninsula, here you will meet a beautiful blend of mountainous terrain and stunning sea views. The peninsula is dominated by the towering Mount Brandon and the Slieve Mish Mountains, where we will climb high to an ancient fort where legendary warriors once battled. To reward yourself after the climb, the lively town of Dingle is a great place to enjoy music and wonderfully fresh seafood.

Heading back up the Dingle Peninsula means braving the famous Conor Pass, the highest mountain pass in Ireland, an iconic, breathtaking and occasionally nail-biting drive. On a clear day from the Conor Pass you can see truly spectacular views, all the way to **Loop Head** in County Clare and even the Aran Islands off the Galway coast. It is a great place to consider how the landscape here has been so shaped by the flow of glaciers during the Ice Age. Around 20,000 years ago, thick sheets of glacial ice moved slowly down into Brandon Bay, scouring the landscape and picking up millions of tonnes of debris. When the ice began to melt around 14,000 years ago, it left behind this rugged and jagged landscape with deep valleys and corrie lakes.

26 | MINARD CASTLE

Minard Castle is believed to have had a comparatively short life for a castle, having been slighted by Cromwellian forces within a century of its construction. It is one of the last FitzGerald castles to have been constructed in Kerry. It was built as a typical four-storey tower house some time in the second half of the sixteenth century, though only three storeys survive today and the castle is in a somewhat precarious condition.

The ruins of Minard Castle stand next to Cill Mhuire Bay, which is of considerable geological interest. The cliffs here are partially formed from 380-million-year-old fossilised sand dunes, and it also boasts one of the finest storm beaches in Ireland, where blocks of sandstone have been gradually shaped and rounded by the relentless action of the ocean over millennia and thrown by storms to form a high ridge at the back of the beach.

Minard Castle

MINARD CASTLE

MAP 6

Coordinates: Lat. 52.126374, Long. -10.110129

Irish Grid Reference: V 55522 99169

Opening hours/entry fees: No entry fees or opening hours applied at the time of visit.

Directions: Minard Castle is a just over a fifteen-minute (13km) drive from Dingle. Head east on the N86 for 10km. Turn right at Kate's Cross, Lispole, signposted An Mhin Aird. Continue on this road for 2.5km and turn left where there is an old sign for Minard Castle. The castle is 400m down this road on the shoreline.

Nearest town: Dingle (13km).

MINARD CASTLE

Cathair Mhurfaí

A large number of stone forts and clocháns can be found on the southern slopes of Sliabh an Iolair (Mount Eagle) overlooking Dingle Bay on the stunning Slea Head, perhaps evidence that the area was well populated and relatively prosperous during the early medieval period.

One of the accessible sites is Cathair Mhurfaí (Murphy's Fort), an oval-shaped cashel that encloses five roughly circular clocháns and a souterrain. The site was considerably reconstructed during the nineteenth century, but it is still certainly worth visiting to enjoy the stunning views over Dingle Bay. A similar stone fort, known as Caherdorgan, is located close to Kilmalkedar (Site 31) at coordinates Lat. 52.179224, Long. -10.339125. This is a circular cashel enclosing five well-preserved clocháns and a souterrain. Like Cathair Mhurfaí, Caherdorgan was also restored and repaired in the nineteenth century. The site also commands fantastic views, and it is a very worthwhile stop on your way to Kilmalkedar.

As well as the numerous stone cashels, this area is also known for the once-grand promontory fort at Dúnbeg, whose remains are precariously perched close to the cliffs above Dingle Bay at the base of Mount Eagle. Sadly, this fort has suffered badly from coastal erosion, with particularly bad collapses in 2014 and early 2018, when storms caused sections of the site to tumble into the Atlantic below. Archaeologists from Ireland's National Monuments Service and the OPW have long known that Dúnbeg is a particularly vulnerable site, and so it was carefully excavated in the late 1970s to retrieve as much information as possible before its inevitable surrender to the relentless elements. The excavations revealed that Dúnbeg had its origins in the Bronze Age period, though it was in use right into the early medieval period, with a number of features including a drystone clochán in the interior dated to the tenth or eleventh century.

FAHAN   MAP 6

Coordinates:
Cathair Mhurfaí: Lat. 52.100902, Long. -10.420640
Caherdorgan: Lat. 52.179224, Long. -10.339125
Irish Grid Reference: V 34149 97109

Opening hours/entry fees: There may be a small charge or donation requested from visitors for Cathair Mhurfaí.

Directions: The Fahan Group is around a 25-minute (14km) drive from Dingle. Head west on the Slea Head Drive (R559), passing straight through Ventry village. About 6km beyond Ventry the parking area for the Fahan Group will be on your left overlooking the sea.

Nearest town: Dingle (14km).

28 | IONAD AN BHLASCAOID MHÓIR

(The Blasket Centre and Dunquin Harbour)

This excellent, bright and airy visitor centre honours the community that called the Blasket Islands their home until the island was finally evacuated in 1953. The centre houses an extensive collection of photographs, writings and storyboards, models, artworks, documentary films and research resources along with a bookshop and cafe. The islands were a beautiful if harsh home, and the stunning scenery and life on the island has inspired a plethora of poets, folklorists, ethnographers and artists over the years. The islands themselves have a rich literary tradition, with writers and storytellers such as Tomás Ó Criomhthain, Muiris Ó

The Blasket Islands

Súilleabháin and Peig Sayers. The exhibition also recreates the interior of a typical Blasket Island dwelling, where you can see the everyday features of the home along with the islanders' names in Irish and English, offering a small but intimate glimpse into their daily life.

You can take a trip to the Great Blasket Island from the picturesque harbour of Dunquin, but please be aware that the terrain of the island can be challenging and the weather changeable, so be sure to wear suitable clothing and good boots. Near the car park above the quay at Dunquin you can enjoy a lovely view over the Blasket Islands. Inis Tuaisceart is the one that most grabs the eye. It is known as the Sleeping Giant, or locally as *An Fear Marbh* ('the dead man'), as it has the distinct look of a man lying on his back.

The stretch of waters between the mainland and the Blasket Islands is known as Blasket Sound, and despite its convenience it has occasionally proved to be a dangerous passage for unwary or unlucky seafarers due to its unpredictable tides and unforgiving rocks. In 1588 five ships from the Spanish Armada sought shelter in Blasket Sound. One of them, the *Santa Maria de la Rosa*, hit the rocks and immediately sank. Only the pilot's son survived. Islanders regularly had to brave the Blasket

The Blasket Centre

Sound in lightweight coracle boats made of tarred canvas over a wooden frame, known locally as *naomhóga*. Looking over the waters towards the islands, the old tune '*Port na bPúcaí*' arrives unbidden, but very welcome, to the mind. This slow air is thought to have originated in the Blasket Islands, where some believe it was inspired by the song of the humpback whale, an occasional visitor to these waters.

Above: The Sleeping Giant, or '*An Fear Marbh*'
Opposite page: Dunquin Harbour

Coordinates:

Visitor Centre: Lat. 52.132286, Long. -10.461605

Dunquin Harbour: Lat. 52.125419, Long. -10.459955

Irish Grid Reference: Q 31459 00653

Opening hours/entry fees: Visit: www.blasket.ie

Directions: Ionad an Bhlascaoid Mhóir is a 40-minute (23km) drive from Dingle. Head west on the Slea Head Drive (R559) through Ventry, around Slea Head and through Dunquin. Turn left at the crossroads at Dunquin Youth Hostel, where there is a sign for Ionad an Bhlascaoid Mhóir. It is 400m down this road on the right.

Nearest town: Dingle (23km).

29 | REASK (RIASC) MONASTIC SITE

The remains of circular clocháns at Reask

Slea Head abounds with the remains of many early monasteries. The ruin of a small monastic enclosure can be discovered at Reask near Ballyferriter. The monastery is enclosed by drystone walls that surround the remains of clocháns, a small stone oratory and a number of cross slabs, including the Reask Stone, which is beautifully decorated with a cross, ornate spiral designs and the letters *DNE*, meaning *Domine*, (Latin for 'O Lord'). Reask was excavated by the archaeologist Tom Fanning, who discovered the foundations of the structures along with a number of graves and some sherds of

Mediterranean pottery that date to around the sixth century. These fragments of pottery are likely to have come from a large amphora-style container that perhaps contained wine or oil, giving evidence of the rather extensive trading network of early medieval Ireland. In more recent centuries, long after the monastery had fallen out of use, the local community still

The Reask Stone

saw the site as hallowed ground and it became a *ceallúnach* – a burial ground for unbaptised children. A tiny figurine of a baby in swaddling clothes was amongst the poignant objects recovered from these small graves.

A number of the important grave slabs discovered during the excavations are on display in the superb **Músaem Chorca Dhuibhne** (West Kerry Museum), situated in the Old Schoolhouse nearby in Ballyferriter.

REASK MONASTIC SITE   MAP 6

Coordinates: Lat. 52.167717, Long. -10.387269

Irish Grid Reference: Q 36718 04393

Opening hours/entry fees: No opening times or entry fees applied at the time of visit.

Directions: Reask Monastic Site is a fifteen-minute (10km) drive from Dingle. Take the Slea Head Drive (R559) north-west (counterclockwise), turning right 1km outside Dingle town, signposted An Mhuiríoch. Continue for 5km along this road and turn left. Continue for another 2km to rejoin the R559 at the Smerwick Harbour Hotel. About 2km after this, turn left at the sign for Reask Monastic Site, which is 350m down this road on the right.

Nearest town: Dingle (10km).

Gallarus Oratory

One of the truly iconic sites of the Dingle Peninsula, Gallarus is a drystone oratory with a corbelled roof. The oratory stands at the south-east side of a large stone-walled enclosure on the lower slopes of Lateevmore, with a vista that overlooks the broad crescent of land surrounding Smerwick Harbour. There is some debate about how old the oratory is, with the most likely possibility being somewhere around the tenth or eleventh century. The church was constructed from a single continuous corbelled vault, with the splayed walls of the base supporting the roof. This style of construction provides Gallarus's distinctive shape; from a distance it appears rather like the hull of an upturned boat.

Just outside the church you can see a *leacht* or altar feature with an early cross slab that bears the Latin inscription *LIE COLUM MEC GR*, which is thought to translate to 'The Stone of Colum, Son of Gr...'.

Gallarus is a very popular site with visitors, but in between the coach tours it is possible to have the church almost to yourself while you soak in the atmosphere.

The *leacht* and cross slab

GALLARUS
MAP 6

Coordinates: Lat. 52.173594, Long. -10.353673

Irish Grid Reference: Q 39314 04880

Opening hours/entry fees: Visit: www.heritageireland.ie/en/south-west/gallarusoratory/

Directions: Gallarus Oratory Visitor Centre is about a fifteen-minute (8km) drive from Dingle. Take the Slea Head Drive (R559) north-west (counterclockwise), turning right 1km outside Dingle town, signposted An Mhuiríoch. Continue for 5km along this road and turn left and then immediately right, signposted for Gallarus at both junctions. Continue on this road for 1km and the entrance to the visitor centre will be on your right.

Nearest town: Dingle (8km).

The remains of an important and extensive early church complex at Kilmalkedar

Kilmalkedar is one of Ireland's most important early church complexes. It takes its name from its founder, Saint Maolcethair, who died in AD 636, though traditionally Kilmalkedar is more associated with Saint Brendan the Navigator. The complex covers an area of over 10 acres and includes a Romanesque church, cross, ogham stone, sundial, Saint Brendan's House and a number of other important ecclesiastical features.

In the graveyard you can see a tall and slender ogham stone that is inscribed ANM MAILE INBIR MACI BROCANN (which has been translated to 'the soul of Mael-Inbir, son of Brocán').

The Kilmalkedar ogham stone

The sundial

Nearby is a large stone cross, and a lovely example of an early medieval sundial.

The beautiful Romanesque church shares many architectural similarities to Cormac's Chapel on the Rock of Cashel in County Tipperary, and it may indeed have been constructed by the same architects and masons. Like Cormac's Chapel, the church at Kilmalkedar is also thought to be mid-twelfth century in date, though the chancel was extended in around 1200. Notable features of the church include the ornate doorway, which is typically Romanesque in design, with three orders decorated with a carving of a human head in the centre, which perhaps represents the founder or local ruler, and zigzag decoration. The projecting antae and the blind arcading on the interior are also classic features of Romanesque architecture. The chancel arch is also finely decorated in the Romanesque style, and the 'alphabet stone' is positioned just next to the arch. This stone is unusual in its use of the Latin text, and it contains the letters DNI, a contraction of 'Domini' (Latin for 'Lord'), along with a Latin cross with scrolled terminals. This stone is thought to be possibly as early as sixth or seventh century in date.

The Romanesque church at Kilmalkedar

The chancel and Alphabet Stone

Saint Brendan's House at Kilmalkedar

A three-storey stone building known as **Saint Brendan's House** stands on private land across the lane from the churchyard. This may have originally been the home of the priest who served the medieval parish church. Nearby to the west is **Saint Brendan's Oratory**, though at the time of my visit in 2017 this site was undergoing conservation works and so, unfortunately, was not accessible. It is a rectangular oratory, similar to that of **Gallarus** though its corbelled roof has collapsed. In a field to the north-west of the main site of Kilmalkedar you can find a fine example of a bullaun stone (at coordinates Lat. 52.185574, Long. -10.338190): further evidence of the remarkable wealth of early medieval heritage in this region.

Kilmalkedar is on the Pilgrim's Path, one of Ireland's most rewarding walking trails. It follows the ancient pilgrim route known as **Cosán na Naomh**. It is approximately 18km (11 miles) in length, and runs from Ventry Strand to the foot of Mount Brandon.

MAP 6

KILMALKEDAR

Coordinates: Lat. 52.184798, Long. -10.337258

Irish Grid Reference: Q 42062 06200

Opening hours/entry fees: No entry fees or opening hours applied at the time of visit.

Directions: Kilmalkedar Church is about a fifteen-minute (9km) drive from Dingle. Take the Slea Head Drive (R559) north-west (counterclockwise), turning right 1km outside Dingle, signposted An Mhuiríoch. Continue for 7km along this road. Turn right at the signpost for Kilmalkedar church and the church will be on your right.

Nearest town: Dingle (9km).

32 | CAHERCONREE

The rampart of Caherconree

The remains of sunken structures visible along the interior of the rampart

According to legend, this fort was constructed by Cú Roi Mac Dáire, a sorcerer king of west Munster. He is said to have humiliated and defeated the legendary warrior Cú Chulainn by carrying off his girlfriend Blathnad and forcing her to become his wife. Blathnad was not impressed with this state of affairs, and so she helped Cú Chulainn gain his revenge by agreeing to signal him at the

Follow the wooden stakes to the fort high on the ridge above

most opportune time to attack, when Cú Roi's defences were at their weakest and his men sleeping. At the appropriate moment, Blathnad poured gallons of milk into a mountain stream, turning the waters white. At this sign Cú Chulainn and his men rushed to the attack and succeeded in overcoming the defences, and slaughtered Cú Roi and his men.

The stunning views from Caherconree

Even without legendary defenders, Caherconree would pose a truly formidable challenge to any attacking force. Situated at the western end of the Slieve Mish Mountains, it is the highest promontory fort in Ireland, at over 625m (2,000 feet) above sea level. A roughly triangular-shaped tongue of land is defended by a wall that measures over 110m (360 feet) long by 5m (16 feet) wide and still stands some 3m (10 feet) high. The site is also naturally defended by the precipitous cliffs surrounding it. A further line of bank and ditch stand outside the wall, but they are much reduced; they would, however, have posed another serious obstacle when they were newly fortified. A number of sunken structures can be discerned along the interior of the rampart.

The views from the fort are truly magnificent, with **Loop Head** visible to the north, the **Blasket Islands** to the west and the MacGillycuddy's Reeks and the mountains of the Cork/Kerry border to the south and east. However, the weather here is very changeable, and you can quickly go from a clear bright day to being enveloped in thick cloud and mist. Treat this site with the precautions that you would any other serious mountain hike: bring appropriate footwear and clothing, water and food, compass and map, and a phone.

CAHERCONREE

MAP 6

Coordinates:
The fort: Lat. 52.197223, Long. -9.862291
Parking: Lat. 52.188044, Long. -9.877383

Irish Grid Reference: Q 72677 06642

Opening hours/entry fees: No opening hours or entry fees apply, but please ensure you only attempt the walk in good weather conditions.

Directions: To get to Caherconree from Tralee head south-west on the N86 for 16km towards Camp and take the left-hand turn just before the small bridge (with an old signpost for Caher Con Rí). Follow this smaller road as it leads you up into the mountains for 4.5km. You will see signs for Caherconree. Pull in off the road in one of the gravel lay-bys and be sure not to block the road. From the road there are way markers to lead you up as far as the fort (at an altitude of 683m). There is a track leading most of the way. Take care as the ground is wet and boggy in places while the last 200m of ascent are on very steep ground. It will take a little over two hours to walk the 4km to the fort and back to the road. This is not a suitable walk for dogs.

Nearest towns: Tralee (22km), Dingle (35km).

NORTH KERRY AND THE MOUTH OF THE SHANNON

The land becomes somewhat less mountainous and rugged as we head into north Kerry, though the cliffs at Bromore are still a hint that the landscape hasn't quite been tamed.

In the medieval period, the fertile lands of north Kerry were part of an important and influential bishopric centred at Ardfert, where you can still discover the legacy of those holy men. The area also has long beaches, like Ballybunion, perfect for an evening stroll as you imagine what life was like in the castle that perches above the golden strand.

The strategic importance of the Shannon can be seen in the many fortifications, such as this battery at Kilcredaun on Loop Head

The River Shannon has always been integral to the story of Ireland. From hidden pools in Fermanagh and the Shannon Pot in Cavan, it flows, ever growing in strength and scale. It was once the highway that brought pilgrims and scholars to monasteries like Clonmacnoise, and the artery that the Vikings exploited to raid deep inland. As well as a routeway, it has often been a boundary, a demarcation line that could only be crossed with blood and might. By the time it reaches its mouth, the River Shannon has travelled for over 360km (225 miles) and passed through twelve counties (Fermanagh, Cavan, Leitrim, Roscommon, Longford, Offaly, Westmeath, Galway, Clare, Tipperary, Limerick and Kerry). The strategic value of the mouth of the river has long been noticed, and a number of early monasteries flourished here thanks in part to the accessibility for pilgrims, and we also see attempts to defend and control access into the river, with a number of castles and fortifications that guard the banks along the Shannon Estuary, dating from the medieval period all the way to the nineteenth century.

33 | ARDFERT

Ardfert Cathedral

The important ecclesiastical centre of Ardfert is associated with Saint Brendan, one of the key figures in the early Irish church. He is best known as Brendan the Navigator, from the stories of his miraculous and fantastical voyages.

The earliest visible structural evidence at Ardfert is thought to date to around the eleventh century. The northern wall of the cathedral incorporates older masonry work that is likely to have been part of an earlier church, possibly the *daimliag* or stone church that appears in historical records of 1046, which was recorded as being struck by lightning in 1152. Part of the foundations of a round tower can also be seen to the south-west of the cathedral. In the twelfth century Ardfert became the head of a powerful diocese that controlled an area corresponding with much of modern County Kerry.

The ornate Romanesque western doorway of the cathedral

Archaeological excavations revealed parts of a large enclosing ditch that once surrounded the early monastery, along with structural features and evidence of other early medieval activity. Over 2,000 burials were discovered by archaeologists, and analysis of these remains has provided much information about the life of the people of Ardfert throughout the medieval period. One of the skeletons from the twelfth century wore a ring that incorporated

The interior of the cathedral

an antique intaglio setting of cornelian and depicted the Roman goddess Minerva. Three glass beads were found around the skull, perhaps evidence of a bishop's mitre. Other burials contained pilgrim badges from Santiago de Compostela, providing insights into pilgrimage and travel in medieval Ireland.

The **cathedral** has been modified over centuries, and encompasses a variety of architectural features. One of the remarkable features of the cathedral is the western doorway, which is heavily ornamented with Romanesque design.

The central doorway is flanked by two pairs of blind arches, creating a five-bay facade, which may be influenced by the French Romanesque style. This doorway would have been part of the earlier church, but it was incorporated into the thirteenth-century redevelopment of the cathedral. Other interesting features in the cathedral include the handsome Gothic sedilia and matching double piscina, where the priest would ritually wash the holy vessels and his hands during Mass. Three great lancet windows in the eastern wall provide light into the choir, with a series of nine trefoil-headed lancet windows in the south wall. With such details, along with ornamentation and flourishes on the capitals and around the windows, the choir of the cathedral has been described as 'one of the most accomplished pieces of Gothic architecture in Ireland'. The cathedral was altered in the late medieval period with the addition of parapets on top of the wall. The cathedral was burned following the defeat of the Earl of Desmond, Ardfert's chief patron, in the 1580s, and it fell out of use, with the exception of the south transept, which was converted into a parish church in the late seventeenth century. The OPW has restored and conserved the structure of the cathedral, and a visitor centre and exhibition are now housed in the former parish church.

Just to the north-west of the cathedral you can find the interesting twelfth-century church known as Templenahoe. The church has Romanesque design, most clearly seen on a particularly well-preserved window in the south wall that bears beautiful decoration of flowers and geometric designs. Just behind this church you can see Templenagriffin, a small fifteenth-century building that takes its name from a carving of intertwined beasts on the window in the northern wall.

The delicately carved Romanesque window in Templenahoe

Situated a short walk down from the cathedral, **Ardfert Friary** is also well worth exploring. The church of the friary originally dates to the thirteenth century. It was founded in *c.* 1253 by Thomas FitzMaurice, the Lord of Kerry. The friary consists of a church with particularly fine lancet windows, along with the remains of a cloister and domestic buildings to the north. In the late sixteenth century, the tower of the friary was used as a barracks for soldiers. However, a local folktale warns of the dangers of interfering with the friary: a farmer is said to have once taken stone from the friary to repair a field wall. That night he was awoken by a ferocious storm that raged until dawn. The next morning he was shocked to find that none of his neighbours had experienced a storm, and that all had passed a peaceful evening, except him. That night his house was again battered by a dreadful tempest that threatened to collapse the building. While cowering in his bed, he remembered taking stone from the friary, so the next morning he quickly loaded a cart and returned all of the stone back to its original position. No supernatural storms blew on his house again.

Ardfert Friary

The interior of Ardfert Friary

Coordinates:

Cathedral and Visitor Centre: Lat. 52.328439, Long. -9.781789
Friary: Lat. 52.330128, Long. -9.774293

Irish Grid Reference: Q 78589 21099

Opening hours/entry fees: Visit: www.heritageireland.ie/en/shannon-region/
ardfertcathedral

Directions: Ardfert Cathedral is about a fifteen-minute (11km) drive from
Tralee. Take the R551 road north-west from the town to the village of Ardfert.
The cathedral is located in the centre of the village. The friary is situated at
the bottom of the hill north-east of the cathedral. Park in the car park for the
cemetery and proceed on foot past the small row of houses and into the park.

Nearest town: Tralee (11km).

34 | RATTOO ROUND TOWER

Rattoo has one of the finest of all of Ireland's round towers. It
stands some 29.5m (97 feet) tall and is made of beautifully
dressed and warmly coloured sandstone, displaying the skill of
master masons. The tower stands on a platform of masonry, and
it is recorded that it once had a causeway leading from its base;
however, land alterations in the late nineteenth century have been
altered the topography so any causeway has since disappeared.

The round-headed doorway is situated nearly 3m (9.5 feet)
above ground level and is 1.6m (5 feet) high. It has a unique
architectural form for a round tower, featuring a semicircular arch
of three stones ornamented with a simple curvilinear motif in
relief, although it is quite weathered today. Rattoo is also unusual
for having a Sheela-na-gig carved on the top left-hand corner of
the frame of the northern window. There are around 80 Sheela-
na-gigs known in Ireland. They are more commonly found at late
medieval castles, tower houses and churches. The exact meaning
or purpose of Sheela-na-gigs is subject to some debate. Some
believe them to have been fertility symbols, while others believe
their presence was meant to ward off evil spirits.

RATTOO ROUND TOWER

The ruins of a medieval church in a well-kept graveyard are next to the round tower. The early monastery is believed to have been originally founded by Saint Lughach, though the church is likely to date to the fifteenth century.

Rattoo Round Tower

RATTOO

MAP 7

Coordinates: Lat. 52.442463, Long. -9.650559

Irish Grid Reference: Q 87838 33587

Opening hours/entry fees: No opening hours or entry fees applied at the time of visit

Directions: Rattoo Round Tower is just over a twenty-minute (18km) drive from Listowel. Take the R553 north-west towards Ballybunion for 7km. At Lisselton, turn left onto the R554 and join the R551 after 3.5km, turning left. Continue for a further 5km, passing through the village of Ballyduff. Turn left at the signpost for Rattoo Round Tower. Drive 1km down this road to the site.

Nearest town: Listowel (18km).

Ballybunion Castle

Though little remains today of Ballybunion Castle, it is believed to have been the seat of the heirs apparent of the powerful FitzMaurice family from the fourteenth century until the middle of the sixteenth century. It stands on the site of an earlier promontory fort, and commands an unusual rocky crag above a golden stretch of sand. The castle is said to have been badly damaged in a raid by Lord Kerry in 1582 and it was given to the Bunnion family, though their lands, including Ballybunion, were soon confiscated and eventually granted back the the FitzMaurice family. Evidence of the turbulent history of the times was discovered when a network of tunnels, thought to be escape tunnels, were found underneath the castle. These were filled in due to safety considerations. Today only the eastern wall has survived the relentless pounding of time and tide, but it is still enjoyable to walk along the beach and consider what life would have been like here at the court of the FitzMaurices, some six centuries ago.

BALLYBUNION CASTLE

BALLYBUNION CASTLE

MAP 7

Coordinates: Lat. 52.511219, Long. -9.677023

Irish Grid Reference: Q 86163 41346

Opening hours/entry fees: No opening hours or entry fees applied at the time of visit

Directions: Ballybunion Castle is about a twenty-minute (15km) drive from Listowel. Take the R553 north-west towards Ballybunion. In the village centre, bear left at the Bill Clinton statue and proceed along Main Street and Sandhill Road. The castle will be on your right where the road meets the beach.

Nearest town: In Ballybunion. Listowel (15km).

36 | BROMORE CLIFFS

The Cliffs at Bromore

The rugged cliffs of Bromore are home to a number of important archaeological monuments, including a good example of a coastal promontory fort. Relatively few of Ireland's 200 or so promontory forts have been excavated, though they are typically thought to have origins as early as the Late Bronze Age or Iron Age, though those few examples that have been excavated have revealed activity as recent as the early medieval period. The jagged coast of County Kerry is very suited to these defensive structures, as in the case here at Bromore, where only one large rampart and ditch was required to make a near-impregnable fortress, thanks to the sheer cliffs on the other three sides. Whether the promontory fort at Bromore was occupied year round, or whether it served more as a refuge or shelter during times of raiding or conflict we do not know. You can see evidence for the early medieval period here by the presence of a ringfort, known as Lidsoonaflan Ringfort, nearby to the south-west. The strategic location of the promontory led to a lookout tower being constructed on it during the Second World War.

The promontory fort at Bromore

The caverns and caves at the base of the cliffs are also an important habitat for wildlife. A colony of Atlantic grey seals live in the Seals' Caves, and the sea stack known as The Devil's Castle is thought to have been the nesting site of the last native Irish eagles. With a lovely coastal walk, where you can enjoy the bright sea pink flowers and the sounds of the Atlantic, a trip to the Bromore Cliffs is certainly worthwhile.

BROMORE MAP 7

Coordinates: Lat. 52.536195, Long. -9.666809

Irish Grid Reference: Q 86949 44020

Opening hours/entry fees: Although no opening hours applied at the time of visit, there is a requirement to pay for parking. Visit: www.bromorecliffs.com

Directions: The cliffs are located north of Ballybunion, approximately twenty minutes' (18km) drive from Listowel. From Listowel head north-west on the R553 and continue onto the R551 when the roads merge. Stay on the R551 through Ballybunion and turn left at the ruined church (signposted for Bromore Cliffs). Continue on this smaller road for 1.5km and the car park will be on your left. There is an information booth with a local map showing the walking routes and points of interest next to a parking meter.

Nearest town: Listowel (18km)

37 | CARRIGAFOYLE CASTLE

Carrigafoyle Castle is a fine example of a late medieval Irish tower house. It was built by O'Connor Kerry in the late fifteenth or early sixteenth century and stands on the edge of the Shannon Estuary. The stonework of the castle is particularly fine, and the tower stands some five storeys tall, with vaults over the second and fourth storeys. The surrounding bawn wall still partly survives, and one of the turrets has been used as a dovecot for pigeons. A small medieval church is situated on the slope to the west, and appears to date to around the same period as the castle.

Carrigafoyle Castle

A view of Carrigafoyle Castle from the church.

The castle dominates the southern bank of the Shannon Estuary, yet its low-lying position left it vulnerable to attack. In 1580 the castle was captured by Sir William Pelham. He besieged the castle and its garrison, which was made up of Irish and Spanish soldiers in the service of the Earl of Desmond. He took the castle after only three days, when he attacked with artillery from the low hill to the west. The artillery made short work of the western wall, and the outnumbered garrison were overrun and massacred. The Earl of Desmond's valuables were plundered and sent as trophies to Queen Elizabeth I.

CARRIGAFOYLE

MAP 7

Coordinates: Lat. 52.569660, Long. -9.494706

Irish Grid Reference: Q 98747 47514

Opening hours/entry fees: No opening hours or entry fees applied at the time of visit, though the interior of the castle may be open during daylight hours in the summer months

Directions: Carrigafoyle Castle is about a twenty-minute (16km) drive from Listowel. Take the R552 north for 12km to Ballylongford village. Turn left in Ballylongford village onto the R551, signposted Ballybunion. Continue for just under 1km and then turn right, signposted Carrigafoyle Castle. Continue for another 2.5km and the castle will be on your right

Nearest town: Listowel (16km).

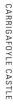

CARRIGAFOYLE CASTLE

Lislaughtin Friary

In 1477, John O'Connor requested permission from Pope Sixtus IV to found this Franciscan friary in his demesne. The Franciscans were founded by Saint Francis of Assisi (who died in 1226). As an order they adhered strictly to vows of poverty and service. The O'Connors had a beautiful processional cross crafted for the friary in 1479. Now known as the Ballymacasey Cross, this ornate cross in the Late Gothic style was rediscovered when it was unearthed in 1871 by a man ploughing his field. The cross was likely to have been buried deliberately to hide it from English soldiers. These were the same soldiers led by Sir William Pelham who had captured **Carrigafoyle Castle** (Site 37) and who then moved to raid the friary here at Lislaughtin. Most of the friars and priests fled, and carried what they could with them. It is possible that the cross was too difficult to conceal and to travel with so perhaps it was hidden with the intention of retrieving it later, or perhaps the one who concealed the cross was captured or killed. It is also possible that it was hidden by one of three elderly men – Donagh O'Hanrahan, Philip O'Shea and Maurice O'Scanlon – who could not, or would not, run. They took refuge in the church, but the sanctity of this holy place did not protect them; they were killed by the English soldiers, who then plundered the friary. However, the raiders never discovered the cross. It remained buried close by until it was

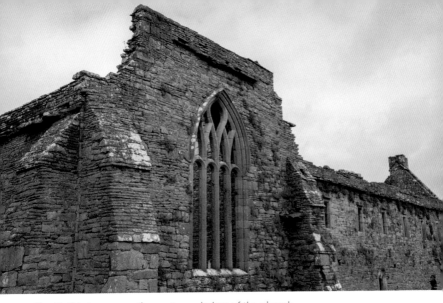

Fine Gothic tracery on the eastern window of the church

unearthed by chance 400 years later. Today, the beautiful cross is on display in the National Museum of Ireland in Kildare Street, Dublin.

The church is one of the better-preserved buildings on site, and has a north transept, a triple sedilia (formal seating for the priests during Mass) and two tomb niches. Other visible features of the friary include the cloister and the partial ruins of domestic buildings, and the original medieval gateway. The sacred ground of the medieval abbey is still in use as a graveyard to this day, and modern headstones stand side by side with more ancient ruins.

LISLAUGHTIN FRIARY

MAP 7

Coordinates: Lat. 52.557120, Long. -9.469537

Irish Grid Reference: R 00354 46084

Opening hours/entry fees: No opening hours or entry fees applied at the time of visit.

Directions: Lislaughtin Friary is about a twenty-minute (14km) drive from Listowel. Take the R552 north for 12km to Ballylongford village. Go straight across at the crossroads in Ballylongford village centre, signposted Lislaughtin. Continue for just over 1km and turn left through the gateway, also signposted Lislaughtin. The friary is 100m down this road.

Nearest town: Listowel (14km)

LISLAUGHTIN FRIARY

39 | FOYNES FLYING BOAT MUSEUM

This small port on the Shannon Estuary was once the hub of early transatlantic air travel, and the excellent Flying Boat and Maritime Museum tells the story with exhibitions, film and lots of interactive activities as well as a full-size replica of a flying boat.

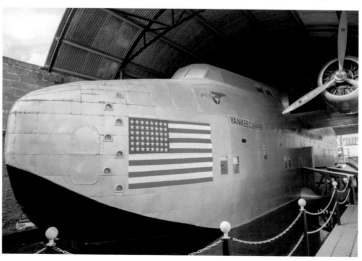

Replica of a flying boat

After Alcock and Brown proved the possibility of non-stop transatlantic flights (see **Derrigimlagh Bog**, Site 51), aviation companies in the United States and Europe began to assess the potential for a regular transatlantic passenger service. During the 1920s and 1930s, land-based passenger planes lacked the sufficient range, so the famous aviator Charles Lindbergh was commissioned to assess suitable locations for a flying boat port in Ireland. His identification of Foynes would result in this small town becoming one of the most important civilian airports in Europe during the 1940s. Work began on the terminal at Foynes in 1935, and services began from 1937.

Four main airlines flew through Foynes: Pan-American Airways, Imperial Airways, American Export Airlines and Air France Transatlantique. They all flew different types of flying boat, including Boeing-314, Sikorsky VS-44, and Latécoère

521. At this time, air travel was extremely expensive, and many of the aircraft were akin to luxury cruise liners. The very top of Hollywood's A-list landed at Foynes, including Humphrey Bogart and Bob Hope. The museum's full-size replica of a B-314 allows you to experience what a journey on one of these marvellous aircraft would have been like.

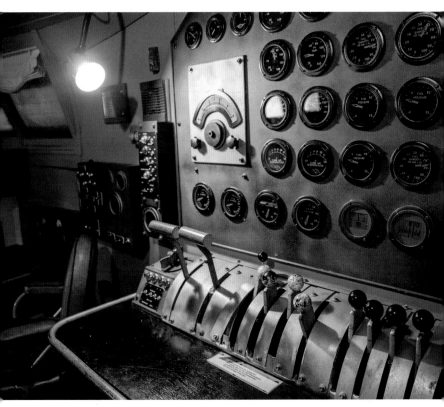

A control station within the flying boat

During the war years, Ireland was a neutral country, but many important politicians and high-ranking military of the United States passed through Foynes. It also became an important conduit for refugees fleeing occupied territories of Europe and North Africa on the way to seek safety and a new life in the United States. You can watch a video on the story in the museum's 1940s-style cinema.

As well as being a true pioneer in air travel, Foynes can also claim to be the place where the world-famous Irish coffee was first created to help comfort passengers during the bleak winter of 1943. You can try the authentic drink for yourself at the Irish Coffee Centre in the museum, and watch a holographic scene that tells the story of the invention of this renowned drink. After the end of the Second World War, the focus turned to land planes, with development of today's airports like Shannon and Dublin. With land planes able to carry more passengers for greater distances, it was the end of the era for the flying boats. The station at Foynes closed in 1946.

Foynes – the Centre of the World!

FOYNES FLYING BOAT MUSEUM MAP 7

Coordinates: Lat. 52.611581, Long. -9.109658

Irish Grid Reference: R 24882 51681

Opening hours/entry fees: Visit: www.flyingboatmuseum.com

Directions: The museum is located on the N69 (Main Street) of Foynes.

Nearest town: In Foynes.

40 | SCATTERY ISLAND

Scattery Island lies in the Shannon Estuary in County Clare. The island was inhabited until the late 1970s, and you can still see the fields, boreens and deserted buildings left by the islanders. Today, it is quite overgrown, though fortunate visitors might catch a glimpse of the resident hen harriers of the island that prey upon the multitude of rabbits that have made the island their home. As well as abundant wildlife, the island is rich in historical sites, with an important collection of monastic and church remains associated with Saint Senan. He was an influential figure in the early Irish Church, and is credited with being the tutor of Ciarán of Clonmacnoise. When he was a very young child, he showed wisdom and erudition far beyond his years and so his mother named him Senan, meaning 'The Old'. He is credited with many miraculous feats. Perhaps the most famous of his stories is the battle with the monster of Scattery Island. In Irish, Scattery Island is called *Inis Cathaigh* (meaning the Cathach's Island). This refers to the legend of the Cathach, a large serpent-like monster that made the island its lair. The Cathach was a menace to all who approached the island, and regularly attacked boats to devour the sailors, who were helpless in the face of the monster's ferocity. Saint Senan was said to have faced the Cathach with his arms spread wide in prayer. He banished the monster to a lake called *Dubhloch*, near Mount Callan, and some believe that it lurks in the dark depths of the lake to this day.

Scattery Island Visitor Centre

Teampall na Marbh

Scattery was raided and eventually settled by the Vikings, until it was recaptured by Brian Boru in AD 977, when Brian's forces stormed the island and slew Ímar and his sons as part of a campaign to drive the Norse from Limerick. However, the island was raided again in 1101 by the famous Magnus 'Barelegs', King of Norway. Despite this turmoil, the monastery on Scattery Island continued to develop and grow in importance, through the continued patronage of the Dál Cais kings.

There are a number of archaeological sites on the island. Near the shore you can see the lower levels of a small tower house, called **Keane's Castle**, which once protected the landing place. A late medieval church known as **Teampall na Marbh** ('the church of the dead') stands further along the path. This rather plain, rectangular church may have been constructed around the same time as the castle as part of sixteenth-century development on the island. The graveyard that surrounds it has a number of interesting headstones and is still in use today.

The main monastic remains can be seen further along the path towards the interior of the island. **Saint Mary's Cathedral** is the largest church on the island. It has distinctive antae (small projections of the side walls beyond the gable walls). The building has been extensively modified throughout the centuries, and it was extended and embellished by Brian Boru and his descendants. The relative grandeur of the building reflects the importance of the Bishop of Inis Cathaigh, who once held sway over a large diocese that incorporated parts of Clare, Limerick and Kerry. A representation of a bishop's head wearing a mitre can be seen on the outer wall at the apex of the eastern window; it is positioned above two snarling animals that may be a fantastical reimagining of aspects of the beast that Saint Senan defeated. The last Bishop of Inis Cathaigh died in 1188, and following the Norman conquest of the region, the once-famed monastery began to fall into decline. The diocese of Inis Cathaigh was broken up and its territories absorbed into the dioceses of Killaloe, Limerick and Ardfert. A small nave-and-chancel church stands immediately north of the cathedral, the Romanesque-style features of it suggesting a twelfth-century date.

Saint Mary's Cathedral and Round Tower

The **round tower** is one of the best examples in Ireland. It stands some 26m (85 feet) tall, and unusually it has its doorway at ground level, one of only two (along with Castledermot in Kildare) to have a ground-floor entrance. The tower is likely to have been constructed some time between the tenth and eleventh centuries. Its conical cap appears stunted, suggesting it may have been damaged in the past, by lightning or strong winds. With the doorway at ground level, it affords a rare opportunity for a visitor to look up all the way to the top, allowing a view of where the floors would once have been secured, as well as the light bleeding in from the small windows.

Saint Senan's Church

Not far to the west of the round tower you can see Saint Senan's Well, which legend says appeared when the saint plunged his staff into the ground whilst praying for water during a drought. The well still features in pilgrimage, and it is visited during the pattern on 8 March, Senan's feast day.

Fragmentary traces of the drystone cashel wall that once enclosed the monastery can be seen to the north. By following along the path to the north visitors can see **St Senan's Church**, a small twelfth- or thirteenth-century church. A smaller church, known as Saint Senan's Bed, adjoins the larger church and it is believed to have been constructed over the grave of the saint. This church has a local tradition that forbids women from entering.

Apparently it holds a curse that any woman who goes inside will never have a happy marriage or bear children. Behind the church you can see an interesting ninth- or tenth-century cross slab, which bears an interlaced Latin cross and an inscription that seeks a prayer for Móenach, teacher (*aite*) of Mugrón.

The highest point of the island is known as *Cnoc an Aingeal* ('the hill of the angel') and it is marked by a small church. According to legend, it was to here that an angel carried Saint Senan to do battle with the Cathach.

The lighthouse and artillery battery

A large artillery battery that once protected the mouth of the Shannon was established on the southern tip of the island. It was built by the British army in 1814, as part of a fortification of Ireland's coastline during the Napoleonic Wars. It once would have housed up to eight heavy cannon, and along with the battery at **Kilcredaun** on **Loop Head** (Site 41), it would have been a formidable obstacle to any hostile ships. A lighthouse stands nearby. As Scattery is in such an important position at the mouth of the Shannon Estuary, there have been a series of lighthouses on the island dating back as far as the 1680s to help to protect shipping. The current lighthouse was built in 1872. Today, the lighthouse is fully automated and solar-powered.

Coordinates: (Kilrush Marina) Lat. 52.635229, Long. -9.494398

Irish Grid Reference: Q 97450 52452

Opening hours/entry fees: Visit: www.heritageireland.ie/en/shannon-region/scatteryislandcentre/

For information, times and fees for the ferry visit: www.scatteryislandtours.com

Directions: Scattery Island is a 2.5km boat journey from Kilrush Marina. The marina is located on Merchant's Quay approximately 500m south-west of Market Square in Kilrush. There are daily crossings to the island between May and September.

Nearest town: Kilrush.

41 | LOOP HEAD PENINSULA

The outstretched finger of the Loop Head Peninsula contains a host of stories to discover. The peninsula forms the northern boundary of the mouth of the Shannon Estuary, and so Loop Head has been an important and strategic location for millennia. This is borne out by a plethora of diverse historical sites.

Loop Head Lighthouse

The breathtaking scenery of Loop Head

Loop Head is important not only to humans: it is one of the most varied natural habitats in Europe with a myriad of rare plants and animals, which can be seen along its coastline. The range of environments, from beaches, cliffs, salt marshes, mudflats and hedgerows are home to a wide variety of flora and fauna. Loop Head is recognised as one of the best locations in the world to see a many different species of resident and migratory seabirds. Despite its relatively small size, the Loop Head Peninsula has

long been a popular place for visitors, an unspoiled paradise that boasts incredible scenery, authentic charm and a warm welcome.

Visitors to Loop Head may wish to start at the **West Clare Railway Museum**. The railway was truly revolutionary for the inhabitants of Loop Head. It brought wealth, because it allowed the export of cattle, horses, pigs and thousands of tonnes of hand-cut turf to markets in Ennis, Limerick and beyond. It also brought thousands of visitors to experience the delights of Loop Head.

The strategic importance of Loop Head is reflected in the ruins of **Carrigaholt Castle**. This handsome tower house still stands proudly on a headland. It is thought to date to around the late fifteenth century, and it was the seat of the MacMahon family, who were chieftains of Corca Baiscinn (a territory roughly comprising southern County Clare).

Carrigaholt Castle

Seven ships from the ill-fated Spanish Armada anchored here in the estuary in September 1588, as they attempted to regroup to sail home following their defeat by the English. The Spanish fleet had been battered by ferocious storms, and the beleaguered survivors anchored in the estuary to carry out running repairs to enable them to get home. Some of the crew attempted to land, though they received little support from the locals, as the English authorities had declared that they would execute anyone who offered aid to the Spanish. Six of the ships set sail again shortly after, though one, the *Annunciada*, was so badly damaged in the storms that it was beyond repair. To stop the *Annunciada* falling into English hands, the crew set her on fire before returning to Spain on the other ships.

The last MacMahon chieftain to occupy Carrigaholt was Teige Caech, or Teige the Blind. He joined the rebellion against Elizabeth I during the Nine Years' War, and with his experienced seafaring fighters, he managed to capture an English vessel in the Shannon Estuary in 1598. Making the most of this turbulent time, he launched a series of raids to capture livestock and loot the lands of those who sided with Queen Elizabeth, including an attack on Donnell O'Brien, brother of the Earl of Thomond. In retaliation, the Earl laid siege to Carrigaholt and executed many of MacMahon's followers. For their role in the rebellion, the MacMahons forfeited their lands, and Carrigaholt was given to their O'Brien enemies. Donal O'Brien inherited Carrigaholt, and he made a number of alterations to the castle. However, by the end of the century, the O'Briens found themselves in political strife, when Daniel O'Brien, Viscount of Clare, supported King James at the Battle of the Boyne. After James's defeat to William of Orange, the O'Briens lost their lands. The land and Carrigaholt Castle were granted to the Burton family who resided in the castle until the nineteenth century. Today, Carrigaholt is a popular place for fishing, water sports, and dolphin watching.

Kilcredaun is located further along the peninsula. It takes its name from Saint Credaun, a contemporary of Saint Senan of **Scattery Island** (Site 40). He is associated with the two churches on the headland. Now in ruins, these churches appear to date to the early medieval period. One was modified in the twelfth century, when a finely decorated Romanesque window was inserted into its wall. When the church fell out of use, it became a graveyard. A holy well is found on the shoreline near one of the churches. This well is said to have miraculous properties. It too is dedicated to Saint Credaun, and its waters are said to cure many ailments. Every high tide the well is filled with salt water, but it refills with fresh water when the tide retreats. A cave close to the well was used as a place of prayer for people with relatives lost at sea. Nearby you can see a coastal battery that dates from the Napoleonic Wars between Britain and France. This battery was constructed in 1814, as part of a large-scale fortification of the British and Irish coastline to prevent a French invasion. It is a twin to the battery on **Scattery Island** and together they formed a formidable challenge to any enemy.

At low tide at **Rinevella Bay** it is possible to see the stumps of Scots pine trees from an ancient forest. The remains of the trees were preserved by deposits of peat and estuarine clay that built up over millennia, though the endless washing of the tides has eroded away the peat, leaving the tree stumps visible at low tide. The trees are part of what would have been an attractive landscape for Ireland's earliest inhabitants. The mixed zones of woodland, estuary and fertile soils would have attracted settlement and activity throughout the prehistoric period. Evidence for this can be seen with the discovery of Neolithic settlements, tombs and artefacts along this coastline. Local folklore tells of a lost village, Cill Stuifín, that is visible off the coast of Rinevella every seven years. Cill Stuifín was said to have been engulfed by waves and drowned. The disaster may be historically documented in the ancient Annals of Ireland, which recount that, in the year 804, 'there happened great wind, thunder and lightning on the day before the festival of Patrick this year, so that 1010 persons were killed in the territory of Corca Bhaiscinn'. Today folklore warns that fairies now inhabit the place, and anyone who glimpses the doomed village will suffer misfortune.

At the tip of **Loop Head** itself you can enjoy a spectacular vista. To the south you can see the relatively calm waters of the Shannon Estuary, in comparison to the north where the restless waters of the Atlantic pound against the spectacular cliffs. With such otherworldly beauty, Loop Head has become the setting for many legends and folktales. The sea stack off the coast is known as Diarmuid and Gráinne's Rock, and is said to be one of the places the young couple took refuge whilst they were fleeing Fionn MacCumhaill; it is also a setting for tales of the legendary warrior Cú Chulainn, who used the sea stack to escape an amorous admirer, the powerful cailleach (wise woman) Mal.

The undisturbed cliffs here are a haven for a variety of seabirds, including kittiwakes, guillemots and razorbills. It is a great place to observe the passage of migratory birds, and to watch the waters for the numerous whales and dolphins.

The lighthouse on Loop Head is one of 70 around the coast of Ireland. There was a lighthouse here as early as 1670 and in those days the signal consisted of a coal fire contained in a brazier on the roof of a single-storey cottage. The present lighthouse became operational in 1854. It was designed by George Halpin, who also designed Kilcredaun Lighthouse. It stands 23m (75 feet) and four storeys high. Changes and improvements were made throughout the nineteenth and twentieth centuries. Today the lighthouse is fully automated, with the last keeper having been withdrawn in 1991.

On the road back to the north-east, the lovely **Church of the Little Ark** is well worth a stop, before enjoying the scenery at the **Bridges of Ross**. This is a natural formation known as a sea arch where the waves have undercut the land to leave a natural bridge-like feature. There were three arches here once upon a time, but two were eroded in the past century and have collapsed into the sea. The cliffs afford an opportunity to view the sedimentary geology of the area, where different layers of rock have been folded and tilted over millions of years. The beautiful scenery around the Bridges of Ross was featured in David Lean's famous film *Ryan's Daughter*, starring Robert Mitchum.

Church of the Little Ark

The coastal path along the Kilkee Cliffs, with Bishop's Island visible in the distance

I highly recommend talking the coastal path from the charming town of **Kilkee** to see the spectacular cliffs and for a view of Bishop's Island. The remains of an early Christian monastery can still be seen on the island, amongst which you can see the ruins of a drystone church that was constructed in a similar style to the famous **Gallarus Oratory** (Site 30) on the Dingle Peninsula in County Kerry. It is likely that these church buildings were associated with Saint Senan's monastery on Scattery Island, on the other side of the peninsula. There is a local legend relating to the name Bishop's Island. In the nineteenth century, a bishop tried to escape the Great Famine by bringing food to the island. He became trapped on the sea stack and starved to death. The sea stack was subsequently named '*Oileán an Easpaig Gortaigh*' ('the island of the hungry bishop').

LOOP HEAD LIGHTHOUSE

MAP 8

Coordinates: Lat. 52.560999, Long. -9.930047

Irish Grid Reference: Q 69159 47213

Opening hours/entry fees: For information about Loop Head, visit www. loophead.ie.

Directions: The Loop Head Peninsula is certainly worth a day trip, and you can find great food and drink (and accommodation) in Kilkee and all along the peninsula. To drive straight from Kilkee to the lighthouse at the tip of Loop Head is approximately 30 minutes straight down the R487. See Map 8 for details of how to see the various stops along the way.

Nearest town: Kilkee (26km).

LOOP HEAD PENINSULA

WILD PLACES: FROM THE CLIFFS OF MOHER TO THE BURREN

The wildness of the Wild Atlantic Way certainly becomes apparent as you explore this elemental, soul-stirring part of Ireland.

The Cliffs of Moher are one of the most instantly recognisable and visited places in the country, but no matter how many times you see photographs or video of the cliffs, no matter how familiar and almost stereotypical they seem, each time you see them with your own eyes you feel smaller, vulnerable, awed by the sheer scale of the truly abrupt terminus to the land.

This part of Clare is rightly famed for its influential music tradition, and you can experience authentic sessions in the wonderful villages and towns like Miltown Malbay, Lahinch, Quilty, Ennistymon and Doolin.

Further north, you enter the unique landscape of the Burren. One of my favourite places on earth, the Burren is like an otherworld. Its cold, grey limestone plateaus are patchworked with green oases and dotted with colourful and delicate wildflowers in the spring and summer. The Burren is home to a vast array of monuments representing almost every era of humanity in Ireland. The Wild Atlantic Way just skirts the very edge of this wonderland, but it well worth taking your time to explore the full region. The town of Ballyvaughan is an idyllic place to base yourself, and it contains another priceless cultural treasure: O'Loclainn's Pub.

The great Seamus Heaney once perfectly described a visit to Clare's Flaggy Shore and the magic of the blustery Atlantic weather in his poem 'Postscript' (1996):

As big soft buffetings come at the car sideways
And catch the heart off guard and blow it open.

The unique landscape of the Burren has been shaped by millennia of human activity

....

42 | THE CLIFFS OF MOHER

The Cliffs of Moher have become one of Ireland's most popular visitor attractions and a truly iconic landmark. The cliffs soar 120m (390 feet) above the roaring Atlantic, and they are so dramatic in their appearance that they featured as the feared Cliffs of Insanity in the popular fantasy adventure film *The Princess Bride* (1987), and in *Harry Potter and the Half-Blood Prince* (2009) as the exterior of a enchanted cave containing a Horcrux.

The visitor centre contains interactive exhibitions that detail the geology and wildlife of the cliffs, with information about the colonies of the tens of thousands of seabirds that make the dizzying cliffs their home. Visitors can enjoy the spectacular Cliff Walk (though please be sure to take the official path as the

The Cliffs of Moher

unofficial path that tracks along the cliff edge is prone to collapse and is highly dangerous). On the walk you will encounter O'Brien's Tower, a folly constructed in 1835 as a viewing area for visitors by the enterprising local landlord Sir Cornellius O'Brien. Local stories tell that he had the tower built as a romantic retreat to impress a local lady he was courting. If the weather conditions are favourable you can enjoy an unforgettable view of the cliffs from the water on a boat tour (boats available from Doolin).

O'Brien's Tower

The name of the cliffs derives from An Mothar, originally known as *Mothar Uí Ruaín* ('the ruin of Ó Ruaín'). It refers to a stone fort that was located near Hag's Head.

The towering cliffs viewed from the Atlantic

Coordinates: Lat. 52.972539, Long. -9.423246

Irish Grid Reference: R 04213 92154

Opening hours/entry fees: The Cliffs of Moher are one of Ireland's most visited attractions, particularly in peak season. I recommend visiting either early in the morning, or after 4 p.m. to enjoy the site after the coach tours leave. Otherwise, you can book your ticket in advance. Visit www.cliffsofmoher.ie.

Directions: The cliffs are located just north of the village of Liscannor. From Lahinch take a right turn just after the Santa Maria Hotel onto the R478 (signposted Cliffs of Moher). Continue on this road for approximately 4km until you reach the village of Liscannor. Continue through the village and follow the R478 past the petrol station. Follow the road as it winds up a hill, passing Murphy's and Considine's pubs. Continue on this road (taking due care of the many pedestrians and cyclists that you may encounter) and the entrance to the car park is on the right-hand side of the road.

Nearest town: Lahinch (10.5km).

43 | CAHERDOONERISH STONE FORT

Caherdoonerish Stone Fort

Set high on a ridge at Black Head, the stone fort of Caherdoonerish commands breathtaking views over Galway Bay and as far as the Aran Islands. Like the majority of stone forts in the region, Caherdoonerish is likely to date to the early medieval period. It has an unusual D-shape plan. In places the drystone walls stand nearly 3.6m (12 feet) high, though most of the walls are in a precarious condition. The name Caherdoonerish derives from the Irish *Cathair Dhúin Irghuis*, which translates to 'the fort of Irghuis'. Irghuis was a chief of the legendary Firbolg. This area abounds in folklore, and the headland is said to be one of the haunts of the banshee Bronach the Sorrowful. As you stand at this atmospheric site and take in the view, it is easy to imagine that the otherworld is truly close at hand.

CAHERDOONERISH   MAP 9

Coordinates:

Fort: 53.146883, Long. -9.258976
Parking: 53.153632, Long. -9.262660

Irish Grid Reference: M 15812 11401

Opening hours/entry fees: No entry fees or opening hours applied at the time of visit.

Directions: Caherdoonerish is set high above Black Head and it is quite a steep climb, so be sure to wear appropriate boots and that weather conditions are good before attempting it. From Ballyvaughan head west on the R477 for 9.5km and I recommend you park just before (or opposite) Blackhead Lighthouse. There is a long looped walk you can take but if you are in a rush I recommend simply walking straight up the steep slope. Beware as it is easy to twist an ankle on the unforgiving Burren limestone. Keep walking upwards for about 30 minutes (that will depend on how many times you stop to take in the sensational views!), across a small lane and continue straight up until you reach the fort. If you have any breath left after the steep walk, the views will take it.

Nearest town: Ballyvaughan (9.5km).

Gleninagh Castle

Hidden away down a secluded and winding track, Gleninagh Castle is an atmospheric place to escape the tourist traffic. It is a fine example of an Irish tower house, and it is thought to date to around the fifteenth century. The castle has a L-shape with the projection containing the entrance and spiral staircase. The tower was well defended with a series of machicolations, musket holes and arrow loops. During its heyday, the tower was likely to have been whitewashed, and the white tower contrasting with the grey rocky shore would have been a strong visual statement on the landscape.

The castle was built by the O'Loughlins, who called themselves the 'Princes of the Burren'. It changed hands a number of times over the centuries but the castle ended up back with the O'Loughlins until it fell out of use as a domestic dwelling in the nineteenth century. When John O'Donovan and Eugene Curry visited Gleninagh during work on the Ordnance Survey in 1839, it was noted that the once-proud castle had been thatched with straw to make a barn for cattle, giving it a 'homely appearance'.

The atmospheric laneway that leads to Gleninagh Castle

A holy well is located close to the castle, and presumably it was the main water source for the garrison. A nineteenth-century account details that the well once contained some unusual features: 'Upon an offset in the wall, within the interior, are human skulls, and round flat stones, resembling cakes of home-made bread.' There is still a tradition of pilgrimage to the well, as it is said to provide a cure for eye ailments.

The well at Gleninagh Castle

MAP 9

GLENINAGH

Coordinates: Lat. 53.136276, Long. -9.205706

Irish Grid Reference: M 19348 10337

Opening hours/entry fees: No entry fees or opening hours applied at the time of visit.

Directions: Gleninagh Castle is just over a five-minute (4.5km) drive from Ballyvaughan. Leaving Ballyvaughan, take the R477 north-west with the coast on your right. Just after a small cottage on the right, there is a laneway leading to the right with iron gates facing you. The castle is about 400m down this laneway. Drive to the end of the very narrow lane and park. You need to walk through a field to reach the castle.

Nearest town: Ballyvaughan (4.5km).

45 | CORCOMROE ABBEY

Corcomroe Abbey

The chancel

Corcomroe Abbey is located in a green valley surrounded by the grey limestone landscape of the Burren. The Latin name for Corcomroe – *Petra Fertilis* (the Fertile Stone) suggests that the land was productive. The abbey is believed to have been founded by Donal Mór O'Brien, King of Thomond, in *c.* 1194. It was home to a small community of monks that originated in the Cistercian foundation of Inislounaght (near modern day Clonmel, County Tipperary). Today, the church is the most significant visible remains of the abbey. It dates to the early thirteenth century, and though smaller than other Cistercian churches, the quality of the stonework and architecture is still very high, particularly at the eastern end of the building where you can see carved capitals with delicate designs of flowers and decorative bases.

Some of the delicate architectural flourishes and detail in the chancel

It is believed that this was the work of master masons known as 'The School of the West'. The roof has fine rib vaulting with an unusual herringbone design that is uncommon in Ireland. You can also see a beautiful example of a sedile with faint traces of paint on the remains of the plaster, and the effigy of King Conor na Suidane O'Brien who was buried here in 1268. On the wall near the tomb you can also see an effigy of an abbot.

In contrast to the elaborate chancel area, the nave of the church is rather plain and austere, and may represent the financial difficulties that Corcomroe faced in later periods. In 1544, following the Dissolution of the Monasteries, the lands and abbey of Corcomroe were in the hands of Murrough O'Brien, a descendant of the O'Brien who founded the monastery some 350 years earlier. Outside the church and in the surrounding fields, you can see partial remnants of other buildings associated with the abbey, like the ruin of a gatehouse and fragments of the precinct walls.

The effigy of King Conor na Suidane O'Brien

CORCOMROE ABBEY   MAP 9

Coordinates: Lat. 53.126468, Long. -9.054296

Irish Grid Reference: M 29472 08923

Opening hours/entry fees: No entry fees or opening hours applied at the time of visit.

Directions: From Ballyvaughan, follow the N67 as it heads north-east until you get to the village of Bealaclugga. Where the road splits into a Y, leave the N67 and bear right onto the L1016 (Abbey Road) for 300m, then turn left (signposted for Corcomroe Abbey). Continue on this road for 1.5km and you will reach the car park for the site.

Nearest town: Ballyvaughan (9km).

46 | OUGHTMAMA CHURCHES

Nestled in a fertile pocket of land at the foot of Turlough Hill, Oughtmama is one of the best examples of early medieval ecclesiastical heritage in the Burren. It is associated with three early saints, each named Colmán. John O'Donovan of the Ordnance Survey described Oughtmama as 'one of the most beautiful of the early Irish Churches I have ever seen', and it truly is an enchanting and atmospheric place.

The two churches within the inner enclosure of Oughtmama

The site consists of two near-concentric enclosures containing three churches. The innermost enclosure surrounds two churches, and a small church lies a short distance away in the outer enclosure. The largest of the three churches has a nave and chancel. This is likely to have been the principal church of the monastery, and probably served as the place of worship for the monks and the lay community. It is likely that it was a single-celled church originally, with the chancel added in a later period. Architectural features in the nave suggest that its origins predate the twelfth century. The small chapel close to the larger church may have had a certain significance for the veneration of a founding saint. The church that is located in the outer enclosure may have been a chapel exclusively for the use of women. In the surrounding fields, archaeologists have identified the traces of a medieval mill race and small paddocks, which provide further evidence of the complexity and importance of this early monastic foundation. The church continued in use up until at least the later medieval period, though it appears that the monastery had lost significance after the foundation of Corcomroe Abbey nearby.

The small church in the outer enclosure

OUGHTMAMA MAP 9

Coordinates: (Churches) 53.117010, Long. -9.038481

Irish Grid Reference: M 30516 07855

Opening hours/entry fees: No entry fees or opening hours applied at the time of visit, but please seek permission to cross the fields.

Directions: From Ballyvaughan follow the N67 as it heads north-east until you get to the village of Bealaclugga. Where the road splits into a Y, leave the N67 and bear right onto the L1016 (Abbey Road), passing through Bellharbour until you get to a T-junction. Turn left (signposted Kinvarra, Galway) onto the L1014 and continue on this road for 1.5km, then turn right. Continue to follow this narrow road as it turns into a boreen. The hills will rise to your left and the ground sweeps down to your right as you continue to follow the road. The churches are at the bottom of a field down to your right. You should just be able to see the tops of the gables of the larger church. Park your car as unobtrusively as possible and walk through the field to the churches (please seek permission if possible).

Nearest town: Ballyvaughan (11km).

GALWAY, CONNEMARA AND THE ARAN ISLANDS

Boats moored alongside the pier at Inis Mór

Galway is a fun and vibrant city, with a long tradition and history to be discovered. Diving into the music and spirit of the city is always a rewarding experience.

The stunning region of Connemara is in some senses like a wilder version of Ireland in miniature, with deep bogs with their shining mirror-like pools of water, mountain ranges and a rugged coast. It is a wild and somewhat desolate area. The interior land of Connemara is difficult to farm, wild and scanty, so the focus has long been on the sea. The Connemara National Park boasts true wilderness. This is an ancient place, with megalithic tombs and Bronze Age alignments marking natural features in the landscape.

The Aran Islands off the coast have inspired many poets, writers and painters through the centuries. They abound with the remains of ancient monasteries founded by early saints, and enormous monumental forts that still hold the capacity to inspire awe in visitors to this day.

47 | DUNGUAIRE CASTLE

Surely amongst the most photographed castles in Ireland, the picturesque Dunguaire Castle has long been a popular stop for visitors. Its location is as strategic as it is scenic, atop a small raised knoll surrounded by the waters of Galway Bay on three sides and connected to the mainland by a narrow causeway. The castle was constructed in *c.* 1520, and is believed to have been built on the site of the *dún* (or fort) of Guaire, a seventh-century king of Connacht. This gives the castle its name, Dún Guaire. The sixteenth-century castle is thought to have been a seat of the Ó hEidhin (O'Hyne) family, who were the regional rulers.

In 1924 Dunguaire Castle was purchased and renovated by Oliver St John Gogarty, a man of incredibly varied talents and interests, who was immortalised as Buck Mulligan in James Joyce's novel *Ulysses*. Gogarty was a well-known literary figure, and the castle became the setting for many meetings of the literary revivalists such as Lady Gregory, W.B. Yeats, George Bernard Shaw and J.M. Synge.

In 1954 the castle was acquired by Christobel Lady Amptill, who completed the restoration started by Oliver St John Gogarty. In more recent years, the castle was purchased by Shannon Development, who have developed the castle into a visitor centre to give you an insight into the life of people who lived and worked for the castle from its foundation to modern times. Popular banquets and entertainment are a regular event in the castle from April to October.

Dunguaire Castle

48 | GALWAY CITY

Galway is one of Ireland's liveliest cities, with a great music scene and terrific restaurants and nightlife. Galway's unique heritage is still a living feature of the city, and even to this day, the legacy of its medieval past is cherished. One of the most famous aspects of Galway's past is the so-called 'Tribes of Galway'. These were fourteen prominent merchant families who were influential in Galway's development, politics and commerce for hundreds of years, particularly from the thirteenth century until the middle of the seventeenth century. The families were Athy, Blake, Bodkin, Browne, D'Arcy, Deane, Font, Ffrench, Joyce, Kirwan, Lynch, Martin, Morris and Skerritt. The majority of the families were of Anglo-Norman descent, and they grew wealthy from trade. They helped to develop Galway into one of medieval Europe's significant trading ports. However, the families suffered significantly after they supported the Irish Confederacy in the rebellions of the middle of the seventeenth century. Galway was besieged by Cromwell's forces and following the surrender of the city, the prosperous merchant families lost much of their possessions and property in confiscations. The families briefly returned to prominence following the restoration of the monarchy with King Charles II, but following their support of King James during the Williamite Wars they lost power once again after King William's victory, and their influence waned. However, even to this day they are recalled in the nickname of Galway's GAA teams – the Tribesmen.

Colourful Quay Street in Galway city

Walking through the streets of Galway, it is possible to catch glimpses of the medieval buildings that are, for the most part, hidden behind modern facades. The origins of the city really began with the Anglo-Norman de Burgh family, when Richard de Burgh was granted lands in Connacht. He defeated the O'Connors, the Gaelic kings of Connacht, in 1235 and built his castle on the site of a former O'Connor stronghold that commanded an important crossing point of the River Corrib. The castle formed the nucleus of the growing town of Galway. Though little exists of the castle today, apart from the remains of the large medieval building known as the **Hall**

The Tribes of Galway are still celebrated in the city

Lynch's Castle

of the Red Earl, which was discovered by archaeologists during work to extend the office of the Revenue Commissioners. This building was probably the great hall of the original castle of Galway. It is associated with Richard de Burgh (d. 1326, grandson of the aforementioned Richard), who was known as the Red Earl, one of the most powerful figures in the region at the time. The hall would have been the centre of administration, justice and power for the city and its hinterland, a place where taxes and duties were collected, and a place of feasting and entertainment. Analysis has revealed a number of architectural phases in the building, showing its adaptation over time. With the decline of the de Burgh family's power and influence, it is likely that the building began to fall into disrepair as the power in the city shifted. The hall was recorded as being in ruins by 1556 and around a hundred years later, it was swallowed up by newer buildings, until it was rediscovered in the late 1990s. The excavations revealed over 10,000 artefacts, and it was decided to preserve the remains and to keep them visible to visitors. It is now open to the public with guided tours available.

Positioned near the centre of the old medieval town at what was once the most important crossroads of the town, **Lynch's Castle** is one of Ireland's best surviving examples of an urban tower house. It was the home of Galway's most prominent merchant family, the Lynches. The building originally dates back to around 1500, though it has been modified many times in its history, particularly in the early nineteenth century. Though many of the features are out of their original position, the fine masonry and carved window mouldings give an insight into the quality of the building. Of particular note are the waterspouts, some of which are gargoyles and which once would have carried the rainwater away from the roof of the building. On the front of the building on the Shop Street side you can see a plaque with the arms of the Lynch family, and on the Abbeygate Street side you can see a plaque with the arms of the FitzGeralds, the most prominent dynasty in late medieval Ireland; a third plaque above one of the doorways has the arms of Henry VII of England. As well as being a luxurious and imposing reminder of the wealth of the family, the castle has a number of defensive features, such as gun loops on the corners and machicolations. Today, Lynch's Castle is home to a bank. Inside the foyer you can see a fine seventeenth-century fireplace that was brought from another medieval building to its present location during renovation work in the 1960s.

St Nicholas' Collegiate Church is the best place in Galway to soak in the medieval atmosphere. The present building was constructed in *c.* 1320, on the site of an earlier church. It was extensively modified in the fifteenth and sixteenth centuries, when the crossing tower was added and the nave aisles enlarged. Other phases of remodelling and renovation were carried out in the seventeenth, eighteenth and nineteenth centuries, though the church retains its medieval ambience. There are lots of intricate details and fascinating carvings to discover. On the south aisle of the church are a number of charming gargoyles, and you can see two carvings of mermaids, one on the north aisle of the church and the other on the gable window in the south transept. A beautiful baptismal font and a number of interesting tomb memorials are well worth examining. More recent memorials are also of note, including the battle standards of the famous Connaught Rangers. It is easy to spend an hour or two taking it all in. Others have done so in the past, including the explorer Christopher Columbus, who is believed to have attended Mass here in 1477 when he stopped in Galway on one of his voyages.

Saint Nicholas' Collegiate Church

The Spanish Arch

The **Spanish Arch** is one of Galway's most instantly recognisable places. It was built in around 1584 next to the mouth of the River Corrib. It once formed part of a sixteenth-century bastion in the city walls, designed to protect valuable merchant shipping in the harbour. It was built by the Mayor of Galway Wylliam Martin and it was originally known as *Ceann an Bhalla* (meaning 'head of the wall'). There is some debate about how it gained the name 'the Spanish Arch'. Some believe it is a relatively recent moniker applied through romantic ideas of the Spanish galleons that used to sail into port here. John O'Donovan of the Ordnance Survey suggested that it may have come through a corruption of the word '*sparra*', meaning 'gateway'. The excellent **Galway City Museum** gives a great overview of the story of Galway. You'll find it just adjacent to the Spanish Arch.

GALWAY   MAP 10

Coordinates: (Galway City Museum) 53.269515, Long. -9.053529

Irish Grid Reference: M 29725 24874

Opening hours/entry fees: Visit:

www.galwaycitymuseum.ie

Directions: I recommend beginning your tour of Galway at the City Museum on Merchant's Road Lower, adjacent to the Spanish Arch.

Nearest town: Galway.

---

49 | INIS MÓR

Ireland's largest archipelago of inhabited islands, the Aran Islands abound with a wonderful array of archaeological and historical sites, and a number of excellent guidebooks have been compiled on the heritage of these fascinating islands alone. However, for the purposes of this guidebook, we will concentrate on the largest of the islands, Inis Mór ('the big island'), and the famous great stone fort of Dún Aonghasa. If you have time, however, I recommend hiring a bicycle and spending a few days on the island, such is the wealth of heritage to discover.

Sunset at Kilronan

This entry is laid out as a trail that leads from the harbour at Kilronan (from where you can hire bicycles, etc.). From Kilronan I recommend heading first to Dún Aonghasa. If you visit the famous fort before 10.30 a.m. or after 3 p.m. you should miss the crowds and have the site almost to yourself. To get there from Kilronan, I recommend you travel generally westward along the coast road. You will first encounter the early monastery known as **Mainistir Chiaráin**, which is associated with Saint Ciarán who studied under Saint Éanna and who would later found the famous monastery at Clonmacnoise. The remains consist of the church (Teampall Chiaráin), numerous cross slabs, a sundial and a burial ground. As you continue along the road you will pass the resident seal colony, and eventually reach Kilmurvy (Cill Mhuirbhigh). From here, simply follow the signs up to the visitor centre at Dún Aonghasa.

Sundial at Teampall Chiaráin

Dún Aonghasa encompasses an area of almost 5.8 hectares (14 acres). The site is defined by a series of three curving walls forming an outer, middle and inner enclosure that terminate at the edge of the dramatic 90m (295 foot) high cliff. Archaeological investigations by Claire Cotter and the Discovery Programme have revealed fascinating insights into the story of this iconic site. The earliest activity found so far by archaeologists dates to the Middle Bronze Age, around 1500 BC. However, the majority of the visible remains had their origin in the later Bronze Age.

It was during this period that the enclosures were first constructed, and evidence for prehistoric structures was found within the middle enclosure. At this period, Dún Aonghasa was

The inner enclosure of Dún Aonghasa

comparable to a high-status hillfort. These were believed to be important places in society, where communal activities would take place, such as inaugurations or religious ceremonies, and a place where agreements could be made or disputes ruled upon and justice dispensed. Undoubtedly, the establishment of a large stone hillfort here would have taken the cooperation and work of a large number of people, and this hints at a strong social cohesion during the Bronze Age. Interestingly, a large amount of evidence of Bronze Age metalworking was discovered during the archaeological excavations. Perhaps at this early period, the manufacture of metal tools was akin to sorcery, a secret skill and knowledge reserved for the select few, to be practised only within certain important, and perhaps sacred, places.

The outer enclosure was first established in around 1000 BC. Though the drystone walls are quite low, the outer enclosure was constructed along the edge of a natural terrace that helped to make it a formidable sight for anyone approaching the fort. The area that the wall encloses is very exposed to the weather, and during the excavations, no evidence of habitation was found within this area. The outer enclosure may have been a place to pen livestock, or it may simply have been constructed to form a mental and physical 'boundary' or separation from the surrounding landscape. A further layer of defence was added by the construction of chevaux-de-frise to surround the middle enclosure of the fort (the best-preserved area can be seen to the west).

The chevaux-de-frise

This was a band of large stones, some up to 2m (6.5 feet) tall, which were stood upright by being wedged and propped up with other large stones. The tightly packed pillars were effective at stopping cavalry, and they even made it difficult for soldiers to advance in a group. As the bedrock of the land makes it difficult to dig, the chevaux-de-frise were a practical and effective alternative to a deep ditch.

During the early medieval period, Dún Aonghasa was transformed with an enormous amount of construction that incorporated the Bronze Age enclosures within massive new drystone walls, which were much higher and broader than the originals, and almost swallowed the older walls within the new fabric. This is clearly seen with the middle enclosure, where the original Bronze Age wall was almost doubled in both width and height. The inner enclosure was also refortified during the early medieval period. At this time, the Aran Islands were a disputed territory, as a frontier point between Connacht and Munster. The redevelopment of the ancient fort was a powerful statement of the dominance and power of the ruling family. Archaeologists also found evidence of early medieval houses within the inner enclosure, along with a brooch pin, a comb and burials, including the remains of two young men, which were dated to between AD 680–950.

Dún Aonghasa was declared a National Monument in 1880, and extensive work was carried out to restore and repair the site. Today, the site is under the auspices of the OPW, and it is one of the most popular visitor attractions in Ireland. It is a truly affecting experience, to stand at the very edge of Europe and look out past the dizzying cliffs to the Atlantic below, knowing that Newfoundland, over 3,000km (approximately 1,900 miles) away, is the next shore. You can discover an introduction to the story of Dún Aonghasa at the visitor centre, and guided tours of the site are available. In a field just behind the area of shops near the visitor centre stands the ruins of a small medieval church called Teampall na Naomh. Another, but more impressive, ruin of a medieval church is located a little down the hill from the visitor centre. This is **Teampall Mhic Dhuach**, named after Colman Mac Duach, a seventh-century saint.

Teampall Mhic Dhuach

The church represents two periods. The nave is thought to date to around the tenth or eleventh century, discerned by features like the primitive lintelled doorway. The chancel is a later addition, and may date to the twelfth or thirteenth century. An impressive cross-inscribed slab stands just outside the church opposite the doorway.

Na Seacht dTeampall

From here, head back to the main road and turn left, heading west towards the important early church site at **Na Seacht dTeampall** ('the seven churches'), which can be found approximately 2km (1.25 miles) west of Dún Aonghasa. There are the remains of a number of buildings, including two churches, the largest being Temple Brecan, and another known as Teampall an Phoill. Temple Brecan was dedicated to Saint Brecan, a disciple of Enda, and the building shows a number of architectural styles, possibly representing modification and reconstruction from the twelfth to the fifteenth centuries. Within the church, high on the southern end of the western wall, if you look carefully you can see an inscription that reads OR AR II CANOIN ('pray for the souls of two canons'). The small graveyard contains interesting graveslabs and features, including a *leaba*, a saint's grave, with a partial graveslab that is inscribed with SCI BRECANI (of Saint Brecan). A number of cross slabs can also be seen, along with fragments of three high crosses. When you are finished at Na Seacht dTeampall, turn back and head east. After 1km or so you will see a sign pointing to **Dún Eoghanachta**, which stands proudly on the high ground above you.

Dún Eoghanachta

Dún Eochla

Follow the small road as it winds upwards, and turn right onto a narrow boreen that leads to the fort (you would be well advised to leave your bicycle unobtrusively as the lane narrows and becomes quite overgrown). The fort is well situated, with stunning views northwards over Na Seacht dTeampall in the foreground and the Connemara coast in the distance. The fort takes its name from the powerful Eoghanacht dynasty that held sway over Munster in the early medieval period. A branch of the Eoghanacht, the Eoghanacht Ninussa, were the rulers of the Aran Islands and the Burren. This circular drystone fort measures approximately 28m (92 feet) in diameter, and is similar to the forts like **Caherdoonerish** (Site 43) in the Burren or **Staigue** (Site 17), **Cahergal** and **Leacanbuaile** (Site 24) in Kerry. There are foundational remains of three structures within the fort. Archaeological investigations at the fort produced radiocarbon dates in the early medieval period around AD 800, though, like the other stone forts of the Aran Islands, it was repaired and reconstructed in the nineteenth century. Following your visit to Dún Eoghanachta, continue heading back eastwards along the main road, and you will see a sign pointing right up a steep hill towards the fort of **Dún Eochla**.

As a complete novice on a bicycle I found the climb to be a pretty gruelling cycle, and had to dismount and push it most of the way. You will be rewarded for your efforts, however, as Dún Eochla is situated at the highest point of Inis Mór, allowing for stunning views over the island. From here you can see the patchwork of fields hemmed by drystone walls, which is such an identifiable feature of the landscape of the Aran Islands. The famous drystone walls of the islands were mainly constructed in the nineteenth century. Prior to this, the land would have been less enclosed and more suitable for grazing, with walls constructed only to protect crops from livestock. The population growth in the nineteenth century created an increased demand for land for tillage to grow potatoes, and defined plots of land became more important than open pasture, leading to the construction of the drystone walls. Before getting to Dún Eochla, you will pass through the enclosure for Dún Aran where you can find a Napoleonic signal tower and, curiously, a fake wedge tomb that has been constructed in recent years (by whom or for what purpose isn't immediately clear). The name Dún Eochla translates to the 'fort of the yew wood'. Like the other stone forts of Inis Mór, the high stone ramparts were reconstructed in the nineteenth century. Avoid the temptation of cycling down the very steep hill back to the main road. When you reach the road turn right and pass back through Kilronan, heading ever eastwards and then bearing south to the promontory fort of **Dún Dúcathair** ('the black fort'). This is a much less visited place than **Dún Aonghasa**, but it is well worth taking the time to see. The fort is protected by sheer cliffs on three sides and an enormous stone rampart that stands 6m (20 feet) high and over 5m (16 feet) thick. Like Dún Aonghasa, the fort of Dún Dúcathair is also protected by a formidable cheval-de-frise. Inside the fort you can see the remains of a number of oval-shaped drystone clocháns, structures that are likely to date to the early medieval period.

From here continue south-east through the village of Killeany and past the small airfield. The Aran Islands played an important role in the development of the early Irish Church. The most prominent of the early ecclesiastics is Saint Éanna (Enda), an influential sixth-century saint who founded a monastery of such renown that some of the most important Irish saints travelled to study there, such as Ciarán of Clonmacnoise, Brendan of Clonfert, who is said to have received Éanna's blessing before embarking on his legendary voyage, Jarlath of Tuam and Colmcille, who was said to be so furious with Éanna's refusal to grant him land on Aran that he cursed the island with 'every want', especially of firewood and turf, so the people of Aran were forever more forced to make fires with dried cow dung. What is left of Saint Éanna's monastery can be discovered at **Cill Éinne** (Killeany) in the south of the island, overlooking the sandy stretch of An Trá Mór.

Cill Éinne

The graveyard that surrounds Teaghlach Éinne is said to be the burial place of Éanna and over a hundred other saints. The church shows at least two phases of development. The eastern gable, with its round-headed window and projecting antae, is likely to be eleventh to twelfth century in origin, while the west and south walls, along with the northern doorway, are likely to be later, perhaps seventeenth century in date. Inside the church you can see bullaun stones and part of a shaft of a high cross, along with a number of grave slabs.

Sunrise at Teampall Bhéanain

The stump of a round tower on the slope below Teampall Bhéanain

The tiny **Teampall Bheanáin** is perched higher up the slope to the west of Teaghlach Éinne. This is a small stone oratory, dedicated to Saint Benan, a disciple of Saint Patrick. It is one of the smallest in Europe, measuring just over 3m x 2m (10 x 6.5 feet) internally. It is also unusual as it is orientated north–south rather than the more traditional east–west of Christian churches. This may be a practical consideration, given the elevated and exposed location of the church. Nearby you can see the foundations of clocháns and part of the enclosure wall that once surrounded the monastery, along with the stump of a round tower below the church. The monastery was raided twice by the Vikings, in the years 1017 and 1081. Sadly, four of the original six churches that once stood here were demolished and quarried to build the nearby Cromwellian fort known as **Caisleán Aircín**, which was constructed in c. 1655, around the same time as the fortification on **Inishbofin** (Site 54).

I had the great fortune of seeing the sun rise from Teampall Bheanáin. The sight of the island slowly being unfurled as the sky lightened from black to rosy pink and gold is a memory I will long treasure.

These are but a few of the heritage highlights of Inis Mór. Both Inis Meáin and Inis Oírr are similarly filled with historical features. On Inis Meáin you can find the great forts of Dún Chonchúir and Dún Fearbha, along with other important early church sites. On Inis Oírr a medieval O'Brien Castle stands surrounded by the stone ramparts of an ancient fort, showing that even centuries after they were first constructed, the mighty stone walls of Árann's forts still provided protection and shelter.

Caisleán Aircín

DÚN AONGHASA MAP 11

Coordinates: Lat. 53.125396, Long. -9.767026

Irish Grid Reference: L 88514 08906

Opening hours/entry fees: Visit: www.heritageireland.ie/en/west/dunaonghasa/
For general information about visiting the Aran Islands, visit: www.aranislands.ie

Directions: The Aran Islands are easily accessible via Aran Island Ferries from Rossaveal in Connemara, and Doolin Ferry close to the Cliffs of Moher. You can also take an eight-minute flight from Connemara.

Aran Island Ferries: www.aranislandferries.com

Ferry from Doolin: www.doolinferry.com

Flights from Connemara: www.aerarannislands.ie

Nearest town: Doolin, Galway.

INIS MÓR

Patrick Pearse's Cottage

This charming cottage in its picturesque location was the summer residence of Patrick Pearse (1879–1916), one of the leaders of the 1916 Easter Rising. The cottage dates to around 1870, its steeply pitching thatched roof and rural setting giving a tranquil and comforting vista. As well as a retreat, Pearse held a summer school here for his pupils from St Enda's in Dublin. One of his former pupils, who attended the summer school in 1915, later wrote of his visits there: 'The Twelve Pins came in sight and Pearse waved his hand here and there over the land, naming lake, mountain and district away to the Joyce Country under its purple mist.' Pearse truly loved this landscape and the folklore and storytelling traditions of the area. It was within this cottage that he penned the funeral oration for O'Donovan Rossa, which finished with the stirring words: 'They think that they have pacified Ireland. They think that they have purchased half of us and intimidated the other half. They think that they have foreseen everything, think that they have provided against everything; but the fools, the fools, the fools! They have left us our Fenian dead, and, while Ireland holds these graves, Ireland unfree shall never be at peace.' This famous oration became a key catalyst in the launch of the Easter Rising.

Pearse was born in Dublin in 1879. He passionately believed in the cause of Irish freedom, and he became one of the most prominent figures in the independence movement. When the Easter Rising began on Monday 24 April 1916, it was Pearse who read the Proclamation of the Irish Republic outside the General Post Office, as he was chosen as the President of the Republic. However, the Easter Rising ended after six days of fighting, when Pearse issued the order to surrender in an effort to stop civilian casualties. Pearse and fourteen other leaders, including his brother Willie, were court-martialled and executed by firing squad. During the War of Independence, the cottage was burned down, though today it has been restored and houses an exhibition with information on the life of Pearse. A wonderful visitor centre has been recently constructed near the cottage, and houses interactive displays that beautifully weave the tale of this important figure in Irish history, and his love of Connemara.

PATRICK PEARSE'S COTTAGE MAP 12

Coordinates: Lat. 53.386263, Long. -9.620002

Irish Grid Reference: L 92258 38530

Opening hours/entry fees: Visit: www.heritageireland.ie/en/west/patrickpearsescottage/

Directions: Pearse's Cottage is about a 90-minute (55km) drive from Galway. Take the R336 west from the city for about 49km, passing through Barna, Spiddal and Costelloe (Casla). About 11km beyond Costelloe, turn left at the T-junction onto the R340, signposted Pearse's Cottage. Continue along this road for 5km. Turn left down a narrow road, again signposted for Pearse's Cottage. The car park and visitor centre are located approximately 300m down this road.

Nearest town: Galway (55km).

51 | DERRIGIMLAGH BOG

This haunting landscape of lowland blanket bog is one of Ireland's most important industrial heritage landscapes, as it was chosen by the Italian inventor Guglielmo Marconi to construct the world's first permanent transatlantic radio station, from where he transmitted the very first transatlantic radio signal in 1907. At its peak, hundreds of workers were stationed in this remote landscape. Unfortunately, the station was burned and largely destroyed during the War of Independence, though the foundations of many of the buildings can still be seen today.

One of the walkways in Derrigimlagh Bog

You can also see a white aeroplane wing sculpture that stands as a memorial to the daring aviators John Alcock and Arthur Whitten Brown, who crash-landed in Derrigimlagh Bog in 1919 at the end of the first non-stop flight across the Atlantic. They had taken off from Newfoundland in a Vickers Vimy biplane and flown for over sixteen continuous hours – over 1,890 nautical miles – above the Atlantic, braving technical malfunctions, fog and inclement weather before reaching Derrigimlagh. They were uninjured in the landing, and as Alcock clambered from the aircraft he proclaimed, 'Yesterday I was in America. I am the first man in Europe to say that.'

The recently installed and well-interpreted series of trails allows for easy access through the bog, and passes by some of the many lakes and still bog pools. I particularly recommend trying the innovative 'historioscope' information points that allow you to view the landscape as it once was during the heyday of the communications centre.

One of the 'historioscopes' at Derrigimlagh

DERRIGIMLAGH BOG   MAP 12

Coordinates: Lat. 53.446568, Long. -10.022536

Irish Grid Reference: L 63231 45839

Opening hours/entry fees: No entry fees or opening hours applied at the time of visit.

Directions: Derrigimlagh Bog is just over a five-minute (4km) drive from Clifden. Take the R431 south for 4km and turn left at the junction signposted for the Marconi Station and Alcock & Brown Landing Point. The Derrigimlagh Discovery Point will be on your right.

Nearest town: Clifden (4km).

The rugged landscape of Connemara

The lane to Clifden Castle, with an ornamental standing stone in the foreground

This Gothic Revival castle was constructed in around 1818 for John d'Arcy. He was a wealthy magnate who founded the nearby town of Clifden with the ambition to create a centre of commerce and industry in this rural and impoverished region in Connemara. He managed to acquire the services of the famous engineer Alexander Nimmo, who was sent to the area in 1822. Nimmo constructed a quay at Clifden and a road to Galway, thus connecting the new town to the outside world. Thanks to the vision of d'Arcy and the expertise of Nimmo, Clifden began to flourish. By the time d'Arcy died in 1839, Clifden had expanded from nothing to a prosperous town with a population of more than 1,000. However, his son and heir, Hyacinth, is said to have lacked his father's vision and drive, and he had many confrontations with his tenants. Hyacinth led the family into bankruptcy in the hard years of the Great Famine in the middle of the nineteenth century, and both the castle and the town were sold to the Eyre family from Bath in England, whose crest is depicted above the entrance. In the early twentieth century, the lands of the castle were acquired by the state and redistributed amongst the tenantry. With no owner, the castle soon fell into disrepair, and many of its fixtures, fittings and useful building materials were stripped and quarried away for use elsewhere. Today the castle is a roofless ruin, and an evocative reminder of the wealth and ambition of John d'Arcy.

Clifden Castle

CLIFDEN

MAP 12

Coordinates: Lat. 53.491917, Long. -10.048344

Irish Grid Reference: L 63543 51031

Opening hours/entry fees: No entry fees or opening hours applied at the time of visit.

Directions: Clifden Castle is just a five-minute (2km) drive from the centre of Clifden. Take the Sky Road west for 2km and the entrance gateway to the castle will be on your left. From here, proceed through the gateway on foot for a further 1km to the castle itself. There is often livestock in the fields so it is not suitable for dogs. You will see a number of standing stones, which appear to be a remnant of nineteenth-century landscaping rather than Bronze Age.

Nearest town: Clifden (2km).

53 | KNOCKBRACK MEGALITHIC TOMB

Knockbrack megalithic tomb

The coastline of Connemara is bejewelled with many megalithic monuments. One of my personal favourites is the tomb at Knockbrack (also known as *Labbadermot,* meaning Dermot's Bed, presumably a reference to the story of Gráinne and Diarmuid, who are said to have sheltered and slept in ancient tombs like this during their escape from Fionn Mac Cumhaill). Though it is uncertain, the remains may represent a wedge tomb dating to the Late Neolithic or Early Bronze Age. The monument consists of a narrow chamber with an east–west alignment and is covered by a large capstone. The tomb is now incorporated into a field boundary, in a beautiful location close to the seashore on the western side of Salerna Bay.

MAP 12

Coordinates: Lat. 53.557234, Long. -10.131604

Irish Grid Reference: L 58974 58639

Opening hours/entry fees: No entry fees or opening hours applied at the time of visit, but please ensure that you ask for permission at the house near the first gateway.

Directions: Knockbrack Megalithic Tomb is just over a fifteen-minute (12.5km) drive from Clifden. Take the N59 north from the town. After 5km turn left onto the road signposted Cleggan/Inishbofin. Continue on this road for 6.5km, passing through Cleggan village. About 500m beyond the village, turn right, signposted Strand. Drive 500m down to the beach. The tomb is in the fields to your right past the northern end of the beach.

Nearest town: Clifden (12.5km).

54 | INISHBOFIN

Inishbofin sunset (courtesy Terry O'Hagan)

The small island of Inishbofin lies around 8km (5 miles) off the coast of Connemara. Its name derives from *Inis Bó Finne*, meaning 'the Island of the white cow'. Though today it is home to around 180 inhabitants, the island is an important area of natural heritage, with resident populations of corncrakes and seal colonies. Inishbofin is separated from the smaller island of Inishark by a narrow channel. Like Inishbofin, Inishark also has a number of interesting heritage sites, and if you have the opportunity I highly recommend a visit.

Historically, Inishbofin is associated with Saint Colman of Lindisfarne, who established a monastery here in the seventh century. According to the Venerable Bede, Colman had left Ireland to become the head of the important Northumbrian Church at Lindisfarne. He became embroiled in the debate over whether the date of Easter should be calculated using the Roman method or the Irish method, and he passionately advocated for the latter at the Synod of Whitby in 664. After he was lost the debate, he left

Cromwellian fort (courtesy Terry O'Hagan)

Northumbria for Ireland, accompanied by both Irish and Saxon monks who supported him. He founded a monastery here on Inishbofin, but soon afterwards his congregation of Irish and Saxon monks fell out, and Colman established a new monastery on the mainland in County Mayo for the Saxons, and ruled both houses until his death in the year 676. Though no traces remain of his early foundation, the present fourteenth-century church is thought to have been established on the site of the earlier monastery. The surrounding graveyard contains the remains of two holy wells, cross-inscribed slabs and a bullaun stone. Traces of the enclosure that once surrounded the early monastery can possibly be discerned to the north.

In later years, the island was part of the holdings of the Earls of Clanricard, though the O'Malley family temporarily gained possession of the island. It is thought that Gráinne Ní Mháille had a castle built on the western side of the harbour (for more on her story, see **Clare Island**, Site 58, and **Rockfleet Castle**, Site 64). Another fort on the opposite side of the harbour is said to have been built by a legendary Spanish buccaneer called Don Bosco, an ally of Gráinne Ní Mháille. According to the story he had a heavy chain pulled across the mouth of the harbour to prevent any boats from entering or exiting without first paying him dues. The strategic harbour of Inishbofin became an important supply base for the western coast during the Confederate Wars of the 1640s. The Earl of Clanricard had a garrison stationed on the island, though after Galway city fell to Parliamentary forces in 1652, Inishbofin became one of the last bases of the Confederate forces. A large Parliamentarian expeditionary force set out to conquer the island in 1653 and forced the garrison into surrender. As part of the terms of surrender, the garrison of 1,000 Irish soldiers left Inishbofin to sail to Ostend, and the Parliamentarian forces took command of the island. They constructed a powerful fort on the site of Bosco's original castle, with artillery bastions that protected the harbour. The fort was converted into a prison to house Catholic priests before they were transported overseas.

This followed the law introduced during Elizabeth I's reign that declared all Roman Catholic priests to be guilty of high treason. Enormous numbers of priests were hunted down, imprisoned and transported to plantations in the Americas or Barbados. This was a marginal improvement, as previously priests were often summarily executed, before the Parliament was strongly lobbied into moderation by Catholic rulers in Europe. In 1657, an order was made for payment of £100 upon the account of Colonel Sadler, the Governor of Galway, for the 'maintenance of such Popish Priests as are or should be confined to the Isle of Buffin, according to six pence dayly allowance, Building Cabbins and the like'. Despite the relatively handsome stipend, from contemporary accounts of Inishbofin, the priests were kept in appalling conditions, close to starvation. It is likely that the majority of the allowance was swallowed up by corruption. By 1662, the fort had returned to its military role and a garrison was kept on the island due to the threat of invasion by the French or Dutch. During the Williamite Wars, a Jacobite garrison was stationed on Inishbofin in September 1690 but surrendered not long after the fall of Galway in July 1691, and the fort was finally abandoned in the early eighteenth century.

Saint Colman's Church (courtesy Terry O'Hagan)

INISHBOFIN

MAP 12

Coordinates:
Island: Lat. 53.614567, Long. -10.210261
Cleggan Pier: Lat. 53.557335, Long. -10.112207

Irish Grid Reference: L 54046 65167

Opening hours/entry fees: For the latest information on Inishbofin visit: www.inishbofin.com

Inishbofin Island Discovery (ferry service): www.inishbofinislanddiscovery.com

Directions: To get to Inishbofin, you must take the ferry from Cleggan Pier, located northwest of Clifden. The ferry leaves Cleggan pier three times a day during peak times and twice a day off-peak (see Inishbofin Island Discovery website for ferry times). Cleggan Pier is a fifteen-minute drive (11.5km) from Clifden. Head north from Clifden on the N59 and after 5.5km turn left (signposted Inishbofin and Cleggan Pier). Continue on this road for just under 6km and follow it down to the pier (which will be on your right). The ferry crossing usually takes around 30 minutes.

Nearest town: Clifden (12.5km).

A view of Diamond Hill from the visitor centre

The Connemara National Park consists of nearly 3,000 hectares of some of the most stunning wilderness in Europe. The park is dominated by the iconic mountain known as Diamond Hill and the slopes of the Twelve Bens, including Bencullagh, Benbrack and Benbaun. The heart of the park is Gleann Mór ('Big Glen'), through which the River Polladirk flows. An exhibition centre near Letterfrack gives great insights into the important natural and built heritage of the region. From the centre, you can find information on a number of fantastic walks and hiking trails through this beautiful National Park. One of the most rewarding is the trail that leads up the 500m (1,640-foot) high Diamond Hill. On the slopes you will encounter the ruins of a nineteenth-century farmstead abandoned after the Great Famine, and a megalithic tomb.

The spectacular scenery is largely the result of those immense master sculptors, the glaciers of the Ice Age that ended around 12,000 years ago. The present parklands once formed part of the **Kylemore Abbey** estate. In the past, the uplands of the park were generally used for sheep grazing, and the lowlands for cattle pasture, with some vegetable crops grown in the more fertile areas. The bog was exploited for its turf, and many of the old turf banks, from which people toiled to cut the fuel for their fires for decades, can still be seen. This is blanket bog and heathland, covered with heather and bog cotton in the summer months, with sundews and butterworts trapping the numerous insects for nourishment. The purple moor grass that is so abundant here colours the hillsides, and some plants more associated with the Arctic Circle and Scandinavia can be found high in the uplands. As well as rich biodiversity in plant species, Connemara National Park is also home to varied bird life, with kestrels, merlin and peregrine falcons, skylarks, meadow pipits, stonechats, woodcock, snipe and chaffinch all to be found here, along with the noisy wren and inquisitive robin. The most famous resident of the park is the charming Connemara pony.

CONNEMARA NATIONAL PARK   MAP 12

Coordinates: Lat. 53.550956, Long. -9.945110

Irish Grid Reference: L 71140 57417

Opening hours/entry fees: Visit: www.connemaranationalpark.ie

Directions: Connemara National Park visitor centre is just over a fifteen-minute (14.5km) drive from Clifden. Take the N59 north towards the village of Letterfrack. The entrance to the National Park will be on your right and is well signposted.

Nearest town: Clifden (14.5km).

56 | KYLEMORE ABBEY

The magnificent Kylemore Abbey was built between 1864 and 1871 for Dr Mitchell Henry, who was from a wealthy family of cotton magnates in Manchester, England. Mitchell had the house constructed in flamboyant baronial style to the design of James Franklin Fuller and Ussher Roberts. Reputedly, it took over 100 men to build it, using granite shipped by sea from Dalkey and Ballinasloe limestone. The house was intended as a gift for Mitchell's wife, Margaret. The couple had fallen in love with the beauty of the valley here they visited during their honeymoon. Sadly, Margaret did not live long to enjoy this idyllic retreat. She fell ill during a holiday in Egypt and died shortly afterwards at the young age of 45. Broken-hearted, Mitchell threw himself into local politics and became an MP for Galway and a founding member of the Home Rule movement. In 1878, he had the beautiful neo-Gothic church constructed as a memorial to his beloved wife, with four different types of coloured marble from the four provinces of Ireland. On his death in 1910, he was laid to rest next to Margaret in the little mausoleum in a wooded glade on the grounds of the estate.

The house and estate was sold to the Duke and Duchess of Manchester. The duke, the impressively named William Angus Drogo Montagu, was a notorious spendthrift, who loved a lavish lifestyle and gambling, and he soon became bankrupt not long after purchasing the estate. The estate was purchased by Benedictine nuns, who needed a base as they were fleeing the dangerous violence of Ypres, Belgium during the First World War. The nuns continued to offer education to Catholic girls, opening an international boarding school and establishing a day school for girls from the locality. Today the house and its beautiful walled gardens are a popular place for visitors to Connemara.

Kylemore Abbey

KYLEMORE ABBEY

MAP 12

Coordinates: Lat. 53.559426, Long. -9.891553

Irish Grid Reference: L 74854 58507

Opening hours/entry fees: Visit: www.kylemoreabbey.com

Directions: Kylemore Abbey is situated on the N59 between Clifden and Westport. It is easily accessible from Shannon, Galway city, Clifden, Cong and Westport. From Clifden, take the N59 for Westport and continue past the entrance to Connemara National Park and through Letterfrack village. Kylemore Abbey will be on your left-hand side, approximately 3km beyond Letterfrack.

Nearest town: Clifden (20km).

MAYO

I have to admit to having a certain favourable bias towards Mayo, as I spent two very happy years living here when I worked as an archaeologist for the county council. The coast of County Mayo is truly beautiful and varied, from rugged cliffs, sheltered coves and deep bogs to the turquoise, almost tropical-looking, waters of Clew Bay abounding with islands set in the shadow of the holy mountain, Croagh Patrick.

There is always something fascinating around every bend in County Mayo

The charming town of Westport has become one of Ireland's most popular places for a break, thanks to its wonderful music scene and hospitality.

However, the weather in Mayo can often be difficult to predict. You may well encounter the famous Mayo mist, especially on Achill Island. The mist wraps you in white, almost ethereal, drifting shrouds that, very thoroughly and evenly, drench you before you notice how hopelessly wet you are. Even on a fine day elsewhere, the weather on Achill and Clare Island does its own thing.

This is the land of Gráinne Ní Mháille, the Pirate Queen, whose deeds and actions have won her a place in history and legend. She commanded these waters, and we will visit a number of her strongholds and harbours. Further north along the coast at Céide you will discover a remarkable prehistoric landscape, and discover the story of how Ireland's first farmers cleared enormous forests to start to change the landscape of Ireland forever.

57 | DOOLOUGH VALLEY

The scenic Doolough Valley

The beautiful Doolough Valley was the scene of one of the darkest tales in Irish history. The province of Connacht experienced the very worst of the Great Famine. In the decade between 1841 and 1851, census records show that the population of Connacht fell

The Famine Memorial at Doolough Valley

by well over 400,000 people. In just ten years nearly one third of the people of Connacht had either emigrated or perished. The rough and largely uncultivated land of County Mayo was especially ill prepared for the devastation of the Famine. Most of the people were employed in agriculture, particularly on small farms, and there was little industrialisation and few large towns. With such a dangerous set of circumstances, the repeated failure of the potato crop caused appalling devastation. Disease and cold winters carried away many of the people, who were weakened by poor nutrition. However, as harsh as the conditions were, they could not compete with the ignorant cruelty of uncompassionate men, who valued profit and their personal ease above the lives of the people.

On 31 March 1849, it was a bitterly cold day in Louisburgh. Hundreds of starving people sought food and shelter in the Westport Workhouse. After expending much of their scant resources and energy to arrive in Louisburgh, they were informed that the relieving officer would not inspect them there; instead, they were ordered to walk to Delphi, a distance of nearly 20km (12 miles), to apply to the Board of Guardians. Heedless of the condition of the starving people, the relieving officer declared that if they did not arrive in Delphi at 7 a.m. the following morning they would be removed from the Relief List. A number died from exhaustion and exposure on that long cold march to Delphi through the mountain passes. Those who arrived for the appointed time had to endure a wait of more than five hours in the freezing weather as the Board of Guardians did not appear until noon, after they had enjoyed a pleasant lunch. They refused to help them and ordered them to return to Louisburgh. Now completely exhausted and battered by icy winds, rain, hail and snow, a number of the starving people collapsed and died on the road back through the Doolough Valley. The contemporary writer and storyteller James Berry described the path from Louisburgh to Delphi as being covered with corpses 'as numerous as sheaves of corn in an autumn field'.

DOOLOUGH VALLEY MAP 13

Coordinates: Lat. 53.666196, Long. -9.781367

Irish Grid Reference: L 82304 69948

Opening hours/entry fees: No opening hours or entry fees applied at the time of writing.

Directions: The simple stone cross marking the Doolough Valley Famine Memorial is situated north of Delphi on the R335.

Nearest town: Delphi (5km).

58 | CLARE ISLAND

Clare Island in Clew Bay possesses a brooding beauty. The history of the island is entwined with that of the O'Malley family, who were lords of Umhall (the lands around Clew Bay) for centuries. The earliest reference to the family comes from the Annals of the Four Masters, which recorded the slaying of 'Donal and Murtough, two sons of Murray O'Malley ... in Cliara' in the year 1235. 'Cliara' was the ancient name for Clare Island. The O'Malleys were feared and respected as a seafaring power. The most famous member of the family is, of course, Gráinne Ní Mháille (or Granuaile), the 'Pirate Queen' who is the subject of many stories and legends (her story is featured in **Rockfleet Castle**, Site 64).

The **tower house** near the harbour was built by the O'Malleys in the sixteenth century. It stands three storeys high and it would once have had a pitched slate roof. The tower house was converted to a police barracks in the early nineteenth century. It was at this time that the decorative slate flashing was added to the defensive bartizans that protect the corners of the tower house. The positioning of the tower house ensured the sheltered harbour was well protected.

The tower house on Clare Island

The martial prowess of the O'Malleys was seen in 1588, when the *Gran Grin*, one of the largest ships in the Spanish Armada, was driven onto rocks off Clare Island. Of the 329 men on board, only around a hundred made it to the shore, where they were immediately captured by Eoghan Dowdarra Roe O'Malley (father of Granuaile). The men of Clare Island held the Spaniards, but when the captives tried to escape by stealing the islanders' boats, the O'Malleys ruthlessly slaughtered them, killing 64, including their leader, Don Pedro de Mendoza.

Clare Island Abbey

Clare Island Abbey is thought to have originated in the middle of the thirteenth century, though it is said that the community of monks was driven off the island by pirates in 1224. The powerful Cistercian foundation at Abbeyknockmoy established a small cell on Clare Island, with a handful of monks to serve the local population.

Some of the wonderful medieval art that has been subject to a delicate conservation process

The interior of the abbey

The building that we see today is a small fifteenth-century Cistercian church, with a small nave and a two-storey chancel with domestic quarters for the monks above it. The ceiling of the chancel is a real treasure, as it is covered with beautiful and intricate paintings, which are some of the finest examples of medieval art surviving in Ireland. They depict fantastical beasts like dragons, and scenes of a cattle raid, a knight on horseback, trident-wielding fishermen, wolves attacking stags, and musicians. They are framed by painted rib vaulting that perhaps echoes the grandiose architecture of Abbeyknockmoy. The paintings have recently been subject to an extensive and delicate conservation programme that has thankfully helped to preserve these remarkable scenes for the future. You can also see a crisply carved plaque with the coat of arms of the Ó Maille (O'Malley) family and their motto, TERRA MARIQ POTENS ('Powerful on Land and Sea'). It is next to a fine canopied tomb – said to be the tomb of the Pirate Queen Gráinne Ní Mháille herself.

I have focused on the medieval monuments of the island as a visit to those will give a visitor a great day trip. However, there are a number of other archaeological monuments and walks to be enjoyed on the island, and it is certainly a rewarding place to explore.

The O'Malley coat of arms

CLARE ISLAND   MAP 13

Coordinates: (Roonagh Pier) 53.762025, Long. -9.902992

Irish Grid Reference: L 71503 85102

Opening hours/entry fees: The key to the abbey can usually be found at the post office nearby.

Directions: Two ferry companies serve Clare Island from Roonagh Pier (near Louisburgh), though please note sailing is subject to weather conditions.

Clare Island Ferry: www.clareislandferry.com

O'Malley Ferries: http://www.omalleyferries.com

The tower house is located in close proximity to the harbour. The abbey is approximately 2km walk from the harbour.

Nearest town: Louisburgh (7km).

The Boheh Stone

The Boheh Stone is a large boulder of outcropping rock that bears some of the finest prehistoric rock art known in Ireland. The rock is covered with petroglyphs, with over 250 motifs evident. Most are in the form of 'cup', 'cup and ring' and 'keyhole' designs. In the early 1990s, Gerry Bracken, a local historian, discovered that on 18 April and 24 August a remarkable sight known as the 'Rolling Sun' can be witnessed from the stone. When viewed from the Boheh Stone, as the sun sets on top of Croagh Patrick, instead of disappearing behind the mountain, it appears to 'roll' down the northern shoulder of the mountain. The dates that you can witness this phenomenon are significant, as they split the year into three equal parts, and perhaps signified the celebration of sowing and harvesting seasons. In later times, the stone became Christianised as it was entwined with the pilgrimage to Croagh

Patrick, and it became known as St Patrick's Chair. The Boheh Stone is part of the Clew Bay Archaeological Trail. If you have the time, I recommend following the trail as there are a number of other fascinating monuments situated around the bay.

The stone is covered with a remarkable array of prehistoric art

BOHEH STONE MAP 13

Coordinates: Lat. 53.747440, Long. -9.553499

Irish Grid Reference: L 97562 78637

Opening hours/entry fees: No entry fees or opening hours applied at the time of writing. For more information on the Clew Bay Archaeological Trail visit: www.clewbaytrail.com

Directions: The town of Westport is around fifteen minutes' drive away. From Westport head south-westwards on the N59 for 6.2km and turn left (following the signs for Clew Bay Archaeological Trail Site 2). The site will be on your right-hand side after 500m (look out for the signage). The stone is behind a house, but the landowner has kindly granted access to visitors.

Nearest town: Westport (8.5km).

60 | MURRISK FRIARY

Murrisk Friary is beautifully situated on the shores of Clew Bay in the shadow of Croagh Patrick. The friary was founded by Hugh O'Malley in 1457 for the Augustinian friars, and dedicated to St Patrick. Murrisk served as the starting point of the Croagh Patrick Pilgrimage, as it contained relics associated with St Patrick, including one of the saint's teeth.

Murrisk Friary in the shadow of Croagh Patrick

The only surviving buildings visible on site are a small church and the remains of the chapter house and dormitory. The chapter house was one of the most important structures in the friary as it was where the monks met to discuss the day-to-day running of the abbey and where the rules of the Order were read to the community of monks working, living and praying in the friary. The dormitory was above the chapter house. The church has quite unusual architectural features, with crenellations or 'battlement' type design, and a beautiful eastern window with delicate tracery in the Irish Gothic style. There are carved faces on the southern and eastern walls of the friary. It is unknown who these faces represent, but it was quite common in the medieval period to display depictions of wealthy patrons of the church on the walls of the building.

Murrisk Friary was suppressed in 1578, but the friars continued on the site until the eighteenth century, presumably due to the relative remoteness

The interior of the friary

of Murrisk and the patronage of powerful Gaelic families. The site at Murrisk is certainly a very interesting example of a later medieval religious house. The site is made even more spectacular by its incredible setting at the foot of Croagh Patrick and on the shores of Clew Bay.

MURRISK FRIARY MAP 13

Coordinates: Lat. 53.782070, Long. -9.639874

Irish Grid Reference: L 91986 82623

Opening hours/entry fees: No entry fees or opening hours applied at the time of writing.

Directions: The town of Westport is around fifteen minutes' drive away. From Westport head south-westwards on the R335 for 9.8km and turn right off the main road, on the opposite side of the road to the car park for Croagh Patrick, and continue up this narrow road to the site. There is an area to park.

Nearest town: Westport (10km).

61 | CROAGH PATRICK

Ireland's holy mountain – Croagh Patrick

Often referred to as 'Ireland's holy mountain', Croagh Patrick has long been the focus for Christian pilgrimage and ritual for generations, but the mountain may have had a sacred aspect that goes much further back into our prehistoric past. Croagh Patrick rises like a monumental pyramid, some 764m (over 2,500 feet) over the southern shores of Clew Bay and Mayo's Atlantic coast. The views from the summit are extraordinary: on some days the waters of the bay are an almost tropical shade of turquoise and blue, adorned with a myriad of emerald-coloured islands.

The earliest known historical reference to Croagh Patrick comes from the seventh-century bishop Tírechán. He described the story of how Saint Patrick spent 40 days and nights on the mountain, following in the footsteps of Moses, Elijah and Christ. Later hagiographical and folkloric tales of Patrick include that the saint climbed the mountain to confront Crom Dubh (the same dark pagan figure that appears as Patrick's adversary in the stories of **Downpatrick Head**, Site 70).

The hinterland of Croagh Patrick has long been an important place. This can be inferred from the number of prehistoric tombs, standing stones and stone rows, and the remarkable **Boheh Stone** (Site 59) that all have association or orientation towards the mountain. It may be that as well as the landscape aspect, the importance of the mountain in the past had quite a practical aspect too. Croagh Patrick is known to have quite extensive gold veins deep within the rock. Perhaps in the Bronze Age, people recognised the mountain as an important source for gold and panned the nearby river for the precious metal.

The statue of Saint Patrick at the base of the mountain

Every year, on the last Sunday in July, known as 'Reek Sunday', over 25,000 pilgrims climb Croagh Patrick to celebrate Mass on the summit. Even to this day some of the pilgrims go barefoot despite the sharp shale rocks. As it is held at the end of July, this tradition might be in some sense a continuance of the important pagan festival of Lughnasa that marked the beginning of the harvest season. A small church was constructed on the summit of the mountain in 1905, with additional wings added in 1962. However, there was a chapel on the summit prior to the construction of the twentieth-century church. In 1838, John O'Donovan of the Ordnance Survey described pilgrims entering the little chapel of Teampall Phádraig on the summit. Archaeological excavations in the mid-1990s discovered the foundations of a small stone oratory-like building, radiocarbon dated to AD 430–890. Workers who built the present church in 1905 discovered human remains while they were digging the foundations. It was thought that the bones were of Robert Binn, known as 'Bob of the Reek', a man who spent fourteen years on the summit, and who earned his living by carrying out penance to the summit in the stead of those pilgrims who were unable to do so themselves. The modern pilgrimage begins at **Murrisk Friary** (Site 60) Walkers can hire sticks and find refreshment at the visitor centre at the base of the mountain.

Do take the time to cross the road from the car park to visit the haunting National Famine Memorial. This striking sculpture by John Behan was unveiled by the then President Mary Robinson in 1997. It represents a 'coffin ship'. The condition of these ships, in which tens of thousands of people emigrated, were appalling: many were substandard vessels and were extremely overcrowded, with a view to making a quick profit. On one of these coffin ships, of the 348 passengers, 117 died at sea; on another, 158 died out of a total of 476.

CROAGH PATRICK   MAP 13

Coordinates: Lat. 53.779028, Long. -9.640212

Irish Grid Reference: L 91948 82256

Opening hours/entry fees: Although there are no entry fees or opening hours that apply to simply walking the mountain, there is a visitor centre where you can find information and refreshments. www.croagh-patrick.com

Directions: The town of Westport is around fifteen minutes' drive away. From Westport, head south-westwards on the R335 for 9.8km and you will see the car park on your left (parking fees apply). The poignant and somewhat ghostly National Famine Memorial is directly across the road from the car park.

Nearest town: Westport (10km).

62 | WESTPORT HOUSE

Westport is one of Ireland's best towns, with a lively traditional music scene, fantastic food and a charming and relaxed atmosphere. Westport developed as a planned town under the auspices of the Browne family, Marquesses of Sligo. The English satirist William Thackeray, who visited Westport in 1842, wrote that 'Nature has done much for the pretty little town of Westport; and after nature, the traveller ought to be thankful to Lord Sligo, who has done a great deal too.' More can be discovered of the story of the town's development at Westport House.

Westport House

Westport House was first constructed by Colonel John Browne, who built on the site of a ruined O'Malley castle. He was originally a lawyer and had served in the army of King James II as a colonel. He was one of the key figures in the drafting of the Treaty of Limerick of 1691 that ended the Williamite War. He owned vast estates in Mayo and Galway, and he and his family were responsible for transforming Westport from a small rural village called Cathair na Mart, into a prosperous and vibrant harbour town.

Westport House was built by 1731 in the Palladian style, to a design by architects Richard Cassels and James Wyatt. It was constructed of fine grey limestone, giving the building an elegant and stately appearance. The house is set in beautiful surroundings, with gardens, terraces, a lake and magnificent views overlooking Clew Bay and the Atlantic. The house has been modified and extended by various generations of Brownes. The Browne family have an ancestry that includes the famous Gráinne Ní Mháille. Several of the splendid rooms inside the house can be viewed by visitors, giving a glimpse of the opulence and taste of the family. The Brownes were awarded the rank of Marquess of Sligo, and the family continued to live in the house until very recently, when it was sold. Today the future of this fabulous building has been secured, and it is a popular place for visitors.

WESTPORT HOUSE   MAP 13

Coordinates: Lat. 53.800137, Long. -9.535768

Irish Grid Reference: L 98858 84476

Opening hours/entry fees: Visit: www.westporthouse.ie

Directions: Westport House is situated on Quay Road just outside the town of Westport.

Nearest town: Westport (on the outskirts).

---

63 | BURRISHOOLE FRIARY

Burrishoole was a Dominican friary originally founded in 1469 by Richard de Burgo. It is said that the friars had not sought permission from the Pope to establish the monastery, and so they were under threat of excommunication. However, in 1486 the Pope ordered the Archbishop of Tuam to forgive the friars.

The Dominican Order first came to Ireland in around 1224 when they established a house in Dublin. The Dominicans had been founded as a mendicant order by Saint Dominic de Guzmán, who died in 1221. The order had an emphasis on poverty, preaching, ministry and opposition to heresy. Following the conquest of Connacht after 1235, the Dominicans began to establish foundations west of the Shannon, and in the fifteenth century they established a number of friaries in rural areas in Connacht, including this one at Burrishoole, which became a busy and prosperous harbour, and Dominican friars from Burrishoole travelled to the continent to work and study.

Burrishoole Friary

The remains today consist of a nave and chancel church with a low and rather squat tower, and a chapel on the southern side, and the eastern wall of the cloister. Interestingly, a fifteenth-century bronze seal was found embedded in a window in the upstairs dormitory.

Following the Dissolution of the Monasteries in the sixteenth century, Burrishoole began to fall into decline, though friars were still reported to be active at Burrishoole into the eighteenth century. It is reported that the roof of the church collapsed in 1793. Today Burrishoole is still in use as a graveyard for the local community, and it is an atmospheric and peaceful place to visit.

BURRISHOOLE   MAP 13

Coordinates: Lat. 53.898947, Long. -9.571578

Irish Grid Reference: L 96691 95513

Opening hours/entry fees: No opening hours or entry fees applied at the time of visit.

Directions: Newport is a five-minute drive away. Head west from Newport on the N59 for 2km, then turn left (signposted Burrishoole Abbey). Follow this narrow road for 1km to the friary. There is a small area to park.

Nearest town: Newport (2.7km).

64 | ROCKFLEET CASTLE

'This was a notorious woman in all the coasts of Ireland.'

Sir Henry Sydney, Lord Deputy, on Gráinne Ní Mháille in 1577.

The strategically positioned Rockfleet Castle

Rockfleet Castle, also known as Carrigahowley, from the Irish *Carraig an Chabhlaigh*, meaning 'rock of the fleet', is a late medieval four-storey tower house thought to have been built in the sixteenth century by the Bourkes, who were the overlords of the region. However, the castle is more famous for its associations with Gráinne Ní Mháille (also known as Gráinne Mhaol, Granuaile or Grace O'Malley). Gráinne is believed to have been born in 1530, and she spent most of her early years on **Clare Island** (Site 58), where she learned the arts of seafaring and command. She was the daughter of Dowdarra Roe O'Malley who controlled the region around Clew Bay. One of the legends about Gráinne is that she was forbidden to sail on her father's ships as her long hair might catch in the ship's ropes and tackle. Not to be deterred, Gráinne cut off all her hair, thus forcing her father to agree to take her on board. This act earned her nickname Gráinne Mhaol (from *maol*, meaning 'bald'). Gráinne's first marriage was to Dónal an Chogaidh Ó Flaithbheartaigh, who was set to inherit the region

The road to Rockfleet Castle

roughly equatable with modern Connemara. Together they had three children, but Dónal was killed in an ambush while hunting in the hills surrounding Lough Corrib. In 1566, Gráinne married the nobleman Risteárd an Iarainn Bourke, known as 'Iron Richard', who is reputed to have worn an old coat of chainmail inherited from his Anglo-Norman ancestors (though an alternative reason for the nickname may derive from his control of the important ironworks at Burrishoole).

Richard was a wealthy man with large landholdings, including the strategically important Rockfleet Castle. They married according to Irish traditional law, though it is said that the marriage was purely one of convenience and strategy for Gráinne. When one year had elapsed, and ensuring her men were in possession of the most strategic assets like Rockfleet, Gráinne divorced Richard in accordance with the law by saying 'Richard Bourke, I dismiss you' and Rockfleet Castle came under her control. She based herself at Rockfleet, and used it to harbour twenty of her ships.

ROCKFLEET CASTLE

The O'Malleys grew in wealth through trade and by taxing all the fishing and trading vessels that sailed in their waters. However, this practice was not universally approved of, and the influential merchant families of **Galway city** (Site 48) protested to the English Crown that the O'Malleys were acting as pirates. Gráinne had a complex relationship with the English authorities. It is said that she carried out many raids along the Irish and Scottish coasts on behalf of the Crown against rebellious lords. However, she was described by Richard Bingham, the infamous Lord President of Connacht, as 'the nurse of all the rebellions in Connacht for the past forty years'. When Bingham captured her sons, Gráinne travelled to London to meet Queen Elizabeth I to petition for their release. It is said that Gráinne refused to bow to Elizabeth, as she did not recognise her as Queen of Ireland. However, the two women appeared to come to an agreement during their negotiations (all of which were conducted in Latin). The outcome was that the tyrannical and cruel Richard Bingham was removed from his position in Ireland, and in return Gráinne swore to cease supporting rebellions and uprisings against the English. However, soon after the meeting, both sides reneged on their promises, and Bingham returned to Ireland, whilst Gráinne supported the Irish rebels during the Nine Years' War. Gráinne is said to have died in Rockfleet Castle in around 1603. She is believed to be buried in the abbey on Clare Island.

ROCKFLEET CASTLE   MAP 13

Coordinates: Lat. 53.896090, Long. -9.627243

Irish Grid Reference: L 93088 95282

Opening hours/entry fees: No opening hours or entry fees applied at the time of visit.

Directions: Newport is a ten-minute drive away. Head west from Newport on the N59 for 6km, then turn left (signposted Carrigahowley Castle). Follow this narrow road to the castle. There is a small area to park.

Nearest town: Newport (7.5km).

65 | ACHILL ISLAND

Achill Island is a truly rewarding place to explore, with a wonderful blend of fascinating heritage and truly breathtaking scenery that includes spectacular sea cliffs, and five Blue Flag beaches, including the stunning Keem Bay. The island has been a source of inspiration for many writers and artists through the years, and it continues to be a popular place for those seeking a deeper immersion into the Irish culture and landscape. This mountainous island is connected to the mainland by the Michael Davitt Bridge, which connects Achill Sound to Polranny. The landscape is dominated by the mountain of Slievemore, and a wealth of historic monuments can be discovered around every corner of the island. The Achill Archaeological Field School has been carrying out vital work investigating and highlighting the heritage of the island.

Kildavnet Church and Graveyard

Kildavnet Church

This area takes its name from *Cill Damhnait*, perhaps referring to the Church of Dymphna, a seventh-century saint who, tradition says, sought shelter here while fleeing from pursuers. Today you can see the ruins of a small late medieval church that is presumably associated with the nearby **Kildavnet Castle**, and a graveyard that straddles both sides of the road. The graveyard has burials from a number of periods, including plots of those who died during the Great Famine. There are also monuments dedicated to significant tragedies in Achill's history, one to a group of more than 30 Achill residents travelling to Scotland who drowned when their boat overturned in Clew Bay. A second monument within the graveyard is a memorial to the ten young emigrants from Achill who tragically lost their lives in a fire at Kirkintilloch, Scotland.

Kildavnet Castle

Kildavnet Castle

This tower house is thought to date to the fifteenth century, and it was built by the O'Malleys to guard Achill Sound. The site is particularly associated with Gráinne Ní Mháille, the famous Pirate Queen (for more on her story please see **Clare Island**, Site 58, and **Rockfleet Castle**, Site 64). The tower house is three storeys and about 12m (40 feet) tall. The ruins of a bawn wall that once surrounded and protected the tower can still be made out.

Keel East Court Tomb

Keel East Court Tomb

It is worth the steep climb up the craggy slopes to the shoulder of Slievemore to visit the court tomb at Keel East. On the day I visited, the hill was shrouded in Atlantic mist, adding an atmospheric sense of mystery but also depriving me of what would surely be beautiful views over the island. The tomb has a roughly circular court area and a three-chambered gallery. It is likely to date back over 5,000 years to the Neolithic period.

Slievemore Deserted Village

The Deserted Village

One of the ruined cottages in the deserted village at Slievemore

A short drive from the tomb, at the base of Slievemore, lies one of Ireland's most poignant historical sites: the ruins of a number of houses that formed a village, once the home of a substantial community. The first edition of the Ordnance Survey, which was produced in 1838, recorded 137 houses, of which around 80 can still be made out today. The majority of these traditional drystone houses were one-roomed cabins, known as 'byre houses', as the inhabitants would have kept their livestock with them within the small houses overnight during winter. Inside many of the houses you can still see the drainage channel that separated the livestock from the dwelling area, and a number of houses still have tethering rings in the walls.

This settlement may have ancient origins, with houses being constructed on top of older dwellings, and archaeological investigation revealed the settlement to date to at least as far back as the twelfth century, though given the proximity of the megalithic tomb at Keel East, it is likely that people lived in the vicinity in the Neolithic period, and recent archaeological discoveries have identified Bronze Age settlement in the area.

Many families left the settlement in the mid-nineteenth century, either from eviction from non-payment of rent through poverty, or through emigration. In the aftermath of the Great Famine, much of the land of Achill came under the control of the

Achill Mission Estate in 1852, a Protestant missionary endeavour that had been established at Dugort some twenty years previously under Rev. Edward Nangle. This led to a reorganisation of the settlement and its field systems. The village became more a base for seasonal booleying, where livestock was moved to mountain grazing during the growing season, allowing the crops to grow undisturbed in the more fertile lowlands, and this practice continued up until the 1940s. Today, the village is an atmospheric place to visit to get a sense of the harsh life of islanders in the nineteenth century.

ACHILL ISLAND   MAP 14

Coordinates:

Kildavnet Church: Lat. 53.883652, Long. -9.944936
Kildavnet Castle: Lat. 53.881031, Long. -9.946218
Keel East Court Tomb: Lat. 53.995531, Long. -10.059032
Deserted Village at Slievemore: Lat. 53.996415, Long. -10.092110

Irish Grid Reference: F 64959 07588

Opening hours/entry fees: Though no opening times or entry fees applied at the time of writing, it is worth visiting the Achill Archaeological Field School website for more information about the island: www.achill-fieldschool.com

Directions: Kildavnet Church and Castle are located on the L1405 in the south of Achill Island. When you cross Achill Sound, bear left onto the L1405 following the sign for *An Chloich Mhóir* and Atlantic Drive. You will arrive at the church after 6.5km, and the castle is just a little further on.

The tomb at Keel East is a 20–30 minute walk up a steep slope: good boots are advised and if it is as misty as it was on the day I visited then you might well get a soaking from all the overhanging foliage. To get there, turn right off the R319 at Keel onto the Slievemore Road (signposted Achill IT Centre and Achill Local Development Company). Stay on the road as it bears right, following the sign for Doogort and Atlantic Drive. Continue on this road and you will see a sign on your right-hand side pointing left for the 'megalithic tomb'. Pull in as unobtrusively as possible and walk through the small gate that leads up the narrow path between the two properties. The path steadily climbs upwards onto the shoulder of Slievemore. There are usually sheep present so it would not be suitable for dogs.

For the Deserted Famine Village, head west from Keel on the R319 to the village of Dooagh. Turn right in Dooagh onto the Slievemore Road and continue up this road for approximately 2.8km. Bear left following the sign for the Deserted Village and park. Walk up the track to the houses.

Nearest town: Mulranny (23km).

ACHILL ISLAND

217

Ballycroy National Park Visitor Centre

The beautiful wilderness of Ballycroy National Park is certainly well worth taking the time to explore, with a visitor centre that tells the story of this landscape of blanket bogs, cliff and river habitats, all dominated by the Nephin Beg Mountains.

Just south of the visitor centre is the Claggan Mountain Coastal Trail, with wooden boardwalks that allow you to traverse the deep sucking bog, covered in bog cotton in the summer with still pools, serenaded by the calls of wading birds. The bog is an ever-evolving and fascinating landscape. It began to form around 5,000 years ago when the soils became much more waterlogged as the climate turned wetter and the first farmers in the Neolithic cleared much of the forests, allowing peat moss to develop. The stumps and gnarled roots of millennia-old trees still fringe the shoreline, remnants of a once-mighty Scots pine forest that thrived here thousands of years ago.

The mirror-like pools of water on the surface of the bog hide a thriving ecosystem, where insects are particularly abundant: from the dreaded ubiquitous midges and whirligig beetles to beautiful dragonflies that dart around with incredible speed and agility. Due to the low nutrient value of the peat, some species of plant like the bladderwort or sundew have evolved to eat insects. The spoon-shaped leaves of the sundew are covered with tiny red tentacle-like protrusions that emit a clear secretion, which insects mistake for nectar. When the insect lands, it becomes 'glued' by the sticky substance. Its struggles cause the other tentacles and leaves to close up over the top of the insect, trapping it while it is slowly digested, providing nutrient to the sundew.

A sundew, one of the insectivorous plants you may encounter in an Irish bog

Though present for millennia, Ireland's bogs are under threat. Vast landscapes of bog in the midlands have been overexploited for turf fuel and large swathes of blanket bog were planted with imported coniferous trees for lumber, causing the fragmentation and drainage of many of Ireland's bogs. Areas such as this at Ballycroy represent some of the best-preserved bog landscapes. Along the Claggan Mountain Coastal Trail you can see the important environment created where blanket bog meets the shoreline, creating a habitat for otters, ringed plover, red-breasted merganser, heron and the endangered curlew.

The Claggan Mountain Coastal Trail

BALLYCROY NATIONAL PARK MAP 13

Coordinates: (Visitor Centre) Lat. 54.024706, Long. -9.823834

Irish Grid Reference: F 80523 09918 **Opening hours/entry fees:** Visit: www. ballycroynationalpark.ie

Directions: Ballycroy National Park Visitor Centre is located just off the N59. From Mulranny simply head north on the N59 for 16km and the entrance to the visitor centre will be on your right. There are a number of walks and looped trails in the park, and the visitor centre can provide you with maps and information.

Nearest town: Mulranny (16km).

67 | FALLMORE CHURCH

This small church on the stunningly scenic Mullet Peninsula is believed to have originally been dedicated to Saint Deirbhile (also known as Deirbhileadh or Dairbhile). The ruins of the church that you see here are believed to be of twelfth-century date. It is built from pink granite. The curving stones that form the lintel of the doorway bear much-weathered designs, at first glance appearing as a series of curved lines, but if the light is kind you can make out a more complex design, which archaeologist Peter Harbison has tentatively suggested may contain a panel depicting the Crucifixion. Inside the graveyard you can see the square foundations of a small structure, believed to have been the tomb shrine of Deirbhile.

Fallmore Church

Saint Deirbhile's Well lies a short distance to the north of the church.

Saint Deirbhile's Well

Deirbhile's Twist, part of the North Mayo Sculpture Trail

Deirbhile was a sixth-century saint and contemporary of Saint Colmcille, who according to legend fled to Fallmore from her home in Meath to escape an ardent admirer. He was said to be besotted with her beautiful eyes, so in desperation she ripped her own eyes out from their sockets to put him off. At this point it appears the horrified suitor finally grasped that Deirbhile wasn't interested and left. A pool of clear water formed where her eyes fell, and Deirbhile bathed the sockets in the water, which miraculously restored her eyes and vision. A holy well stands on the site where she bathed her eyes not far from the church, and local tradition still maintains its waters are a cure for eye complaints. A pilgrimage takes place annually to the well on 15 August on the feast day of Saint Deirbhile. The story of Deirbhile is also commemorated nearby in Deirbhile's Twist, a striking artwork in stone that is part of the North Mayo Sculpture Trail.

Coordinates:
Fallmore Church: Lat. 54.095865, Long. -10.106436
Deirbhile's Twist Artwork: Lat. 54.095529, Long. -10.085569

Irish Grid Reference: F 63604 18229

Opening hours/entry fees: No opening times or entry fees applied at the time of writing.

Directions: Fallmore Church is located near the very bottom of the beautiful Mullet Peninsula, approximately 25 minutes' drive from Belmullet. From Belmullet, head south onto the Mullet Peninsula on the R313 for about 16.5km. At the village of Aghleam turn right towards the coast road (signposted *Bóthar an Chósta*) and take the first left turn after 200m. Continue on this road for 750m and bear right when the road splits into a Y. Continue on this road for 1.8km and turn right at the crossroads (signposted *Teampall Naomh Dheirbhile*). The church will be on your right after 300m.

Nearest town: Belmullet (20km).

68 | CÉIDE FIELDS

For millennia, the bleak blanket bog along the wild coast of North Mayo hid a fascinating system of field walls, enclosures and monuments that were created over 5,000 years ago in the Neolithic period. The walls were first noted by a local schoolteacher, Patrick Caulfield. His son, the archaeologist Seamus Caulfield, carried out a groundbreaking programme of excavation and survey that has revealed one of the most significant prehistoric landscapes in Ireland.

This landscape is of great importance; although a number of Neolithic tombs can still be seen around the country, there are few places where an entire managed agricultural landscape dating back to this period still exist. This gives incredible insight into the farming practice and daily life of Ireland's earliest farmers. From the complex of field systems we can infer that they were created by a highly developed society and must have involved close cooperation by a large number of people to fell the forests and build the walls. Their religious beliefs can be seen in the megalithic

CÉIDE FIELDS

One of the walkways running parallel to the Neolithic field wall at the Céide Fields

The breathtaking coastline of North Mayo

tombs that were also discovered during the survey, along with a number of houses that give an indication of how they lived.

A number of the fields are very large by contemporary Irish standards, with enclosed areas of up to several hectares in size, and may have been used as cattle pasture. Analysis of the pollen trapped within the ancient soil indicates that some of the smaller fields, like the ones close to the visitor centre, may have been used to grow cereal, conceivably early species of wheat, like emmer. During the Neolithic period the climate would have been both drier and warmer than now. Once the forests of pine, birch, hazel and oak had been felled, this landscape was ideal for agriculture. Over millennia the climate has changed, and become both colder and wetter, allowing for the development of the blanket bog

that has sealed and preserved much of this fascinating ancient landscape. The award-winning visitor centre and excellent OPW guides help to tell this remarkable story.

CÉIDE FIELDS

MAP 15

Coordinates: Lat. 54.308174, Long. -9.456516

Irish Grid Reference: G 05242 40909

Opening hours/entry fees: For opening times and entry fees visit: www. heritageireland.ie/en/west/ceidefields/

Directions: The Céide Fields are located on the R314 (the main Wild Atlantic Way) between Belderrig and Ballycastle. From Ballycastle follow the R314 north-west and you will reach the site after 8km. There is ample parking at the excellent visitor centre.

Nearest towns: Ballycastle (8km), Belderrig (7km).

CÉIDE FIELDS

Doonfeeny Standing Stone

The area around Doonfeeny is an important early medieval landscape, with a number of ringforts and archaeological monuments. Perhaps the most striking is the tall, slender pillar of stone that stands proudly on a green hill overlooking the Atlantic. It was likely to have first been erected in the Bronze Age, perhaps to mark a territorial boundary, or perhaps to mark the area as sacred. Although we may never know for certain the true intention of those who erected the stone, it still undeniably creates a powerful visual signpost in the landscape. It stands some 5m (nearly 15 feet) tall, making it one of the tallest standing stones in Ireland. Like so many prehistoric ritual sites, it was appropriated in the early days of Christianity, and two crosses were carved into the stone, a single-line Latin cross with forked ends and horizontal base placed over a double-line Maltese type cross with a curved 'bird's-head design' line. The crosses may date to as early as the sixth or seventh century, or perhaps even earlier. From the site you can see the sea stack known as Dún Briste at **Downpatrick Head** (Site 70), a site associated with the legends of St Patrick. It is enticing to consider that the 'real' Patrick may have seen this tall stone with his own eyes. It is not a great distance to Foghill, believed to be Foclut, the area that he described in his writings where he was held as a slave as a young man. The stone would have certainly already been standing for thousands of years before Patrick's time, and may have still been a distinctive marker on the landscape. If a young Patrick did see the stone, did he know what it symbolised? Or was it just another unknowable symbol in the strange pagan land in which he found himself?

The crosses carved into the surface of the stone

DOONFEENY

MAP 15

Coordinates: Lat. 54.298589, Long. -9.403342

Irish Grid Reference: G 08683 39773

Opening hours/entry fees: No entry fees or opening hours applied at the time of writing.

Directions: Doonfeeny is a short five-minute drive from Ballycastle. Simply head north-west on the R314 for a little over 2.5km, pass straight through the crossroads and take the next turn left up a narrow road (with grass growing in the middle of it). Follow this road for approximately 500m and you will see the tall stone pillar on your left, and the ruins of a church on your right. There is just enough room to pull in the car on the left.

Nearest town: Ballycastle (3km).

DOONFEENY STANDING STONE

Standing close to the edge of the cliff at Downpatrick Head to see the entirety of the breathtaking sandstone pillar of Dún Briste at Downpatrick Head is a truly knee-wobbling experience, as the Atlantic roils and boils far below. The sea stack was once connected to the mainland by a sea arch, until it collapsed in the medieval period.

A number of archaeological monuments have been identified on Dún Briste, including a promontory fort, and the remains of buildings that may be from the medieval period. On the mainland, the remains of a church and a series of penitential stations point to the importance of Downpatrick as a Christian place of pilgrimage. This area is imbued with the story of Saint Patrick, and a statue to him can be seen on the headland. There are many folkloric stories about this area. One of the tales tells of the powerful pagan king Crom Dubh, who challenged Patrick and tried to hurl the saint into a fire. Before he could be seized, Patrick scratched a cross onto a stone and flung it into the flames, causing the fire and the

Left: Monument to Saint Patrick at Downpatrick Head

Opposite page: Dún Briste

ground around it to collapse into the sea and forming the feature known as *Poll a' Sean Tine* ('the hole of the old fire'). In terror at this demonstration of power, Crom Dubh retreated inside his fort on the edge of the mainland. Patrick followed him and struck his staff on the causeway, forcing it to collapse and forever trapping Crom Dubh inside his ruined fort on Dún Briste.

During the Second World War (or 'the Emergency', as it was known here), a lookout post was constructed here to keep watch for shipping or submarines that might stray into Ireland's neutral waters and a large ÉIRE sign was created from white stones to warn aircraft away from crossing into Irish airspace.

DOWNPATRICK HEAD MAP 15

Coordinates: Lat. 54.322856, Long. -9.345851

Irish Grid Reference: G 12502 42365

Opening hours/entry fees: No entry fees or opening hours applied at the time of writing.

Directions: Downpatrick Head is just ten minutes' drive north of Ballycastle. From Ballycastle, head north on Dominick Street for just over 4km and take the left-hand turn at the crossroads (signposted for Downpatrick Head). Simply follow this road for just under 2km all the way to the car park.

Nearest town: Ballycastle (6km).

---

71 | RATHFRAN FRIARY

Rathfran Friary was founded for the Dominican Order in *c.* 1274 by William de Burgh on a strategic location near the mouth of the Cloonaghmore River as it flows into Killala Bay. It is a tranquil place for a monastery, as it is well sheltered from the prevailing winds by low hills. It may have been founded on the site of an important pre-Norman Irish fort, as the name Rathfran derives from the Irish *Rath Brandubh* ('the fort of Brandubh'). This was clearly an important and perhaps even sacred landscape for millennia. Megalithic tombs, such as the **wedge tomb** that can be accessed easily from the R314 road, offer evidence of the sacred aspect of this region. Along with the megalithic tombs, stone

Rathfran Friary

A megalithic tomb near Rathfran

circles and Bronze Age burial monuments known as barrows are also to be found in the vicinity, along with evidence of early medieval settlement with numerous ringforts or raths nearby.

Despite the strategic location and relatively fertile lands, the friary struggled financially in the fifteenth century as it was recorded in 1458 that the friary was impoverished. A series of indulgences were offered for those who would donate money or labour, and the offer was successful as some renovation and construction was carried out on site in the late fifteenth century, with the addition of some of the lancet windows and modifications to the nave. In 1513, the Annals of Ulster record that Edmond de Burgh was slaughtered in the friary by his cousins, the sons of Walter de Burgh. This shocking murder broke all the laws of sanctuary.

The visible remains on the site consist of a church with a chapel to its south and two ranges of domestic buildings to the north, which appear to date from the sixteenth century. The church has an interesting panel depicting the Crucifixion over the western door. You can also see the remains of the cloisters and a series of other buildings but they survive only as low foundation walls. You can see the remnants of what would have been a particularly large east window in the church, but it is said that all the delicate stone tracery was shattered and destroyed in 1839 during the *Oíche na Gaoithe Móire* ('the Night of the Big Wind'), which wreaked devastation across this region, wrecking more than 40 ships and killing hundreds when buildings crumbled and roofs collapsed.

After the Dissolution of the Monasteries under Henry VIII in the mid-sixteenth century, the friary was granted to Thomas de Exeter, only to be burned by Sir Richard Bingham in 1590. Following the destruction of the friary, the lands were granted to Thomas Taaffe, but friars continued to serve in this area until the eighteenth century.

There is a local belief that the nearby **Summerhill House** was constructed from stone plundered from the friary. The house is said to have been cursed because of this despoilment of the holy site, and ill luck fell on all who lived there, perhaps the reason why the house now lies in ruin.

Summerhill House

72 | KILLALA ROUND TOWER

The region of Killala Bay is absolutely saturated with important early Christian sites, and this landscape has long been associated with Saint Patrick. The round tower of Killala is the last surviving remnant of a once-important monastery, traditionally said to have been founded by Patrick himself, though the name Killala derives from *Cill Alaid*, 'the church of Alad'. Killala became a diocese after the Synod of Ráth Breasail in 1111.

Although it appears to dominate the town from a distance, up close it can be difficult to get a full sense of the round tower as it is so hemmed in by buildings. It stands approximately 26m (85 feet) tall, and it is built of finely dressed limestone, with the arch of the doorway lined with distinctive pale sandstone that contrasts against the dark limestone of the main fabric. The doorway is positioned 3m (nearly 10 feet) off the ground, and looks out to the south-east, towards Saint Patrick's Cathedral. This is one of Ireland's smallest cathedrals, and it was built in the late seventeenth century, with the tower and spire added in the nineteenth century. It is likely to stand on the site of an early medieval predecessor. The distance between the cathedral and the round tower gives an idea of the area encompassed by the inner enclosure of the early monastery.

Killala round tower

The town of Killala was the site of the first action of the French army of General Humbert that had landed in Kilcummin Harbour to support the 1798 Rebellion. Humbert quickly defeated the small number of local yeomen who resisted, and marched his forces through Killala to win an initial victory near Castlebar where a combined force of French soldiers and Irish rebels defeated and routed the more numerous British militia, in an action that became popularly known as the 'Castlebar Races'. After the victory, Humbert declared a 'Republic of Connacht', but elsewhere the 1798 Rebellion was already all but crushed. Humbert was defeated at the Battle of Ballinamuck and taken prisoner. Killala was retaken shortly afterwards in a decisive victory for the British.

KILLALA   MAP 15

Coordinates: Lat. 54.212905, Long. -9.220476

Irish Grid Reference: G 20408 30029

Opening hours/entry fees: No entry fees or opening hours applied at the time of writing.

Directions: The round tower is located on Steeple Hill in the centre of Killala.

Nearest town: In Killala.

---

73 | MOYNE FRIARY

The extensive ruins of Moyne Friary

The cloister

One of the largest Franciscan friaries in Ireland, and certainly amongst the most impressive, Moyne is believed to have been founded for the Franciscan Order in around 1455. The extensive ruins at Moyne include a large nave and chancel church with a tall tower, particularly fine cloisters, and domestic buildings such as the kitchen and refectory where they ate in silence whilst a friar read aloud from the bible, standing in the small recess called a *pulpitum*.

You enter the friary through a finely carved western doorway that appears to be later, perhaps seventeenth-century in date. The nave was extended with the addition of an aisle. If you look carefully at the remains of the plaster on the western nave wall you can see an etched graffiti depiction of a seventeenth-century ship, perhaps reflecting the role of the sea and trade in this coastal setting.

As well as the religious buildings of the friary, evidence of other important buildings, such as the mill, give an insight into the

Moyne Ship

Moyne Ship
(highlighted)

economy and practicalities of a large monastery. With good land holdings, and with the ideal location of Moyne, the friars could enjoy a relatively rich and varied diet. Their well-tended gardens provided vegetables, their orchards fruit, and there were fishponds and the nearby shore provided crustaceans and shellfish.

However, the grand Irish Gothic-style architecture exudes a rather brooding and somewhat dark atmosphere, perhaps a result of the terrible events that happened in the friary in the sixteenth century. During a campaign against rebel insurgents in 1579, English soldiers arrested a number of friars and local men and brought them all into the friary. One of the local men was accused of plotting against Queen Elizabeth. He was allowed to make confession to a friar before he was hanged from the friary tower. The soldiers then quickly seized Fr John O'Dowd, the friar who had taken the confession of the doomed man. They demanded to be told all that was confessed in case the executed man had imparted any knowledge of a plot. In accordance with his vows, and to guard the sacrament, Fr O'Dowd refused to break the seal of confession. The soldiers tortured him cruelly: ropes were bound around his forehead and temples and slowly tightened by the turning of a stick. Despite the agony Fr O'Dowd still refused to speak, until his skull finally burst under the pressure.

Just a few short years later, in 1582, the friars were tipped off about an impending English raid. The community quickly gathered their valuables and made their escape on boats, with the exception of an old lay brother, Felim O'Hara, who volunteered to stay behind in an attempt to protect the friars' property. When the friars returned some days later, they found the friary badly plundered, and the butchered body of Brother Felim lying in front of the high altar. In 1590, as part of his vicious campaign, Sir Richard Bingham raided and burned the friaries of Moyne, **Rathfran** and **Rosserk**. After these outrages, the friary and its land were granted by Queen Elizabeth to Edward Barrett, though a small community of friars continued to worship here as they rented the church and a few small buildings from Barrett. By the end of the eighteenth century, the community had diminished and ceased to worship at Moyne.

MOYNE FRIARY MAP 15

Coordinates: Lat. 54.201711, Long. -9.183342

Irish Grid Reference: G 23242 28770

Opening hours/entry fees: No entry fees or opening hours applied at the time of writing.

Directions: Moyne Friary is a very short drive (five minutes or so) from Killala. Head south-east from Killala on the R314 for just over 1km, and then turn left (signposted for Moyne Abbey). Stay on this road for approximately 2km and you will see a signpost pointing left (the sign will be on your right). Please park carefully in front of the wall, taking care not to block the road or the gates. There is a small stile next to the gate: climb the stile and follow the rough path that runs parallel to the wall (the bungalow house will be on your right). Take note of the Beware of the Bull sign and if livestock are in the field be sure to seek permission before entering. Not suitable for dogs.

Nearest town: Killala (3km).

Rosserk Friary

Rosserk is one of my personal favourites among Ireland's late medieval abbeys. Beautifully situated on an estuary of the River Moy, the friary was founded for the Franciscans around 1440, but, unlike nearby **Moyne**, it was established for the Third Order of Franciscans. This was a congregation of men and women, many of whom were married but wanted to live a life of religious service according to the teachings of Saint Francis. The rules demanded simplicity in dress and diet, regular prayer, periods of fasting and abstinence and a prohibition on bearing arms.

A unique depiction of a round tower on a pillar of the piscina, perhaps representing the tower of nearby Killala?

ROSSERK FRIARY

The friary is very well preserved, and consists of a church with a slender central tower and transept, and a small cloister with domestic buildings to the north, which include a chapter house, dormitories, refectory and kitchen. The church has a beautiful four-light east window in the choir, and a sedilia and double piscina can be seen on the southern wall. The piscina is worthy of close inspection: it has a depiction of two angels, and the instruments of the Passion. Notably, one of the uprights has a unique carving of a round tower, a possible depiction of the nearby tower at Killala.

Depiction of angels on the piscina

ROSSERK FRIARY MAP 15

Coordinates: Lat. 54.171255, Long. -9.143712

Irish Grid Reference: G 25376 25317

Opening hours/entry fees: No entry fees or opening hours applied at the time of writing.

Directions: Rosserk Friary is approximately fifteen minutes' drive from Ballina. Head north from Ballina on the R314 for approximately 6km and turn right at the crossroads. Continue on this road for approximately 2km until you get to the next crossroads and take a left (signposted Rosserk Abbey). Continue on this road for just over 1km and take the next right (signposted Rosserk Friary). Follow this small road for 1.5km down to the site. There is a small area to park.

Nearest town: Ballina (11km).

75 | BALLINA

Bustling Ballina is located at the mouth of the River Moy near Killala Bay, a location that allowed it to develop as a port and market town. Now the largest town in County Mayo, it has a number of places of interest to discover. Just next to the imposing neo-Gothic edifice of Saint Muredach's Cathedral, you can see the ruins of an Augustinian abbey that was founded here in 1427. On a sandbank in the port you can see the SS *Crete Boom*, a ship made of steel and reinforced concrete that was launched in 1919. Concrete ships were trialled around the end of the First World War. They were initially popular as the construction materials were relatively plentiful and cheap, but they proved to be enormously expensive to operate and maintain. In 1937, the Ballina Harbour Commissioners purchased the now decrepit SS *Crete Boom* with the intention of sinking it at the mouth of the river as a barrier to prevent sand building up in the harbour, but, distracted by the outbreak of the Second World War, they never carried out the work and the ship slowly sank into the centre of the river. It was finally moved in 1974 to its present location on the west bank of the Moy.

The concrete ship, SS *Crete Boom*

There are some fine period buildings in the town. Inside the former Provincial Bank you can find the **Jackie Clarke Collection**, a fantastic historical resource that is based on the amazing assemblage of over 10,000 historical items and documents relating to Irish history and the struggle for independence, all collected by local businessman Jackie Clarke and bequeathed to Mayo County Council. The collection includes artefacts and correspondence associated with figures like Theobald Wolfe Tone, Michael Collins, Douglas Hyde, Michael Davitt and Jeremiah O'Donovan Rossa, along with newspapers, rare books, posters, political cartoons and an original copy of a 1916 Proclamation.

On the outskirts of the town on Primrose Hill stands a megalithic tomb known as the **Dolmen of the Four Maols**. According to legend, the Four Maols were four brothers – Maol Cróin, Maol Seanaidh, Maoldalua and Maol Deoraidh – who murdered a bishop named Cellach. According to the story, they were put to death and quartered at Ardnaree, the Hill of Executions, on the eastern side of the river, and buried here. Sadly, surrounding development has impinged upon the aspect and atmosphere of this important site, but it is still well worth seeking out for its strange story.

The excellent Jackie
Clarke Collection

The Dolmen of the Four Maols

BALLINA

MAP 15

Coordinates:

Jackie Clarke Collection: Lat. 54.253180, Long. -8.557648
Dolmen of the Four Maols: Lat. 54.107063, Long. -9.165735

Irish Grid Reference: G 24640 19009

Opening hours/entry fees: Visit: www.clarkecollection.ie for the Jackie Clarke Collection. No entry fees or opening hours applied to the Dolmen at the time of writing.

Directions: The Jackie Clarke Collection is on Pearse Street in the town. The Dolmen of the Four Maols is less than five minutes from the town centre. Head south from Ballina on the N26 and turn right over a level crossing (the dolmen is signposted) and continue for approximately 400m. The dolmen is on the high ground on your left-hand side just after the retail park.

Nearest town: In Ballina.

SLIGO

Taking in the stunning view from Knocknarea

The coast of Sligo has become world-renowned for its wonderful waves that are every surfer's dream, and the lively towns and sandy beaches are a fun and life-affirming place to explore.

However, the beautiful landscape offers ancient tales, and the cairn-topped mountains of Sligo are truly monumental. Sligo's mountains and coast were clearly sacred to our Neolithic ancestors, and we will visit the important passage tomb cemetery at Carrowmore, climb the steep slope of Knocknarea Mountain to visit *Miosgán Meadhbha*, the final resting place of the legendary warrior queen Maeve, and seek out ancient tombs hidden in forest glades.

We will explore the vibrant town of Sligo, to discover its medieval heritage and travel to Drumcliff to see an early monastery with high crosses, a round tower, and the tomb of the great writer W.B. Yeats who rests 'under Benbulben's bare head'. We will also take a voyage across Donegal Bay to visit the remarkable island monastery of Inishmurray. Sligo truly has a wealth of fascinating places just waiting to be discovered.

76 | EASKEY CASTLE

The surfer's paradise of Easkey is a lovely laid-back village on the coast of west Sligo. The town is named after the Easkey River, and it has become one of the most popular places in Ireland for water sports and as home to the Irish Surfing Association it is renowned around the world for perfect surfing conditions.

Standing proudly alongside Easkey Pier, the castle (also known as Roslee Castle or O'Dowd's Castle) is thought to have first been constructed by Oliver McDonnell in 1207. Oliver was a Scottish gallowglass warrior and a Lord of the Isles that lie between Antrim and Scotland. He came to Easkey to marry an O'Dowd, who were the traditional rulers of this area that was once known as *Tír Fhíacrach Múaidhe*. A record from 1618 declared that King James I granted Daniel O'Dowd 'two castles, a kitchen, a bake house within the bawn of Roslee'. However, following the Williamite Wars in the final decade of the seventeenth century, the castle was granted to a Williamite soldier named Ormsby. The castle has suffered from the relentless battering of Atlantic weather, and only one tower still stands.

Easkey Castle

A terrible tragedy happened in the Atlantic off the coast of Easkey on 2 July 1940, when a British ship, the *Arandora Star*, was torpedoed by a German U-boat. The ship was packed with 1,500 internees, people of Italian and German birth who had been settled in the United Kingdom but who, after the outbreak of war, were seen as a possible threat; they were rounded up to be deported to Canada, far from the front line of a potential German invasion. Over 800 people lost their lives when the ship sank, including Matteo Fossaluzza, a 43-year-old man from Cavasso Nuovo in Italy. His body washed ashore here, and it was temporarily buried in Roslea Cemetery before reaching its final resting place in Saint Pancras Cemetery in his former home of London.

EASKEY CASTLE   MAP 16

Coordinates: Lat. 54.291818, Long. -8.956494

Irish Grid Reference: G 37764 38533

Opening hours/entry fees: No entry fees or opening hours applied at the time of writing. For more information about Easkey visit: www.easkey.ie

Directions: The castle is located next to the charming village of Easkey. From Ballina head north-east on the N59 for just over 19km then turn left (signposted for Easkey). Follow this road for 7.5km and you will reach the castle and pier.

Nearest towns: Ballina (27km), Sligo (42.5km).

---

77 | KNOCKNAREA

County Sligo is particularly rich in megalithic monuments, and many of them are located in the Cúil Irra Peninsula, and focused towards the cairn-topped mountain of Knocknarea that so dominates the landscape. Legend has it that the great stone cairn known as *Miosgán Meadhbha* is the final resting place of the famous warrior queen Maeve, one of the chief protagonists of the epic *Táin Bó Cúailnge*. She is said to have been buried standing upright in her armour, still facing her ancient Ulster enemies. The cairn measures almost 60m (197 feet) in diameter, and stands some 10m (33 feet) high. Although it has never been excavated, it is thought that the cairn may cover a large Neolithic passage tomb.

The great stone cairn known as *Miosgán Meadhbha*

As well as the great cairn, a number of monuments, also believed to be passage tombs, are evident on the summit of the mountain, and arranged in a roughly linear pattern north and south of the great cairn. The summit is enclosed by steep cliffs on the northern, western and southern sides, and extensive stony banks along the eastern side. This demarcation perhaps signified that the enclosed mountain summit was in itself a sacred space. A number of hut sites have been identified on the southern slopes of the mountain. Whether these represent permanent settlement or were used as temporary accommodation during ceremonies is unknown. The mountain and its cairn appear to be the focal point of a number of prehistoric tomb sites in the Cúil Irra Peninsula, along with other sites at **Carrowmore** and **Carns Hill**, forming one of Ireland's most important and striking prehistoric landscapes.

The wonderful view from the summit of Knocknarea

The walk up Knocknarea offers some of the most spectacular views in Ireland, as the beauty of County Sligo and its Atlantic coastline opens out around you. The walk up to the cairn takes roughly 30 to 45 minutes. It's relatively steep to begin with and good footwear is advised, but the summit is broad and flat, allowing you a leisurely stroll while you take in the stunning scenery. Please do not be tempted to climb or interfere with the cairn as, despite its size, it is a vulnerable archaeological site of great antiquity and importance.

KNOCKNAREA

MAP 16

Coordinates: (Car park) Lat. 54.253180, Long. -8.557648

Irish Grid Reference: G 62637 34566 **Opening hours/entry fees:** No opening times or entry fees applied at the time of writing.

Directions: Knocknarea is well signposted and is approximately a fifteen-minute drive from Sligo: head west from Sligo on the N4 and turn right onto the R292 Knappagh Road. After 3km turn left (signposted Knocknarea). After 1.2km turn right at the T-Junction (again following the sign for Knocknarea) and continue on this road for approximately 2.5km, finally turning right again when you see the sign for Knocknarea Mountain car park.

Nearest town: Sligo (7.5km).

Carrowmore is part of an extensive and important prehistoric landscape in the shadow of the mountain of Knocknarea

The landscape of the Cúil Irra Peninsula west of Sligo town is one of the best places in Ireland to encounter wonderful prehistoric megalithic tombs, and the Carrowmore passage tomb cemetery is an integral part of this incredible series of monuments. Here at Carrowmore, clustering in the shadow of **Knocknarea**, you can find the densest concentration of Neolithic tombs in Ireland. The tombs are laid out in a rough oval with a diameter of over a kilometre at the broadest part. It has been speculated that the concentration of tombs of Carrowmore may reflect a segmented society, with different tribes owning their own tomb. Of the 60 or so monuments thought to have originally been on the site, only 31 are still visible today.

The monuments at Carrowmore may be some of the earliest versions of Neolithic passage tombs. Charcoal found within one of the tombs produced radiocarbon dates of 5400 BC and 4600 BC but there is much debate about whether these early dates represent the construction and use of the tomb or earlier pre-tomb activity, or even that older, perhaps sacred, material was placed in the tomb as part of some kind of ritual practice, perhaps honouring the ancestors. Recent studies by Stefan Bergh and Robert Hensey have established that the cemetery was in use from at least as early as 3775–3520 BC. However, the tombs of Carrowmore are quite different in many ways from the likes of Newgrange and the other famous passage tombs of the Boyne Valley. The tombs here are on a much smaller scale, and their small chambers were not designed for access, unlike the more elaborate tombs of Brú na Bóinne. Instead of an accessible passageway, these tombs tend to have a rudimentary passage that did not reach the edge of the monument and therefore may not have been designed to allow access. Rather than neatly arranged kerbs, the tombs of Carrowmore are typically surrounded by a circle of boulders. Excavations suggest that the tombs were also different as many appear not to have been covered by a great mound of earth or stone, though the central chamber itself may have been covered.

Tomb 7 at Carrowmore

The largest tomb at Carrowmore is Listoghil. Material from Listoghil produced dates of 3640–3380 BC. This is the only tomb at Carrowmore to have megalithic art, with very faint concentric circles carved onto the south-eastern corner of the roof slab of the tomb. A number of smaller passage tombs and boulder burials surround Listoghil, and when you are at the site it is hard not to appreciate the landscape that appears to loom around you. Most of the tombs at Carrowmore were investigated in the nineteenth century, and produced artefacts like prehistoric pottery and bone or antler pins as well as the cremated remains of those interred within the tombs.

CARROWMORE   MAP 16

Coordinates: Lat. 54.251010, Long. -8.518971

Irish Grid Reference: G 66197 33671

Opening hours/entry fees: Visit: www.heritageireland.ie/en/north-west/carrowmoremegalithiccemetery/

Directions: Carrowmore is very well signposted: head south-west from Sligo on the N4 and turn right onto the R292 Knappagh Road. After 1km turn left on Larkhill Road. After 450m take the third exit on the roundabout, taking you to the right on the Ballydoogan Road (Carrowmore will be signposted). Continue on this road for a further 600m and turn left, following the sign for Carrowmore. This road will bring you to the site (after approximately 1.5km). There is an exhibition centre run by the OPW and guided tours of the monuments are available.

Nearest town: Sligo (5km).

---

79 | SLIGO

Surrounded by the Ox Mountains to the south, Knocknarea to the west, Benbulben to the north and the long expanse of Lough Gill to the east, the historic town of Sligo developed around an important crossing point of the Garavogue River, on an ancient routeway between Connacht and Ulster. The name Sligo is derived from *Sligeach*, meaning 'a shelly place', a reference perhaps to the abundance of shellfish. From as early as the Mesolithic period, people collected shellfish along the Sligo coastline, leaving behind the many piles of discarded shells, known as middens, which still surround Sligo Bay.

A Royal Charter was conferred on Sligo in 1290, granting it 'Borough' status and giving it the right to hold markets and charge tolls. This regular and lucrative income ensured that the town

Sligo Abbey

was economically viable for the Anglo-Normans who settled here. Thanks to its strategic location, Sligo had developed sufficiently by the early fifteenth century to contain a thriving port, a castle, Dominican abbey, a hospice (providing accommodation for pilgrims and visitors) and the parish church of John the Baptist, which later became **Saint John's Cathedral**. Unfortunately, medieval life was difficult and uncertain, as Sligo was burned and plundered a number of times during a series of wars and dynastic struggles. However, the settlement of Sligo remained resolute, and each time it was destroyed, it was quickly rebuilt.

Today there are comparatively few remains of the once proud medieval town, though **Sligo Abbey** is still an atmospheric place to experience Sligo's story.

The abbey was founded in 1252 for the Dominican Order by Maurice FitzGerald. The Dominicans were known as 'The Black Friars' due to the black cloaks the monks wore over their white habits. This period of Irish history was extremely turbulent as the resurgent Gaelic tribes sought to drive out the Anglo-Norman colonies. Sligo was burned to the ground by the warlike O'Donnells in 1257, and the unrest led to the FitzGeralds abandoning Sligo forever by the beginning of the fourteenth century. Throughout all of this upheaval and violence, the abbey remained untouched, and when the powerful Richard de Burgo, Earl of Ulster, took control of Sligo in the fourteenth century, he restored the castle and work continued without hindrance in the abbey. Through his patronage the abbey grew in stature and prestige, and it became the burial place of the elite of the region, like the O'Rourkes, Lords of Breffni. However, in the year 1414 disaster struck when a candle accidentally started a fire that became an inferno. The blaze destroyed the friars' living quarters and badly damaged the church. Immediate efforts were made to restore the abbey, and the Pope granted an indulgence to all who would help to restore it. The powerful local magnates, the O'Connors and O'Rourkes, provided most of the financial aid for the restoration. The magnificent east window and the distinctive central tower date to this period of reconstruction and renewal.

A new threat to Sligo Abbey arose in the middle of the sixteenth century, when King Henry VIII began the Dissolution of the Monasteries. However, as the abbey was deep within Gaelic-controlled lands, it remained untouched for decades, until 1595 when Sir George Bingham, President of Connacht, launched a number of attacks on Sligo Castle, which at that time was occupied by the O'Donnells. Bingham used Sligo Abbey as a barracks for his troops, and had his men pull down and use the beautifully ornate wooden rood screen to construct a battering ram to attack the castle.

The cloisters of Sligo Abbey

Remarkably, despite the chaos of these tumultuous days, a small group of the friars still remained at the abbey. However, by 1608, only one, Father O'Duane, remained in Sligo. He died later that year. Hope returned to the abbey when Father O'Crean, a Sligo Dominican who had been in Spain, returned to form a new community. He was aided by the new elites of society, and nobles like Eleanor Butler, the Countess of Desmond, who erected the O'Connor Memorial in the South Wall of the church. This proved to be a brief period of peace: the seventeenth century quickly became one of the most violent in all of Irish history. In July 1642, in retaliation for the events of the Rebellion of 1641, Sir Frederick Hamilton, commander of the garrison of Manorhamilton, descended on Sligo and burned most of the town, including the abbey, where he butchered the friars who remained there.

By the early eighteenth century, it appears that the friars had finally completely left the abbey. The abandoned abbey became the property of Lord Palmerston and portions of its walls were dismantled and quarried as a convenient source of building materials and stone. At this time, Sligo returned to prosperity, and became well known as a centre of commerce, law and justice. During the nineteenth century, the town began to evolve and

The statue of one of Sligo's most celebrated sons, W.B. Yeats

the winding medieval street pattern was supplemented with new streets and streetscapes. Throughout the town's history, the port and river have always been a constant vital artery flowing through Sligo. Both have greatly influenced the town and its people.

Sligo also has an incredible cultural legacy, which includes music, art and literature. It was home and a place of childhood holidays to the famous brothers, painter Jack Butler Yeats and poet William Butler Yeats. As well as the abbey, the town has a number of highlights, including the stately nineteenth-century **Cathedral of the Immaculate Conception**, **Saint John's Church** with its medieval roots and fine Cassels architecture, and a plethora of great traditional pubs.

SLIGO MAP 16

Coordinates: Sligo Abbey Lat. 54.270560, Long. -8.469629

Irish Grid Reference: G 69425 35882

Opening hours/entry fees: For information about Sligo Abbey visit: www. heritageireland.ie/en/north-west/sligoabbey/

Directions: Sligo Abbey is located on Abbey Street near the centre of Sligo town. Opening hours and entry fees apply.

Nearest town: In Sligo.

The Neolithic court tomb at Deerpark

Set high in the hills with expansive views over Lough Colgagh and the surrounding landscape, an ancient court tomb at Deerpark (also known as Magheranrush megalithic tomb) can be found. Court tombs are thought to be one of the earliest types of megalithic tomb built in Ireland, and typically date to the Neolithic period, over 5,000 years ago. As their name implies, they usually feature a large courtyard area that was usually in front of a covered gallery that contained human remains, often in two or more chambers. The galleries or chambers were usually covered with a large cairn of small stones – though often, as with this example at Deerpark, the cairn has long since been removed. Deerpark is also very unusual amongst Irish court tombs as the court is in the centre of the monument, rather than being positioned at the front. It has been suggested that the tomb originally had only one gallery on the western side, and that the eastern gallery was added at a later time. This may hint at the joining of two tribes into one larger group, with the tomb then becoming a shared sacred space.

Court tombs are almost solely found in the northern half of the island, and Sligo has a number of fine examples (such as **Creevykeel**, Site 83). With its beautiful views over the landscape, and with the great cairn of Knocknarea so visible on the horizon, it is hard to beat the atmospheric setting at Deerpark.

Court tombs like this one at Deerpark were constructed by some of Ireland's first farmers.

DEERPARK COURT TOMB MAP 16

Coordinates: Lat. 54.282105, Long. -8.375705

Irish Grid Reference: G 75209 36762

Opening hours/entry fees: No opening times or entry fees applied at the time of writing.

Directions: To find the site, from Sligo take the R278 heading east for approximately 6km (a nine-minute drive). The site is signposted (as both Giant's Grave and Deerpark Court Tomb) from the road at the second right-hand turn after Calry, down a small track (with a cattle grid at the gate). Leave your car at the car park for the forest park and follow the main track through the trees; you'll find the site after about a fifteen-minute walk.

Nearest town: Sligo (7.5km).

81 | DRUMCLIFF

The important early medieval monastery of Drumcliff, now divided in two by the busy main road, is thought to have been founded in around AD 574 by Saint Colmcille. Here you can find the remains of an early monastery with a round tower and high crosses. It continues to be an important place of worship and burial to this day.

Only approximately a third of the round tower still survives. It is likely to date to some time in the tenth or eleventh century. According to historical records, the tower was struck by lightning in 1396, and that may have caused some of the damage, though by its roughly level appearance it may have been partially demolished (or at least reduced to make it safe) in the nineteenth century. The tower is built from limestone boulders, roughly coursed and interspersed with undressed field stones. The masonry work

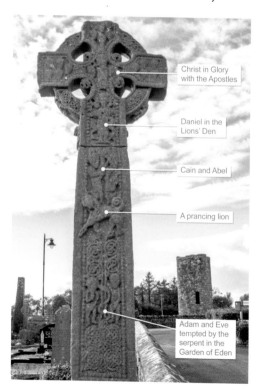

Christ in Glory with the Apostles

Daniel in the Lions' Den

Cain and Abel

A prancing lion

Adam and Eve tempted by the serpent in the Garden of Eden

Drumcliff High Cross east face

appears to be of a lower quality than other round towers – such as **Rattoo**, Kerry (Site 34) or **Killala**, Mayo (Site 72) – and this is certainly a possible reason as to why little remains of the tower today.

Drumcliff's fine sandstone high cross was erected in AD 1000. It is beautifully decorated, and like the majority of Ireland's high crosses it depicts some of the key stories from the Old and New Testaments. The **east face** depicts Christ in Glory with the Apostles at the head of the cross, below which are representations from the Old Testament, with Daniel in the Lions' Den, then Cain killing Abel above a rather charming lion that looks ready to pounce, and Adam and Eve being tempted by the serpent in the Garden of Eden. The serpent is beautifully carved, sinuously coiled around the apple tree. Below is a delicate interlaced ornament. The **west face** depicts the Crucifixion at the centre of the head of the cross, below which are scenes from the New Testament, with

Crucifixion scene

Two unknown figures

Christ being mocked by his captors

A camel

The naming of John the Baptist

Drumcliff High Cross west face

The round tower at Drumcliff in the shadow of Ben Bulben

two unknown figures, then a depiction of Christ being mocked by his captors, then a rather strange camel (which some believe to be a Bactrian camel, perhaps evidence of north Asian influence). The camel stands above a scene that shows the naming of John the Baptist. Again, the bottom of the shaft is intricately carved with interlaced design. The sides of the cross continue some of the interlacing, along with strange and somewhat whimsical creatures. A plain shaft of another cross is also incorporated into the churchyard wall. Eagle-eyed visitors may also spot evidence of another high cross inside the church. In the northern wall of the interior porch area you can see a piece of the shaft of a high cross with interlace design beside the gravestone to Elizabeth Soden; a second fragment is set into the west wall of the nave next to the west door. These pieces were presumably discovered broken on site, and were incorporated by the builders of the Church of Ireland church in the early nineteenth century.

The churchyard at Drumcliff has the honour of being the final resting place of William Butler Yeats (1865–1939). W.B. Yeats had an incredibly prolific career as a writer of the highest distinction, and served two terms in the Seanad. He died in Menton, France, on 18 January 1939. He was buried after a discreet and private funeral in France, as his final request was: 'If I die bury me up there at Roquebrune, and then in a year's time when the newspapers have forgotten me, dig me up and plant me in Sligo.' His wish was eventually granted and in September 1948, his remains were reburied here at Drumcliff. The words of his epitaph are taken from the last lines of 'Under Ben Bulben', one of his final poems: 'Cast a cold eye on life, On death. Horseman, pass by!'

The grave of W.B. Yeats

Saint Columba's Church of Ireland church, Drumcliff

Coordinates: Lat. 54.326103, Long. -8.495382

Irish Grid Reference: G 67784 42061

Opening hours/entry fees: Although you can visit the round tower and churchyard free of charge at the time of writing, there is an exhibition and more information inside the church. Visit www.drumcliffechurch.ie to find out more.

Directions: Drumcliff is very easy to find from Sligo. Simply head north on the N15 for 7.5km (approximately ten minutes) and you will reach Drumcliff. The church (and parking) is on the right-hand side.

Website: www.drumcliffechurch.ie

Nearest town: Sligo (7.5km).

82 | LISSADELL HOUSE

This fine early nineteenth-century country house is located on the shores of Sligo Bay. It was designed in an austere Greek Revival style by architect Francis Goodwin for Sir Robert Gore-Booth, and it is said to be one of the last houses in Ireland to have been constructed in the neoclassical style. The house is particularly notable as it was the childhood home of the poet and suffragette Eva Gore-Booth and her sister Constance Markievicz, who later became a famed revolutionary and politician, and one of the key protagonists in the pursuit of Irish independence. W.B. Yeats immortalised the sisters and Lissadell House in poetry.

The light of evening, Lissadell,
Great windows open to the south,
Two girls in silk kimonos, both
Beautiful, one a gazelle.

('In Memory of Eva Gore-Booth and Con. Markiewicz', from *The Winding Stair and Other Poems*, 1933).

Today the current owners continue to restore the house and its gardens, with a number of woodland trails. The two-acre Alpine Garden in particular is a wonderfully charming place, and well worth a visit.

Lissadell House

LISSADELL HOUSE

MAP 16

Coordinates: Lat. 54.346943, Long. -8.580280

Irish Grid Reference: G 62273 44402

Opening hours/entry fees: Visit www.lissadellhouse.com

Directions: From Sligo, it is about a 25-minute drive. Head north on the N15 towards Drumcliff. At Drumcliff turn left onto the L3305 (signposted for Carney). In the village bear left (following the sign for Lissadell House) and continue on this road. Turn left at the small Lissadell Church. Follow the driveway to the parking area for the house. Entry fees and opening hours apply (see their website for more details).

Nearest town: Sligo (15km).

LISSADELL HOUSE

83 | CREEVYKEEL COURT TOMB

Creevykeel is one of Ireland's finest examples of a court tomb, a type of funerary monument that dates to the Neolithic period. As the name implies, they usually feature a large courtyard area that was in front of a covered gallery that contained human remains, often in two or more chambers. The galleries or chambers were originally covered with a large cairn of small stones or earth. Creevykeel appears to have developed over time, with evidence of a number of modifications and extensions to the tomb, possibly reflecting changing ceremonies or societal beliefs.

Creevykeel was excavated in 1935 by the Harvard Archaeological Expedition. They discovered four groups of cremated human remains, two in each of the chambers at the front of the tomb, but no human remains were discovered in the chambers at the back of the tomb. They also found fragments of pottery, polished stone axe heads, stone tools, including a large flint knife, scrapers and flint arrowheads, and four quartz crystals.

The court tomb at Creevykeel

Creevykeel is one of Ireland's finest examples of a court tomb

Due to the stone walls that enclose the site, it is difficult for the visitor today to get a true sense of how the monument was positioned to sit within the landscape. Creevykeel was reused for different purposes throughout history. Artefacts and evidence of early medieval activity were discovered, and you can still see the outline of a cereal-drying kiln that was placed in the side of the stone cairn.

CREEVYKEEL MAP 16

Coordinates: Lat. 54.439167, Long. -8.433718

Irish Grid Reference: G 71899 54564

Opening hours/entry fees: No opening hours or entry fees applied at the time of writing.

Directions: Creevykeel is very easy to find and is about a 25-minute drive from Sligo. Simply travel north around 23km from Sligo on the N15 towards Lifford. You will see the site signposted, with a small car park on the right-hand shoulder of the N15, just approximately 1.5km north of the village of Cliffony.

Nearest town: Sligo (25km).

---

84 | INISHMURRAY

The island of Inishmurray lies off the coast of County Sligo in Donegal Bay. This relatively small island was inhabited until it was finally evacuated in 1948. At that time, 46 people lived on Inishmurray in a small and self-reliant community that survived by fishing, farming and burning seaweed to extract the valuable iodine. Inishmurray was also famed for its production of poteen, an illegal industry that managed to thrive despite many attempted raids by the Royal Irish Constabulary. The ruins of the islanders' homes still lie along 'Green Street' and are a poignant reminder of the community that once lived here. The island is an important sanctuary for birds and other wildlife, and in late spring the island becomes covered in heavenly swathes of bluebells.

The island is also home to a beautifully preserved early monastery, believed to have been founded by Saint Molaise. Two

The names of the island's families painted on one of the cottages deserted after the evacuation of Inishmurray

of the island's churches are named after the saint: Templemolaise and Teach Molaise. Inishmurray is also connected to the famed Saint Colmcille (who founded the nearby monastery at **Drumcliff**, Site 81). According to tradition, the two saints had an uneasy and difficult relationship. Colmcille is said to have left Inishmurray after a disagreement with Molaise following the construction of a church.

Inishmurray was one of the first sites to be attacked by the Vikings, when they carried out a raid in AD 795, and it was attacked again in 807, when it was 'burned by the heathen'. However, the monastery continued, and much of the remains we can see today date to the ninth and tenth centuries. Most of the monastic remains are located near the centre of the island within a large oval drystone enclosure known as **the Cashel**.

The enclosure measures over 50m by 40m (164 by 131 feet) across, and the drystone walls are 4m (13 feet) thick and stand to a height of 3m (10 feet). There is some debate as to whether the Cashel predated the monastery, or whether it was built later, perhaps as a defence against further Viking raids following the

The large monastic enclosure known as the Cashel

shocking attacks of 795 and 807. The strong walls of the enclosure protect a group of churches and clocháns. The earliest of these churches is **Teach Molaise**, believed to be the shrine chapel of the founder of the monastery. Radiocarbon dating has revealed that this small chapel may date to as early as the eighth century. It is likely to have housed the tomb and relics of Saint Molaise. An oak statue, believed to be a medieval depiction of Molaise, stood on the altar until it was moved to the National Museum of Ireland in 1949. An iron bell and a crozier, thought to have formed part of the statue, were removed from Inishmurray by the nineteenth-century antiquarian collector Roger Chambers Walker. They now form part of the Duke of Northumberland's private collection. The largest church within the enclosure is **Templemolaise** (also known as *Teampall na bhFear*, meaning 'the men's church'). This is a pre-Romanesque church, and dates to around the ninth or tenth century. The clocháns may also date to around this period, and may have served as accommodation for the monks or perhaps for visiting pilgrims.

The island also has a fascinating collection of cross slabs and bullaun stones, a number of which are located within the Cashel. Along with these, Inishmurray has a number of drystone altars known as *leachta*.

One of the outdoor altars or '*leachta*' on Inishmurray

Though these features may have their origins in the early monastery, they were still used as part of the pilgrimage that took place on the island until relatively recent decades on the Feast of the Assumption, 15 August. The largest altar is notable for the numerous rounded stones known as *Clocha Breacha* ('the speckled stones'). These are said to be cursing stones. According to tradition, if an islander wanted to encourage misfortune and disaster upon an enemy or rival, they would undertake a nine-day ritual, which included periods of fasting. They would then go around the altar 'widdershins' (anticlockwise, against the course of the sun). While going around the altar they would rotate the *clocha breacha* three times while repeating their curse. However, this practice was fraught with danger. If the curse was unjustified it was said to backfire on the curser.

Templenaman lies outside the Cashel alongside the road to the village. This church has been dated to the medieval period. It is also known as *Teampall na mBan* ('the women's church') and the island's women were buried within this graveyard, whilst the men were buried within the Cashel until the evacuation of the island in the 1940s. Within the small enclosure of Templenaman you can also see another *leacht* with a fine cross-inscribed slab inserted into it.

Templenaman

Inishmurray is a real favourite of mine, and certainly one the very best highlights of Ireland's Wild Atlantic Way; however, it is not easy to get to, being entirely dependent upon weather conditions. If you plan to visit Inishmurray please note that it is a very delicate and important habitat for nesting seabirds and other wildlife so please take every precaution to avoid disturbing them. The ruins themselves (including the abandoned early modern settlement) are fragile so please don't climb on the walls or light fires. There are no facilities at all on the island, so I recommend bringing water, sun cream and waterproofs. Good boots are highly recommended. There is no harbour, and you have to disembark by jumping onto rocks at Clashymore, so it may not be suitable for everyone. The boat journey takes around an hour each way, and perfect weather is required to land on the island. There are no regular ferry services, but boats can be chartered from Rosses Point or Mullaghmore.

INISHMURRAY

MAP 16

Coordinates:

Mullaghmore Pier parking: Lat. 54.466672, Long. -8.447982
Island: Lat. 54.431227, Long. -8.656485

Irish Grid Reference: G 57427 53851

Opening hours/entry fees: Although no entry fees or opening hours apply as such to Inishmurray, visiting the site is highly dependent on weather conditions and it is only suitable during certain weeks of the year because of nesting birds. You will need to charter a boat to visit the island and prices vary. Try: www. seatrails.ie or www.inishmurrayislandtrips.com

Directions: To get to the pier at Mullaghmore from Sligo (a 30-minute drive), head north on the N15, through Drumcliff and Grange, until you reach Cliffony. At the crossroads in the centre of Cliffony, take the left turn onto the R279 (signposted for Mullaghmore). Follow this road all the way to the pier. There are a number of options for boat hire for the island (two websites are provided above).

Nearest town: Park in Mullaghmore. Sligo (27km).

INISHMURRAY

DONEGAL

Donegal is undoubtedly one of the most beautifully scenic regions in the world, but in comparison to Kerry, it is largely, bafflingly, overlooked by visitors. That makes for an even better experience for those who take the time to visit Ireland's north-west, as you will be rewarded with beautiful scenery, pristine beaches, charming towns and villages and fascinating heritage.

The breathtaking Glengesh Pass in County Donegal

The coastline here is more rugged and unforgiving than that of Sligo, with Europe's highest sea cliffs at Slieve League offering unmatched vistas and scenery. This region has one of Ireland's largest Gaeltacht areas, so it is the perfect place for those who want to immerse themselves in the Irish language, music and traditions.

Donegal is the birthplace of Saint Colmcille (also known as Columba), one of Ireland's most important early saints, who established monasteries in Ireland and Scotland. Donegal is also the setting for romance and tragedy, as the heartland of the doomed rebellion during the Nine Years' War and the place from where the Earls took flight in the aftermath, at the dawn of the seventeenth century.

The Poisoned Glen, at the foot of Errigal

On our journey through Donegal, we will visit the ruins of castles that are still locked in a battle they are destined to lose, as the remorseless Atlantic chews away at their foundations. We will visit places of pilgrimage that have been sacred for millennia at Glencolmcille, and go through the breathtaking Glengesh Pass to the heritage town of Ardara to see the wealth of heritage that surrounds it. We will climb up to a legendary fort with commanding views and travel up the beautiful, and almost otherworldly, Inishowen Peninsula to find the tomb of a warrior sportsman and to discover unique high crosses and early medieval art. We will end our journey at Malin Head, Ireland's most northerly point.

Errigal

The fragile ruin of Kilbarron Castle

Though little remains standing of the late medieval castle of Kilbarron it is still well worth a visit for its stunning setting and its important role in Irish history. The castle is believed to have been first built by the O'Scingins in the early thirteenth century. In the middle of the fourteenth century, it passed through marriage into the O'Clery (Uí Cleirigh) family. Many members of the family served as the *ollamh* to the O'Donnell chieftains. The role of the *ollamh* was akin to a chief adviser, but he also acted as the official keeper of the O'Donnell genealogy and history, and was the source of knowledge on boundaries, tributes and taxation. The *ollamh* was also a poet and, in a sense, a medieval version of a public relations officer for the O'Donnells. In return for these services, the O'Clerys were rewarded with high noble status, and substantial wealth and influence. They were able to develop Kilbarron Castle into a splendid home that was well protected by strong stone walls and by the steep cliffs that surround three sides of the promontory on which it is built. The O'Clerys were well known throughout Gaelic Ireland for their hospitality and learning, and two of the O'Clerys produced historical works of the highest importance. Lughaidh O'Clery compiled the 'Life of Red Hugh O'Donnell', and Michael O'Clery, who was born in Kilbarron Castle, was the chief compiler of the Annals of the Four Masters.

KILBARRON CASTLE

With the defeat at the Battle of Kinsale in 1601, the O'Donnells, along with the other Ulster power, Hugh O'Neill, fled Ireland in what became known as the Flight of the Earls. This was a devastating blow to the O'Clerys, who lost their benefactors and chieftains. Following their victory, the English pushed ahead with the Plantation of Ulster, and the O'Clerys were forced to surrender their lands, including Kilbarron Castle, in 1609. The castle began to fall into dilapidation, and today only fragments survive of this once-fine house, which was once the key seat of learning and education in medieval Gaelic Ireland.

As the ruins are in a precarious state, access to the castle itself is restricted; however, the castle can be viewed from its best advantage by taking a walk that leads from Creevy Pier past the castle and alongside spectacular cliffs. The local community is currently carrying out important work to understand and conserve what remains of this important monument.

KILBARRON CASTLE   MAP 17

Coordinates:
Parking: Lat. 54.530410, Long. -8.251474
Castle: Lat. 54.534709, Long. -8.249095

Irish Grid Reference: G 83923 65177

Opening hours/entry fees: No opening hours or entry fees applied at the time of writing, but please visit the Kilbarron Castle Conservation Group on Facebook to discover news on local events and to learn more about their efforts to conserve this important monument: www.facebook.com/kilbarroncastleconservationgroup/

Directions: There is no direct road access to Kilbarron Castle. Instead, park at Creevy Pier and take the short cliff walk. Good boots are recommended as the ground can be waterlogged in places. Not suitable for dogs as livestock are present in the fields. Creevy Pier is a short (eight-minute) drive from Ballyshannon. Head north-west from Ballyshannon on the R231 for around 5km (you will pass Creevy National School as you go). Continue on the R231 and take the left-hand turn onto the L2385 (signposted for Creevy Pier Hotel, and Creevy Shore Walk). Simply take this turn and follow the narrow road down until you reach the car park before the pier. The path for the shore walk is just above the car park.

Nearest town: Ballyshannon (6km).

Donegal Castle

Donegal Castle was the stronghold of the O'Donnells of Tirconell. The region of Tironnell takes its name from the Irish *Tír Chonnaill*, deriving from Conall, a son of the legendary High King Niall of the Nine Hostages. The leading families of the region, including the O'Donnells, O'Dohertys and O'Boyles, were collectively known as the *Cenel Conaill*, the 'Race of Conall'. In the period between the thirteenth and seventeenth centuries, there was an unbroken line of O'Donnell chieftains and kings. Unlike the traditional view of monarchy, the chieftain was not always by right of primogeniture: instead, the ruler was selected by the nobles, based on their fitness to rule. The oldest part of the castle is the **O'Donnell Tower**, thought to have been constructed by Red Hugh O'Donnell I, who died in 1505.

The English Lord Deputy Sir Henry Sidney, who visited the castle in 1566, described it as follows: 'It is the greatest I ever saw in Ireland in an Irishman's hands, and it would appear to be in good keeping; one of the fairest situate in good soil and so nigh a portable water as a boat of ten tonnes could come within twenty yards of it.'

The Great Hall of Donegal Castle

The last O'Donnell resident in the castle was the famous Hugh Roe O'Donnell, 'Red Hugh II', who was one of the key leaders of the rebels in the Nine Years' War. After the defeat of the rebel forces at the Battle of Kinsale in 1602 (see **Kinsale**, Site 1, for more information), he sailed to Corunna in Spain where many of the Irish chieftains and their families were seeking exile. He travelled to Valladolid to plead with the Spanish king for assistance to defeat the English in Ireland, only to be fobbed off by King Phillip III, who promised help but never acted upon it. Hugh died in 1602 and was buried in Simancas Castle, far from his home in Donegal. Some believe that he was poisoned by the Anglo-Irish double agent James Blake. With the death of Hugh, the long line of O'Donnells as chiefs and kings of Tirconnell came to an end.

The castle became the possession of Sir Basil Brooke in 1616. He carried out large-scale renovations to make it more fitting for an English gentleman's home. The beautifully decorated Jacobean-style fireplace on the first floor of the tower and the fine mullioned windows date to this period. So too does the Jacobean manor house that adjoins the castle. Sir Basil Brooke was succeeded by his son Henry, who led a successful defence of Donegal Castle during the Rebellion of 1641. Though he temporarily lost possession of the castle in 1651 to the Marquess of Clanricarde, he quickly regained control with the support of Sir Charles Coote.

The castle had been abandoned as a residence by the eighteenth century and began to fall into disrepair and ruin. It came into the possession of the OPW in 1898 and the O'Donnell Tower has been largely restored. The interior has many interesting period features and an exhibition detailing the history of the castle and the region.

A staircase in Donegal Castle

The ruins of a **Franciscan friary** can also be seen on the shore of the bay just outside the town to the south. It was founded by the O'Donnells in the fifteenth century, but little remains of the original friary today. It is noteworthy as the home of the Franciscan friars who produced the Annals of the Four Masters (for more on this important work, see **Kilbarron Castle**, Site 85).

DONEGAL CASTLE MAP 17

Coordinates: Lat. 54.654926, Long. -8.110147

Irish Grid Reference: G 92912 78542

Opening hours/entry fees: Visit: www.heritageireland.ie/en/north-west/donegalcastle/

Directions: The castle is located on Castle Street near the centre of Donegal town. Park on street (charges may apply) or in one of the town centre car parks.

Nearest town: In Donegal town.

DONEGAL CASTLE

87 | SLIEVE LEAGUE CLIFFS

As the highest sea cliffs in Ireland, the Slieve League Cliffs are as dramatic and spectacular as the Cliffs of Moher, though much less visited. They rear up more than 600m (1,967 feet) from the waters of the Atlantic. The walk to the cliffs offers truly breathtaking views over to the mountains of County Sligo, with Donegal Bay and the turbulent waters of the Atlantic far below you. The cliffs were once a place of pilgrimage, and feature in the story of Saint Brendan as the place near where Mernóc saw the Delightful Island in the *Navigatio Brendani*. The fragmentary remains of a drystone church known as Hugh MacBrick's Church, a cross-inscribed stone and a number of penitential stations along a narrow ridge are all that can still be seen. The remains of a signal tower can also be found along the cliffs. This dates to the early nineteenth century and formed part of the British coastal defence during the Napoleonic Wars. This particular tower is recorded as having

The Slieve League cliffs

been constructed by 1804 at a cost of £696. The tower was part of a chain of communication. They worked on a signalling system using ball-and-flag methods to transmit messages from station to station, quickly raising the alarm when enemy vessels were spotted. A tall wooden mast was positioned on the seaward side of the signal tower where the flags and balls would be hoisted so that the next signal tower could see the message and pass it on to the next along the chain. However, the defeat of Napoleon at the Battle of Waterloo in 1815 largely made these coastal defences redundant, though a number still survive to give an insight into this period of European history.

A small car park and viewing area can be reached by driving through the gate along a very narrow (and somewhat hair-raising) road, I personally prefer to leave the car in the lower car park to enjoy a relaxed walk to the top. Boat trips are now available from Teelin Pier, providing a stunning view of the majestic cliffs as they soar above you.

Coordinates: (Bunglass Point) Lat. 54.627067, Long. -8.684319

Irish Grid Reference: G 58370 76566

Opening hours/entry fees: No opening hours or entry fees applied at the time of writing; however, a visitor centre is planned to be developed in the near future. For the latest local information about the cliffs, visit: www.sliabhliag.com

Directions: Approximately 30 minutes' drive from Killybegs. Take the R263 west from Killybegs for about 15km (seventeen minutes) and you will reach the village of Carrick. Continue through the village until you see the left-hand turn signposted for L1095 Sliabh Liag, Bunglass. Take the left turn and follow that road as it leads you south-west to the village of Teelin. In Teelin you will see a right-hand turn signposted for the Bunglass Slieve League Viewing Point. Follow the sign and continue up this narrow road until you reach the car park for the cliffs. You can leave the car in the lower car park, or open the gate (and be sure to close it immediately behind you) and follow the narrow track up to the viewing point. This can be a little hairy as there isn't much room to pull over for cars coming down the hill, and occasionally it can be difficult to turn in the upper car park if it is particularly busy.

Nearest town: Killybegs (22km).

A cross-slab on the *turas* of Glencolmcille

There is a wealth of heritage to be discovered in this scenic valley that shelters underneath Glen Head in the westernmost reaches of County Donegal. According to legend, this is where Saint Colmcille battled and defeated a host of devils and demons. A *turas* or pilgrimage is held here every year on Colmcille's Day, 9 June, where pilgrims visit each of the fifteen penitential stations that are set out along the valley. These penitential stations are quite varied: some are beautifully carved cross-inscribed slabs, while others are simple cairns, some of which are megalithic tombs. The *turas* begins at St Columba's Church of Ireland church (I recommend parking opposite the church). Just west of the church is the remains of a megalithic tomb, thought to be a Neolithic court tomb. This is the first station of the pilgrimage.

One of the tombs at Malin More

When you enter the field, walk to the far end of the tomb, where there is a small structure built into the cairn. The pilgrims would kneel here to pray. The second station is approximately 100m (328 feet) to the west of Station 1. This beautiful cross slab stands up from a *leacht*, a drystone altar. The other stations continue to lead westward some distance from the first two. Information about the location of all the stations can be found locally, it would take at least three to four hours to go through the full pilgrimage. The other stations include simple cairns and *leachta*, some with cross slabs, a small drystone church known as Saint Colmcille's Chapel and the holy well known as Tobar Cholm Cille.

The quite remarkable concentration of megalithic tombs in this region attests to the importance and perhaps sacred nature of this landscape. Perhaps the most striking collection can be found just outside Glencolmcille, where a series of six portal tombs straddle a rough line measuring around 100m (328 feet) long on pastureland below a ridge in the **Malin More** valley. The first tomb you encounter is the best-preserved and most impressive example. These monuments are portal tombs that date to the Neolithic period. Typically, the burial chambers were formed of large flat roofstones that were supported on two tall uprights, and a backstone. The chambers are believed to have been originally covered by a cairn or mound of earth, though in most cases the covering is missing, leaving only the iconic shape of the portal tomb visible. These monuments, also known as dolmens, are often imbued with folklore and mythology, bound in tales of druids or legendary heroes. In the case of the largest of the portal tombs at Malin More, it is said that Diarmuid and Gráinne sought shelter within during their escape from Fionn MacCumhaill.

GLENCOLMCILLE

MAP 17

Coordinates:

Station 1 of the *turas*: Lat. 54.710329, Long. -8.723070
Malin More tombs: Lat. 54.689630, Long. -8.774938

Irish Grid Reference: G 53221 84592

Opening hours/entry fees: No opening hours or entry fees applied at the time of writing to the *turas* or the Malin More tombs. For more information about the wealth of heritage in the area visit www.gleanncholmcille.ie

Directions: Head north-west from Killybegs for approximately 25km (30 minutes) on the R263.

Turas Colmcille Station 1: The first stop of Turas Colmcille is at Saint Columba's Church of Ireland, just to the north-east of the centre of Glencolmcille on the L5055. There is an area to park just opposite the church.

Malin More tombs: To find these megalithic tombs, head west on the R263 from Glencolmcille, past the Glencolmcille Folk Village (a lovely pit stop). After 3km (1.8 miles) you will come to Malin More. Drive through the crossroads and take the first left turn up a narrow boreen. The first tombs are located in the field immediately after an abandoned farmhouse. There are often sheep in the field so please take every precaution to close all gates behind you, and do not bring dogs into the field.

Nearest towns: Glencolmcille (on the outskirts), Killybegs (25km).

89 | KILCLOONEY DOLMEN AND ARDARA

The Kilclooney Dolmen

Crossing from Glencolmcille to Ardara you pass through the breathtaking Glengesh Pass and down to the charming and historic town of Ardara. There are a number of interesting places to see nearby, including the Kilclooney Dolmen, one of Ireland's best examples of a Neolithic portal tomb. It consists of two chambers that once would have been covered by an enormous cairn that was destroyed in antiquity. The larger chamber is formed by a 4.2m (14-foot) long capstone that rests on two tall portals that stand approximately 1.7m (5½ feet) tall, and a backstone with a stone pad. The smaller, second chamber is built to the same design although the capstone has slipped somewhat.

The Kilclooney Dolmen truly is an evocative landmark. It is possible to imagine that this monument, when covered by a large cairn, was a strong statement of identity, strength, territorial boundaries and belief, in Neolithic Ireland. Permission must be sought before visiting the Kilclooney Dolmen. I recommend you call into the Dolmen Centre nearby for more information on it and on the heritage of the area, such as the portal tomb, the nearby court tomb, Inishkeel island and the spectacular Doon Fort. The fort is currently not generally accessible as it is in a vulnerable condition. However, the local community, Ardara GAP Heritage and History Group, is working hard to ensure that this incredible monument is preserved for future generations. If you would like more information on Doon Fort please ensure that you ask at the Dolmen Centre as access to the island may not be possible.

Doon Fort

The tidal island of **Inishkeel** is situated just to the north of Ardara, off the coast of Portnoo.

The island is home to an important early monastic site, associated with the sixth-century saint Conall Caol, whose relic, the *Bearnán Conaill* ('Conall's gapped bell') is now on display in the British Museum. Today you can see the remains of two churches and a number of early grave and cross-inscribed slabs, enclosed by a post-eighteenth-century stone-walled graveyard. The island has long endured as a place of pilgrimage. A story from local folklore tells how the Protestant landowner of the island grew irritated with pilgrims disturbing his land, and so one day in anger he dismantled the cairns that marked the penitential stations and threw the stones into the sea. Using a sledgehammer he also smashed an oval-shaped stone that was used in a ritual and flung the broken fragments into the ocean. That night, there was an enormous storm with waves that rose so high they broke over the roof of his house on the island. When the storm abated the next day, he was amazed and terrified to find all the penitential stations had been re-formed in their original positions, and the stone that he had smashed stood proudly where it had before, with no trace of his vandalism beyond slight seams in the rock. On seeing this miracle, he immediately regretted his temerity and moved to live on the mainland for the rest of his days, only returning to the island to make sure the paths were kept clean and tidy for pilgrims to conduct their rituals. Inishkeel is accessible only at very low tides, and you must be extremely cautious about staying too long on the island should you get cut off by the next tide. To visit Inishkeel, I recommend asking in the Dolmen Centre about the best times to access the island.

Inishkeel Island

DOLMEN CENTRE, ARDARA

MAP 17

Coordinates: Lat. 54.822556, Long. -8.437326

Irish Grid Reference: G 71938 97280

Opening hours/entry fees: Visit www.dolmencentre.com

Directions: From Ardara, simply head north on the R261 and you will find the Dolmen Centre on your right after 7km.

Nearest town: Ardara (7km)

The area around Gartan in County Donegal is deeply imbued with tales of Saint Colmcille. A fine heritage centre tells the story of the life of the saint, and at Churchtown you can see the remains of an early monastery, which tradition states was founded in the home of Colmcille's family, Ráth Cnó. This area was once a notable place for pilgrimage as part of the *Slí Cholmcille* or Saint Columba's Trail.

The *Leac na Cumha*, or Stone of Sorrow, is covered in cup marks, a form of prehistoric art

Saint Colmcille (also known as Columba) is one of the most important and revered of Ireland's saints. He is thought to have been born around AD 520, and according to tradition he was born here on this large flat stone known as *Leac na Cumha*, the Stone of Sorrow. He was the son of a noble family, the *Cenel Conaill*, with lineage from the legendary Niall of the Nine Hostages. Colmcille studied under Saint Finnian at Clonard and Mobhi at Glasnevin, and he became one of the key figures in the early Irish Church, with important foundations attributed to him at Derry, Durrow in County Offaly, Kells in County Meath and Swords in County Dublin. However, in around the year 560 he became embroiled in Ireland's first documented copyright dispute. He had secretly copied a psalter at the scriptorium of his former teacher Saint Finnian. Colmcille was determined to keep the copy, but

Finnian challenged his right to do so. The hostilities grew to the point where the High King Diarmait Mac Cerbaill interceded and pronounced the first copyright judgement in Irish history: 'to every cow belongs her calf, therefore to every book belongs its copy'. Colmcille disputed this decision, and agitated with his powerful family to challenge the king. The dispute escalated dangerously and broke out into warfare at the Battle of Cúl Dreimhne, traditionally believed to be in the region of **Drumcliff** (Site 81), County Sligo, in the year 561. Many were slaughtered. Threatened with excommunication for his role in the crisis, Colmcille agreed to go into exile to Scotland, to win for Christ as many souls as had been lost in the battle. According to legend, overcome by sadness and loneliness at the thought of leaving his family and monastery behind, Colmcille returned to the stone where he was born, to sleep the night before he departed. Colmcille would go on to have as great a legacy in Scotland as in Ireland, and founded the important monastery on Iona, amongst other foundations. According to folklore anyone who wishes to overcome loneliness, grief or sorrow will be healed by lying on the stone, and this became a tradition in more recent centuries as people emigrating from the region spent the night here before embarking at the port of Derry.

The stone is part of what appears to be a megalithic tomb, another example of the Christianisation of a prehistoric monument

A large cross was erected here by the Adairs of **Glenveagh** (Site 91) in 1911, to mark the site where Colmcille was born, but despite its associations with Colmcille and Christianity, the *Leac na Cumha* is covered in prehistoric art known as cup marks, and is thought to form part of a megalithic tomb, possibly a wedge tomb dating to the early Bronze Age. This is another fascinating example of the continuing nature of the sacred landscape and the Christianisation of prehistoric monuments.

You can find **Saint Colmcille's Abbey** close to Lacknacoo. Not much remains of the early foundation associated with Colmcille, but you can see the ruins of a fine medieval church, some interesting crosses and a holy well.

The large cross erected by the Adairs of Glenveagh to mark Colmcille's birthplace

LACKNACOO MAP 18

Coordinates:
Lacknacoo: Lat. 5.008385, Long. -7.916282
Saint Colmcille's Abbey: Lat. 5.015288, Long. -7.907447

Irish Grid Reference: C 05404 17883

Opening hours/entry fees: No opening hours or entry fees to Lacknacoo or the abbey applied at the time of writing. For information about the Heritage Centre visit www.colmcilleheritagecentre.ie

Directions: To find Lacknacoo: from Letterkenny, head south-west on the R250 past Newmills Corn & Flax Museum (also well worth a stop if you have time), then bear right onto the R251 (signed for Colmcille Heritage Centre, Glebe Gallery and Glenveagh National Park). Continue on this road through Church Hill, then bear left onto the smaller road that is signposted for Colmcille's Birthplace, Abbey & Cross, and Gartan. Continue on this road past the entrance to the Glebe Gallery. Just past the gallery, be careful to follow the road as it bends right at a Y-junction with a minor road. After 400m you will see a left-hand turn, with a sign for Colmcille's Birthplace. Take the turn and you will find a small car park with a short lane leading to the site. When you have visited Lacknacoo, retrace your steps back to the road junction and then turn left, following the sign for Saint Colmcille's Abbey for approximately 1km. You will see the remains of the abbey on your left. The Colmcille Heritage Centre is also nearby, situated just outside Church Hill on the shores of Lough Gartan. The centre includes an audiovisual exhibition about the life and influence of Saint Colmcille, and information about the heritage of the area.

Nearest town: Letterkenny (17km)

Glenveagh Castle

Like **Kylemore Abbey** (Site 56), the handsome neo-Gothic castle at Glenveagh owes its appearance to Victorian Romantic imagination rather than medieval origins. The castle is surrounded with stunning gardens that contrast beautifully with the rugged natural setting. The castle was designed by architect John Townsend Trench and built between 1867 and 1873 for John George Adair. He was known as a ruthless landlord, who perpetrated the Derryveagh Evictions, one of the most notorious evictions of the nineteenth century, when he expelled nearly 250 tenants off his land so their poverty would not compromise his view of the landscape. This knowledge of their harsh origins lends a poignancy to the beauty of Glenveagh and the castle grounds.

In 1938 Glenveagh was purchased by Henry Plumer McIlhenny of Philadelphia, whose grandfather was an Irish immigrant who became extremely wealthy through his ingenious invention of the gas meter. McIlhenny served in the American Navy during the Second World War, after which he used the castle as a second home. Many famous film stars holidayed in Glenveagh Castle at this time, including Charlie Chaplin, Clark Gable and Greta Garbo. McIlhenny gifted Glenveagh Castle and gardens to the Irish state in 1979, while retaining the right to live there for his lifetime. He had previously sold the bulk of the estate lands to the state in 1974/75, to enable the creation of Glenveagh National Park, the second largest national park in Ireland. The park is comprised of over 16,000 hectres of truly stunning scenery, with rugged hills, lakes, glens, woods, herds of red deer and reintroduced golden eagles. The estate also includes the two highest mountains in Donegal, Errigal and Slieve Sneacht. Today visitors can enjoy a fine visitor centre, the castle and gardens and a number of walking trails.

The beautiful scenery of Glenveagh National Park

Not far from the castle, on the road between Falcarragh and Kilmacrenan, a small bridge, known as the Bridge of Tears, also bears testament to harsh and tragic life in Donegal's history. It was where many took their farewells from their families before crossing the bridge towards emigration to the United States, Australia or elsewhere, from where many would never return to their homes in Ireland. A stone near the bridge reads in Irish: 'Friends and relations of the person emigrating would come this far. Here they parted. This spot is the Bridge of Tears.'

The gardens at Glenveagh

The Bridge of Tears, a place of many partings

GLENVEAGH NATIONAL PARK

MAP 18

Coordinates: Lat. 5.059368, Long. -7.939387

Irish Grid Reference: C 02053 20984

Opening hours/entry fees: Visit www.glenveaghnationalpark.ie

Directions: From Letterkenny, head north for 12km on the N56, through the village of Kilmacrenan. Turn left onto the R255 (signposted for Glenveigh National Park, Gweedore and Dunlewy). Stay on the R255 for 6km, continuing on when it merges with the R251 (signposted for Gaoth Dobhair). Simply follow this road on to the visitor centre. There's plenty of parking space. After the visitor centre you have the option of taking one of the many trails or taking a shuttle bus directly to the castle.

Nearest town: Letterkenny (23km).

92 | RAY CHURCH

This post-medieval church, also known as Raymunterdoney Old Church, is thought to stand on the site of an early medieval monastery associated with Saint Fionán, a contemporary of Colmcille. The church that we see today is thought to date to after 1622. The church itself is rather plain, with four large round-headed windows and a pointed doorway.

Ray Church

The remarkable
cross at Ray Church

However, the church is remarkable as it is dwarfed by a 6m (approximately 20-foot) tall high cross. The head of the cross is surrounded by a ring, and the cross bears a resemblance to Saint John's Cross on Iona, possibly a reflection of the links between the church and Colmcille's foundation there. The cross was moved to its present position inside the church in the early 1980s, prior to which it lay broken in the churchyard. Folklore has it that the cross was shaped in the hills to the south, and it was intended to be shipped to the monastery on Tory Island, but Saint Colmcille realised that he had forgotten his prayer book. He promised the cross to whichever of his followers would return to get his book for him. Fionán returned to the hills and found the book being kept dry and safe by a crow that had its wings spread over the book to protect it from the rain. He returned the book to Colmcille, and much to the famous saint's chagrin, Fionán claimed his prize and had the cross erected in his small monastery here. At the base of the cross you can see early medieval millstones, perhaps further evidence of an early medieval monastery that may once have been in this location.

A darker local tradition tells that this church was once the site of a bloody massacre known as *Marfach Ráithe*, when Cromwellian soldiers slaughtered the entire congregation attending Mass in the church. The victims were said to have been buried in a mass grave nearby.

RAY CHURCH MAP 18

Coordinates: Lat. 5.147205, Long. -8.070289

Irish Grid Reference: B 95566 33337

Opening hours/entry fees: No opening hours or entry fees applied at the time of writing.

Directions: Ray Church is close to the small town of Falcarragh. Follow the N56 heading roughly north-west from Falcarragh. After 3km, turn left, following the signpost for Ray Church. Continue on this small road as it turns into a boreen and it will lead you all the way to the church.

Nearest towns: Falcarragh (4.5km), Letterkenny (40km).

---

93 | DOE CASTLE

Doe Castle is attractively, and strategically, positioned on a promontory in Sheephaven Bay. The castle is believed to have been built in the early sixteenth century, and it was the setting for much tumult and intrigue throughout its history. Some of the shipwrecked sailors of the Spanish Armada are said to have been given refuge here in 1588.

The name Doe is thought to derive from the Irish '*tuath*' (territory). This may come from the family MacSuibhne na dTuath who constructed the castle and who once held this territory, their name eventually being anglicised to 'MacSweeney Doe'. They came to Ireland as Scottish gallowglass mercenaries who had fought their way to prominence and favour with the powerful O'Donnells of Ulster. The castle was originally constructed by the foster father of Red Hugh O'Donnell.

Doe Castle

The tower house stands 17m (55 feet) tall. It is well defended, but it also has a number of elegant features (some added in later periods) to showcase the taste and wealth of the occupants. The tower house is surrounded by a substantial and strong bawn wall that is well protected by the sea on three sides and a deep rock-cut fosse or ditch on the landward side, making the castle an extremely difficult proposition to attack.

As you enter inside the gate you can see the entrance to an underground tunnel that runs back underneath the causeway to a sally port that opens into the fosse. Using this, the defenders of the castle could launch rapid counterattacks on any besieging force, while leaving the main gate of the castle sealed and protected. Like all castles, the main gate was perhaps the weakest part of the defences. Although a square tower protects the southern side of the gate, it is clear that later alterations to the castle may have removed part of the formidable defences that presumably once existed here. As well as attacks from the land, with its position on a promontory the castle was also vulnerable by sea, and indeed in 1543 members of the family were captured in a raid by the O'Malley's of Mayo (see **Clare Island**, Site 58, and **Rockfleet**

Castle, Site 64, for more on their story). A circular tower, known as the Hanging Tower, has a number of gun loops to offer defence against attacks from the water.

The MacSuibhne had lost nearly the entirety of their possessions and lands in the years that followed the Flight of the Earls. When the Rebellion of 1641 erupted they quickly joined in and managed to recapture Doe Castle. It was to here that Owen Roe O'Neill sailed from Dunkirk in 1642, when he left his exile in France to return to lead the Ulster Army of the Irish Confederates in the rebellion in Ireland.

Doe Castle guards a strategic position in Sheephaven Bay

However, within a few short years the castle was recaptured by the English and it became a garrison for the Crown forces, before it became the home of the Vaughan family. Under their stewardship, a large building was constructed at the base of the tower house with the family coat of arms and initial above the doorway. General George Vaughan Hart (1752–1832) was part of the British army during the American War of Independence. After he retired from the army, he returned to represent Donegal as a Member of Parliament in London. It was George who carried out much of the renovation, restoration and alterations to the castle. The castle was a family home until it was finally abandoned in 1843. It is now under the auspices of the OPW.

This is one of the most attractive examples from Ireland's more than 2,000 tower houses. The tall, pale and elegant tower, surrounded by water on three sides, gives a romantic vista into the story of Ireland's medieval past.

DOE CASTLE MAP 18

Coordinates: Lat. 5.135126, Long. -7.864323

Irish Grid Reference: C 08701 31998

Opening hours/entry fees: Visit www.heritageireland.ie/en/north-west/doecastle/

Directions: From Letterkenny, head north on the N56, through Kilmacrenan and Terlin. Shortly after Terlin turn right onto the R245 (signposted for Carrigart, Downings and a brown sign for Doe Castle). Follow the R245 for 3km and turn left (signposted for Doe Castle). Follow this narrow road for about 850m and then turn right at the T-Junction (again signed for Doe Castle). Follow this lane down to the small parking area for the castle.

Nearest town: Letterkenny (28km away).

94 | GRIANÁN OF AILEACH

This beautifully positioned and impressive drystone fort was once the ancient royal seat of the Uí Néill kings of Aileach, one of the most powerful and influential of Ireland's early medieval dynasties. It stands high on Greenan Mountain overlooking the valleys of the Foyle and Swilly rivers. The circular fort has a diameter of 23m (76 feet), with impressive drystone walls that stand 5m (16 feet) high. The parapets of the walls can be reached by a series of steps and terraces.

The annals record that the fort was destroyed and laid waste in AD 676 and again in 1101, when the King of Munster, Muirchertach Ó Briain, destroyed the fort and ordered his soldiers to carry away a stone each in revenge for the devastation of his ancestral home at *Ceann Córadh* at Killaloe thirteen years before. The fort was reconstructed from a ruinous condition in the 1870s by Dr Walter Bernard, the Bishop of Derry.

Beyond the stone fort there is evidence that this spectacular location has been an important place for millennia. A well dedicated to Saint Patrick can be found on the southern side of the hill, and the stone fort is surrounded by a series of three enclosing banks and ditches, though these are difficult to discern today. These may represent the remains of a hillfort dating to the late Bronze Age or early Iron Age. Further indication of ancient activity here can be found with the tumulus recorded on the hill to the south-east of the drystone fort, a feature which may represent the remains of a cairn or possibly a Neolithic passage tomb, given its elevated siting in the landscape.

The entrance into the stone fort

Traces of the enormous enclosures can still be seen surrounding the Grianán

The fort is deeply imbued with mythology. One of the legends tells of Dagda, the king of the magical Tuatha Dé Danann, whose son Aodh was killed by a man named Coirgean in a fit of jealousy. Instead of killing him on the spot, Dagda placed a *géis*, an unbreakable quest, on Coirgean that meant he must carry Aodh's body until he found a flagstone big enough to cover the slaughtered god. Coirgean carried Aodh for miles, until he climbed this hill and found the right stone. He buried Aodh beneath it, and then promptly dropped dead from exhaustion. To mark the burial place of his son, Dagda had a palace constructed on the hilltop and held fairs in celebration of Aodh's life.

Another tale recorded in the wonderful National Folklore Collection (www.duchas.ie) tells of a man who was on the run from English soldiers. He sought to escape by climbing the steep slopes of the Grianán of Aileach, but he saw the soldiers had the hill completely surrounded and cut off. In desperation, he looked around for a place to hide, and noticed that a small doorway had strangely appeared. The door was ajar and a passageway behind it appeared to lead into the side of the hill. With the soldiers closing in, the man had no choice but to venture down the passageway, and closed the door behind him. Outside he could hear the confused soldiers searching for him, then angrily leaving the hill empty-handed, but rather than risk going back outside, he chose to follow a dim light and venture deeper down the dark passageway. As he walked along the passage the light grew steadily stronger, until he came out into a large hall where he saw a king sleeping on a chair, flanked by his court and bards, with thousands of warriors all slumbering around him. He implored the slumbering host to rise up and to attack the English. At the sound of his voice, the strange king opened his eyes and said, 'The time has not yet come,' and went to sleep again. It is said they still slumber under the hill, until a day when a woman lights four fires, one north, one south, one east and one west and a final one on Mount Errigal. Then she will sound a great horn on Aileach. As the note ends seven doors will open in the ground and the host will charge from the side of the hill. They will race around the country to set Ireland free.

GRIANÁN OF AILEACH

MAP 18

Coordinates: Lat. 5.024599, Long. -7.426812

Irish Grid Reference: C 36644 19748

Opening hours/entry fees: No opening hours or entry fees applied at the time of writing.

Directions: From Letterkenny follow the N13 as it heads roughly north-eastwards towards Derry. Stay on this road as it goes towards the Inishowen Peninsula and turn right when you see An Grianán Hotel (with a sandstone church in front of it). Go up this road (passing the church and hotel on your left immediately after the turn) and continue up the hill. Turn right at the T-junction. Follow this small road as it winds uphill, until you see a small laneway on your left with a sign pointing to the Grianán of Aileach. Take this left turn and follow the lane uphill to reach the parking area. From here, take a moment to enjoy the stunning views before walking up the trail towards the fort.

Nearest towns: Derry (18km), Letterkenny (28km).

The high cross at the entrance to the churchyard at Cooly

On a hill overlooking the town of Moville and Lough Foyle, the modern rectangular graveyard wall at Cooly surrounds the remains of an early church site believed to have associations with Saint Patrick, but which may have been founded by Saint Finnian, an important early Irish saint and the contemporary of Saint Colmcille (see **Lacknacoo**, Site 90, for more). At the gate to the churchyard you can see a tall, simply carved high cross. Within the grounds are the ruins of two church buildings, and a small stone chapel known as the Skull House as it served as a tomb shrine associated with Saint Finnian. Other indications of the early origins of the site are a basin stone, a cross-inscribed stone (both adjacent to the Skull House), and near the south church you can see a cross-inscribed slab and stone cross.

The Skull House, a tomb shrine associated with Saint Finnian

COOLY ECCLESIASTICAL SITE

MAP 18

Coordinates: Lat. 5.188803, Long. -7.061642

Irish Grid Reference: C 59816 38368

Opening hours/entry fees: No opening hours or entry fees applied at the time of writing.

Directions: Cooly is less than a five-minute drive from Moville. Head south-west on the main street (R241) of Moville and continue onto the R238. After 400m turn right, then continue up this small road for 1km. Take a slight right and continue for approximately 250m until you see the churchyard with its distinctive cross.

Nearest town: Moville (1.6km).

Clonca Church

Clonca in the far north of the Inishowen Peninsula was once another important early medieval monastic centre, believed to have been founded by Saint Brodan, though today the only surviving church is seventeenth century in date. The church is a rather plain gable-ended church with a small cross on the top of the eastern gable. The church building contains clues to the earlier foundation within its fabric: the large lintel is likely to have been taken from an earlier building. This lintel is decorated with figures though the depiction is badly weathered and difficult to discern. A small bullaun stone inside the church gives further evidence to the early origins of the site, but most noteworthy in the interior of the church are the two sixteenth-century graveslabs affixed to the wall. The most decorated of these reads 'Fergus Mak Allan Do Rini in Clach Sa Magnus Mec Orristin Ia Fo Trl Seo' which translates as 'Fergus MacAllan made this stone; Magnus Mac Orristin under this.' The depiction of a sword alongside a hurley and sliotar illustrates how sport was entwined with warrior culture in medieval Ireland.

A depiction of a sword, hurley and sliotar on a late medieval graveslab

Only one of the high crosses still stands today. It is around 4m (13 feet) tall, and two thirds of the damaged head of the cross has been largely replaced by concrete. The cross is of uncertain date, but it has some interesting designs, with both faces having intricate interlacing ornamentation. At the head of the shaft on the eastern face is a depiction of the Feeding of the 5,000 with loaves and fishes, and on the western face you can see two lion-like creatures, above two seated figures midway down the shaft. The two seated figures may represent Saints Paul and Anthony.

The second cross is a little more difficult to find as it has long since collapsed. To find it go through the field from the standing cross, walking near the fence back towards the road and keeping the hedge boundary of the field with the church in it on your right-hand side. You'll soon find the large fragments of the high cross lying on the ground. It looks to have been a large ringed cross, ornamented with curving decoration.

CLONCA CHUCH

MAP 18

Coordinates: Lat. 5.268661, Long. -7.175211

Irish Grid Reference: C 52587 47086

Opening hours/entry fees: No opening hours or entry fees applied at the time of writing.

Directions: Clonca Church is certainly worth a visit, if just for an excuse to drive around the beautiful Inishowen Peninsula! It is relatively straightforward to find and less than a ten-minute drive from Carndonagh. From the town, head east on Church Road (R238) towards Gort Road. Then bear left, staying on the R238. At the roundabout, continue straight onto Newpark Road (driving past the Supervalu supermarket that will be on your right-hand side). Stay on this road for 5.5km, then take a left (signed for Culdaff). Continue on this road for just over a kilometre until you come to a crossroads. Go straight through the crossroads and you will see a small area to pull in the car just beyond the first house, which will be on your right. There is a small gate and laneway leading to the church behind the house.

Nearest town: Carndonagh (7.5km).

97 | CARNDONAGH

The small town of Carndonagh at the north of the Inishowen Peninsula is home to one of Ireland's most distinctive high crosses, along with unique and fascinating sculpture. Relatively little is known about the history of the important early medieval monastery that presumably was once centred in the vicinity of where the eighteenth-century Church of Ireland church stands today.

Underneath a small shelter beside the road you can see the high cross flanked by two small stelae or pillar stones. Both of these pillar stones are decorated on all sides. The **northern pillar stone** has a human figure on the eastern face. This figure either wears some kind of helmet with a chinstrap, or he has an almost Elvis Presley style quiff, and a beard. He holds a sword and a small round shield that look to be Viking in style. The northern face of this pillar has a bird of prey catching a fish in its talons, while the western face has a depiction of King David playing a lyre. The **southern pillar** has a human face near the top of the pillar on the eastern side and a human head emerging from a fish's

A warrior depicted on the northern pillar stone

mouth on the northern side, perhaps a depiction of the story of Jonah and the whale. On the western face you can see a figure with crossed arms holding a book and bell with a crozier underneath, presumably a depiction of an ecclesiastical figure or saint. On the southern face is a figure with the ears of a horse or donkey, perhaps representing the ancient legend of Labraid Loingsech (a king who was cursed with the ears of a horse). In ancient Ireland a king had to be perfect in both appearance and judgement, so his affliction was a deadly secret. Each year he would have his hair cut, with the unfortunate barber being selected by lot. After the king's hair was cut, the barber was immediately put to death to prevent him from revealing the secret of the horse ears. One year, a poor widow discovered that her only son had been selected to cut the king's hair. She begged the king not to execute her son, and the king agreed on the condition that the son swore an oath to keep his secret. It is said that the secret of the king's ears was such a burden for the son that he became sick and deeply troubled. A druid advised him to tell his tale to the first tree he met, and in doing so, the son was cured. Unfortunately, soon after, a harper cut down this very same tree to make a new harp. Whenever he played the harp, the instrument

A figure with horse's ears on the southern pillar stone

sang out 'King Labraid has horse's ears!' It caused such a sensation that King Labraid had no choice but to reveal his secret to the world.

The high cross, known as **Saint Patrick's Cross**, is a unique and charming example. The eastern face has elaborate interlacing decoration at the head of the cross ending in birds with interlocking beaks; the shaft depicts a cheerful and almost alien-looking Christ flanked by four smaller figures. The base of the shaft has a panel with three human figures facing to the left. The western face of the cross is covered with broad interlace ornamentation. There has been considerable debate about the dating of the cross and pillar stones, but from the artwork a date around the early ninth century may be a reasonable estimate.

Saint Patrick's Cross

A number of other important early medieval sculptures can be discovered in the adjacent churchyard. The doorway of the church appears to be a reused medieval door, with a traditionally fifteenth-century pointed head. Lying on the ground next to the church wall is a lintel from an early church, the decoration of which appears to be twelfth century or earlier in style. It depicts a wheeled cross in the centre, with four, possibly five, figures on the left and interlacing ornament on the right.

The Marigold Stone

Within the churchyard you can also see the **Marigold Stone**. The eastern face depicts a Crucifixion scene with Christ on a Greek cross. The representation of Christ appears to be quite similar to that on Saint Patrick's Cross. The foot of the cross descends in interlacing pattern ending in a small Latin cross at the base. Two strange figures face each other on either side of the shaft of the cross. The western face depicts a marigold or a seven-rayed star, with two figures again facing each other either side of the stem. These figures each appear to be holding a crozier, suggesting that they may be depictions of bishops or saints. Below them is a Maltese-style cross in sunken relief within a circle.

CARNDONAGH

MAP 18

Coordinates: Lat. 5.268661, Long. -7.175211

Opening hours/entry fees: No opening hours or entry fees applied at the time of writing.

Irish Grid Reference: C 46339 45013

Directions: Carndonagh is the main town of the Inishowen Peninsula, and is easily reachable from both Donegal and Derry. The cross and sculptures are located just off the main R238 road, with a small area to park. The cross and stone pillars are under a small wooden shelter. The Marigold Stone and decorated lintel can be found in the adjacent churchyard.

Nearest town: Carndonagh.

98 | FORT DUNREE

This rocky promontory has long been an important strategic location as it guards the entrance to Lough Swilly, one of Ireland's three fjords, and an important harbour.

In 1798, off the coast of Lough Swilly, ships from the Royal Navy defeated a French fleet bringing troops to Ireland. During the fighting, the British captured Theobald Wolfe Tone, one of the key leaders of the rebellion. He was taken to Letterkenny, then to Dublin where he faced trial by court martial. During the trial he made a defiant speech:

> I entered into the service of the French republic with the sole view of being useful to my country. To contend against British Tyranny, I have braved the fatigues and terrors of the field of battle; I have sacrificed my comfort, have courted poverty, have left my wife unprotected, and my children without a father. After all I have done for a sacred cause, death is no sacrifice.

He requested to be shot as a soldier but this was denied, and he was ordered to be hanged like a common felon. In a last act of defiance, Wolfe Tone took his own life in his cell.

Fort Dunree

The promontory was refortified in the early nineteenth century as part of the renewal of coastal defences during the Napoleonic Wars. Later, a new fort was constructed here in 1895, and during the First World War, a boom was placed across the entrance to the harbour to prevent German U-boats from attacking the fleet.

After Ireland gained her independence, the British retained control of Lough Swilly as a Treaty port. It was handed back to Ireland in 1938. During the handover ceremony, by coincidence Sergeant O'Flynn of the Royal Artillery who lowered the British flag and Sergeant McLaughlin of the Irish Army who raised the Irish flag were brothers-in-law. Today, the fort is now a military museum with exhibitions on the armaments that once protected Lough Swilly, and information on the natural heritage of the area.

The formidable defences of Fort Dunree

FORT DUNREE MILITARY MUSEUM MAP 18

Coordinates: Lat. 5.196552, Long. -7.553423

Irish Grid Reference: C 28487 38920

Opening hours/entry fees: Visit: www.dunree.pro.ie

Directions: Fort Dunree is a fifteen-minute (11km) drive north of Buncrana. From Buncrana, head north on the R238 and turn left at Saint Mary's Catholic church onto the Cockhill Road (signposted Ballyliffin, Carndonagh, Clonmany). Drive a short distance and take the first left turn onto Gleann Aibhinn (a very large grey house is on the corner). Follow this relatively narrow road for about thirteen minutes (10km) and you will pass through an old military gate with a sentry post. Continue on and you will arrive at the site. There is ample parking.

Nearest town: Buncrana (11km).

Carrickabraghy Castle

This small tower house is thought to date to the sixteenth century. It stands on a high rocky promontory overlooking the pebble-strewn seashore. In 1600, it is recorded as the home of Phelemy Brasleigh O'Doherty. In 1608 Sir Cahir O'Doherty, the last Gaelic Lord of Inishowen, used Carrickabraghy as a base to launch his attack on the fort at Culmore. His attack failed, and he was captured and decapitated at Doon Rock near Kilmacrennan. Following the failed insurrection, in 1611 Carriackabraghy, along with most of the Inishowen Peninsula, was granted to Sir Arthur Chichester. He installed a Lieutenant Hoan, who was 'bound to rebuild the castle. He hath already finished a good bawne of lyme and stone'.

As a result of its exposed location and the relentless ravages of the Atlantic storms, little remains of the castle today, though through the hard work of the local community the process of conserving what remains is under way. Donations to the Carrickabraghy Restoration Society are most welcome.

The walls of Carrickabraghy Castle

CARRICKABRAGHY CASTLE

MAP 18

Coordinates: Lat. 5.315720, Long. -7.373064

Irish Grid Reference: C 39873 52346

Opening hours/entry fees: No opening hours or entry fees applied at the time of writing, but visit the website of Carrickabraghy Restoration Society: www. carrickabraghycastle.com for further information and if you wish to make a donation towards the restoration.

Directions: The castle is located at the north-western end of the Isle of Doagh, not far from the village of Clonmany. From Carndonagh, head north-west on the R238 for approximately 7.5km. Turn right, signposted for Doagh Isle and the Famine Village Visitor Centre (an interesting stop if you have the time), and bear left to continue past the sign that points right for the Famine Village, simply continue along this road until you come to the castle. Park just after the buildings and before the shingle beach.

Nearest town: Carndonagh (18km away)

The nineteenth-century signal tower at Malin Head

The three-storey signal tower at Malin Head was built in 1804–5, around the same time as the tower on the cliffs at **Slieve League** (Site 87). Following its use as a signal tower for the British army, it later became a meteorological station in around 1870, before returning to its original use as a signal station, this time on behalf of Lloyds of London. It became derelict following its service as a post office telegraph station in 1910. In 1901, Guglielmo Marconi established a radio signal station adjacent to the signal tower, and a year later he succeeded in sending the first commercial radio message from Malin Head to the ship SS *Lake Ontario*. For more on the story of Marconi, see **Derrigimlagh Bog** (Site 51).

This area is associated with the goddess Banba. According to legend, Banba was the first person to set foot in Ireland before the Great Flood. She was part of the Tuatha Dé Danann, and along with her sisters Ériu and Fódla, she forms the triumvirate of Ireland's goddesses.

Due to the unparalleled views, a Second World War watchtower was also established here by the Irish army to look out for enemy shipping, submarines or aircraft. At the request of the Allied Forces, a large ÉIRE sign was placed on the headland as a visual geographical aid to warn Allied aircraft not to stray over neutral Ireland.

The ÉIRE sign on Malin Head

Alongside Malin Head's important role in the history of communications, this region is a truly spectacular landscape with a number of walks and trails that highlight the important natural

The trail along the stunning coast at Malin Head

heritage of Malin Head. I recommend following the trail west towards the cliffs, past the deep crevice known as Hell's Hole. Due to the combination of warm ocean currents, cool coastal water and fresh water that drains from Lough Foyle and Lough Swilly, there is a high degree of marine biodiversity here. It is also an important resting place for migrating birds before they cross the broad Atlantic between Europe and the Americas.

Ireland's most northerly point is a truly breathtaking place and a fitting end to our journey along Ireland's Wild Atlantic Way.

MALIN HEAD

MAP 18

Coordinates: Lat. 5.380701, Long. -7.374659

Irish Grid Reference: C 39687 59509

Opening hours/entry fees: No opening hours or entry fees applied at the time of writing.

Directions: Malin Head is around a 20–25 minute (16km) drive from Carndonagh. From Carndonagh head north and east staying on the R238. After approximately 3km, turn onto the R242 and head north, passing through the village of Malin. Simply follow the R242 all the way to Malin Head. You will see the signal tower on the high ground. There is signposted right turn that brings you up to a small parking area.

Nearest towns: Carndonagh (16km), Malin (12km).

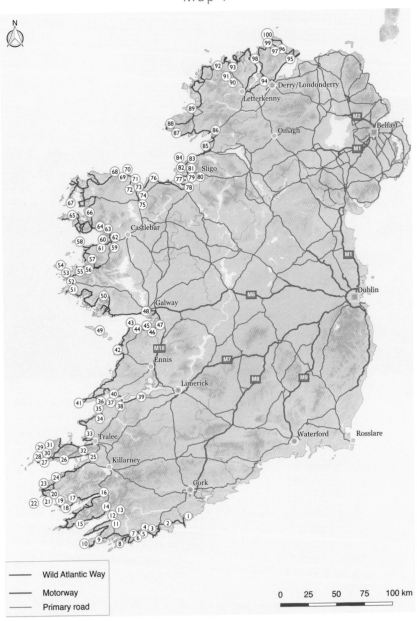

Wild Atlantic Way

Motorway

Primary road

0   25   50   75   100 km

Map 2

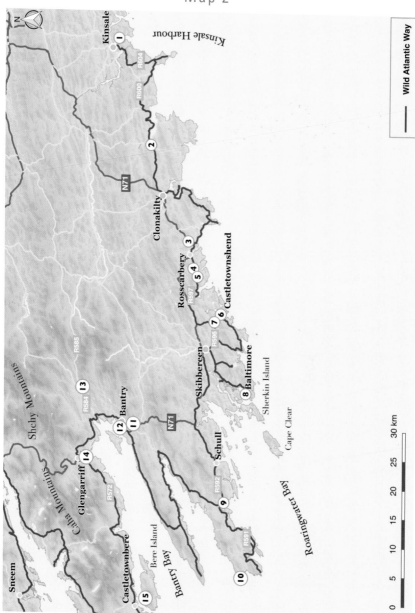

Wild Atlantic Way

0   5   10   15   20   25   30 km

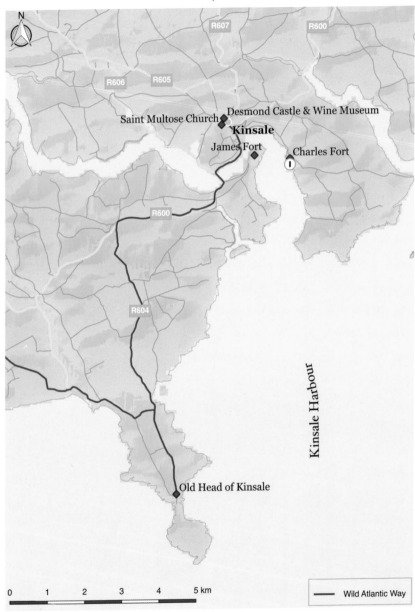

Map 3

Map 4

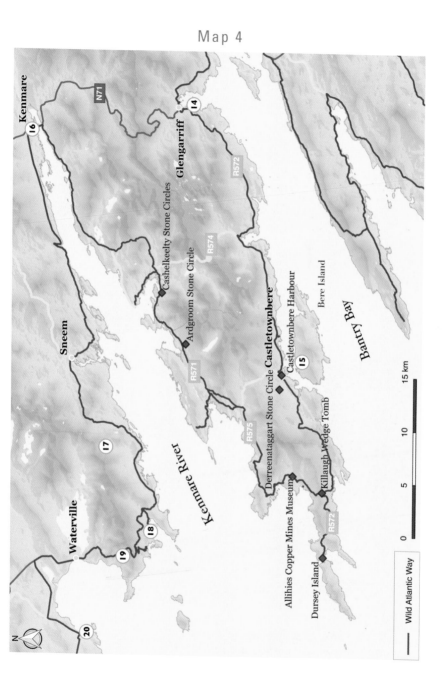

Map 5

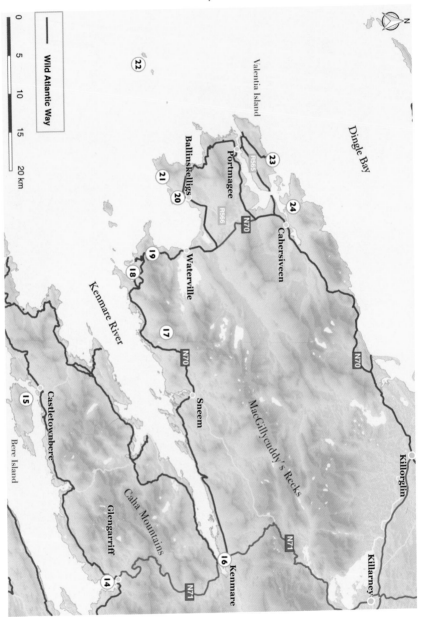

Map 6

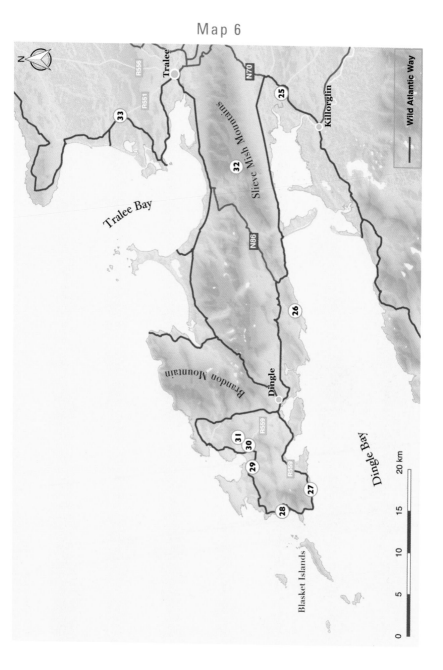

Map 7

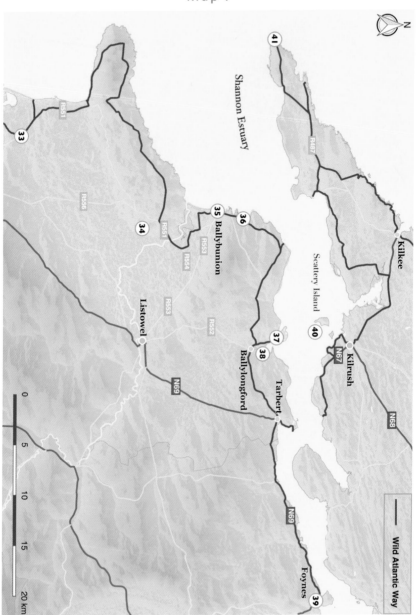

Map 8

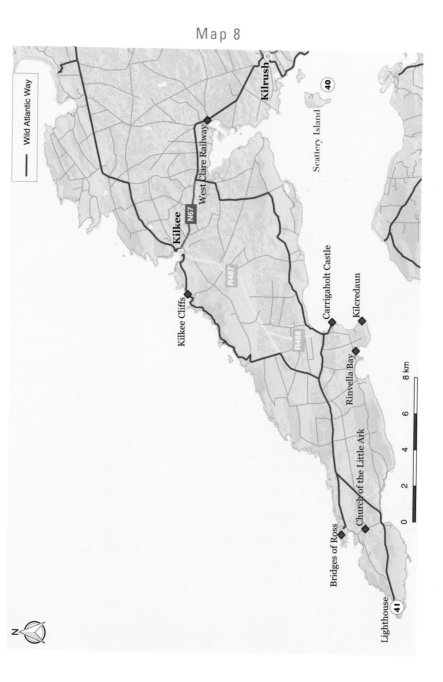

Map 9

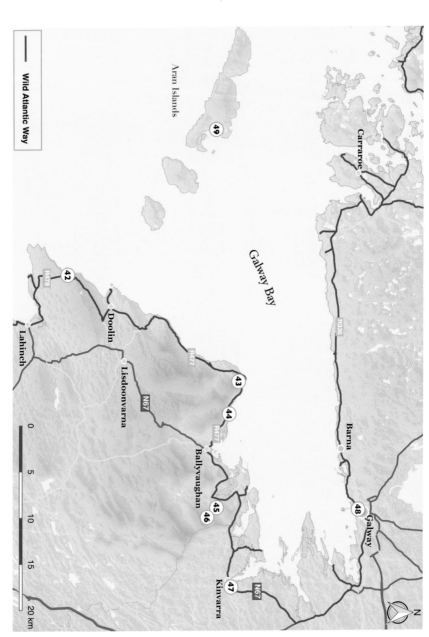

Wild Atlantic Way

Aran Islands

Galway Bay

Carraroe

Barna

Galway

Lahinch

Doolin

Lisdoonvarna

Ballyvaughan

Kinvarra

R478

R477

N67

R477

N67

R336

42

43

44

45

46

47

48

49

0 5 10 15 20 km

N

Map 10
Galway city

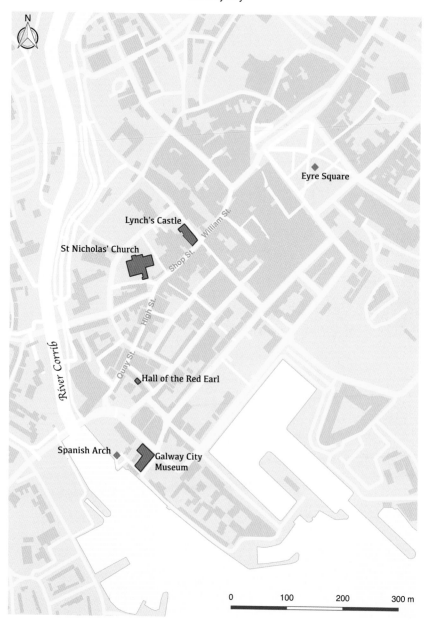

Map 11

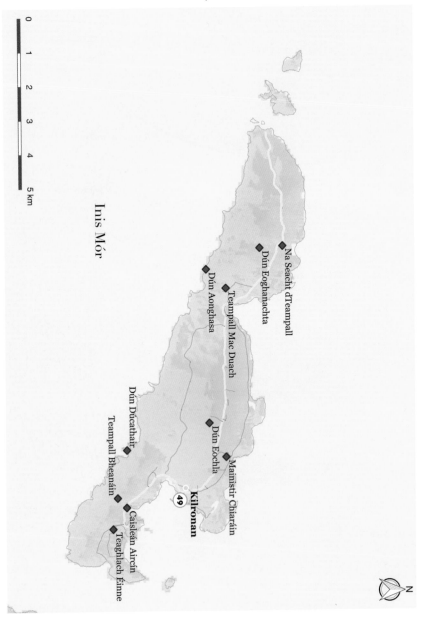

Inis Mór

Na Seacht dTeampall

Dún Eoghanachta

Teampall Mac Duach

Dún Aonghasa

Dún Dúcathair

Teampall Bheanáin

Dún Eochla

Mainistir Chiaráin

Caisleán Aircín

Teaghlach Éinne

Kilronan

49

0 1 2 3 4 5 km

N

Map 12

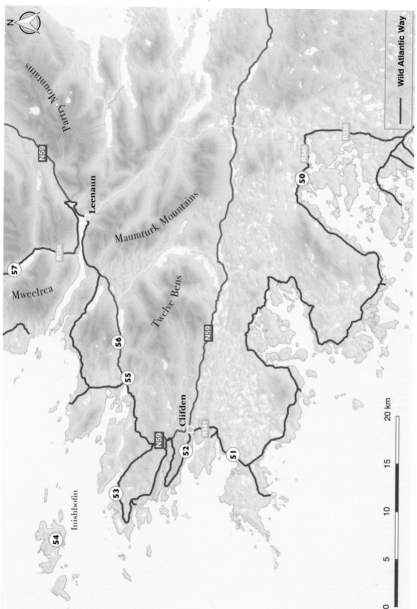

Wild Atlantic Way

0 5 10 15 20 km

Map 13

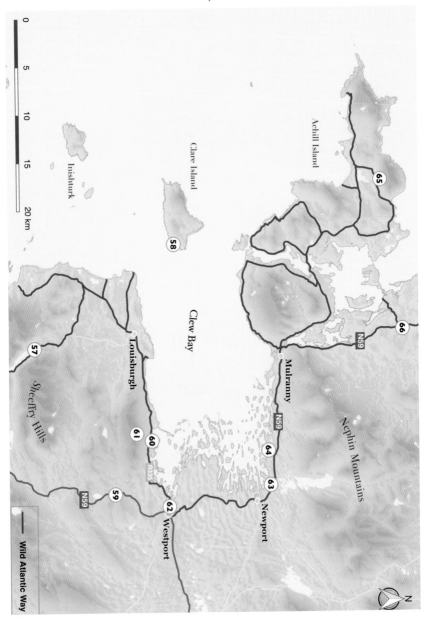

Map 14

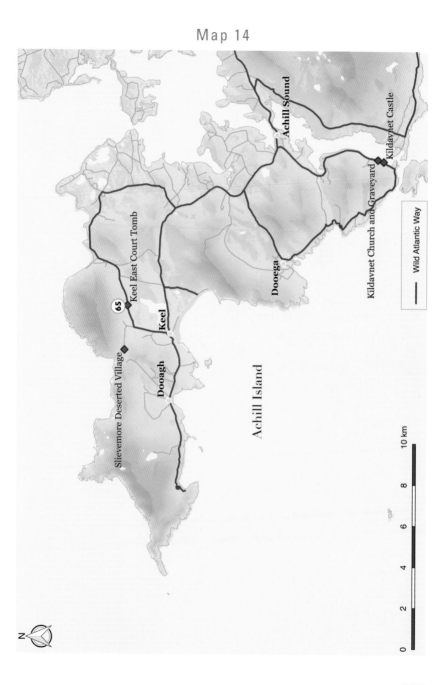

Achill Sound

Kildavnet Castle

Kildavnet Church and Graveyard

Keel East Court Tomb

65

Dooega

Keel

Slievemore Deserted Village

Dooagh

Achill Island

— Wild Atlantic Way

N

0   2   4   6   8   10 km

Map 15

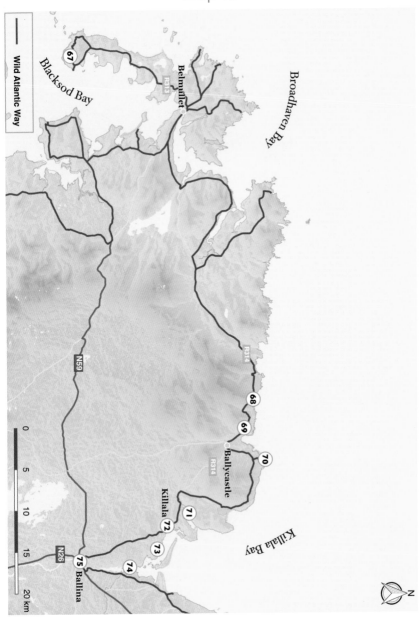

Wild Atlantic Way

Blacksod Bay

Belmullet

R313

Broadhaven Bay

N59

R314

Ballycastle

R314

Killala Bay

Killala

N26

Ballina

0 5 10 15 20 km

N

Map 16

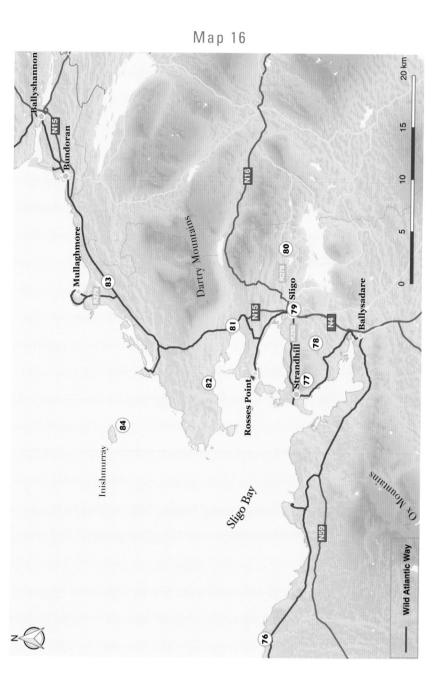

Map 17

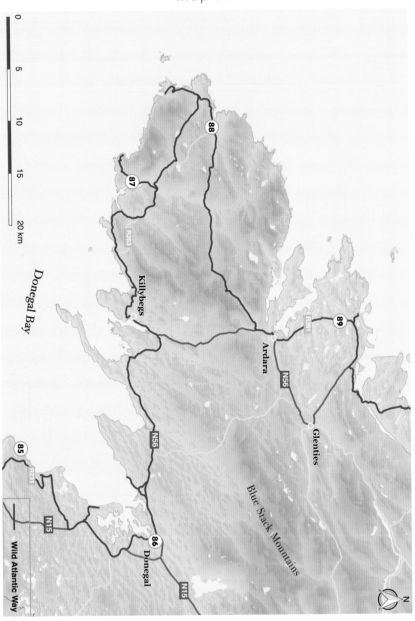

Site Map 18

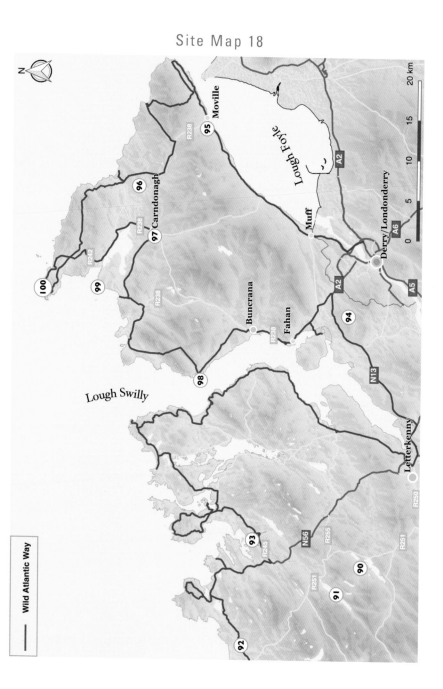

GLOSSARY

aisle: A side division, usually in relation to the nave of a church.

antae: Projections of the side walls beyond the eastern and western gables of early medieval Irish churches.

apse: The semicircular, or occasionally polygonal, end of the chancel of a church or cathedral.

bailey: A defended enclosure, usually in association with a motte. It often protected the ancillary structures related to the fort.

barbican: An external defensive structure, usually attached to the gate of a castle or walled town.

barrow: Circular ditched enclosure, often with an earthen mound in the centre, which covers a burial. Usually dates to the Bronze Age.

base batter: A sloping face on the exterior of castle walls, town walls or occasionally churches.

bawn: A fortified, walled enclosure that usually relates to a later medieval castle or tower house.

bullaun: A large stone with one or more circular depressions carved into it. Often related to early medieval monastic sites; they may have served as holy water fonts, or may have had a more practical purpose similar to a large pestle and mortar for grinding herbs or minerals.

burgage plots: Land and buildings in a town held in tenure by a noble or lord and rented out.

cairn: A man-made drystone mound, often covering the chambers of a megalithic tomb.

calefactory: A comparatively comfortable room within a medieval monastery, warmed by a fire.

cashel: A stone-built circular enclosure, usually dating to the early medieval period. A variation of a ringfort.

chancel: The eastern end of a church, usually where the altar is located.

chapter house: The building or room in a monastery where the monks assembled for meetings and readings.

chevaux-de-frise: A defensive obstacle that prevents or constrains enemy movement.

choir: The area of a church reserved for monks, friars or clergy. Usually located close to the chancel.

cist: A stone-lined grave or chamber, usually dating to the earlier part of the Bronze Age.

cloister: A covered passageway forming a square in medieval monasteries.

corbelled roof: A stone roof constructed from horizontally laid rows of stones with each row projecting inwards more than the row below.

court tomb: A megalithic tomb type that usually features a large courtyard area in front of a covered gallery that contained human remains, often in two or more chambers. The galleries or chambers were originally covered with a large cairn of small stones or earth.

crossing tower: A tower, often housing a belfry, marking the point where the nave and chancel meet. Usually in association with medieval churches.

cruciform: In the shape of a cross.

cup mark: A form of prehistoric art consisting of small artificial depressions carved or pecked into stone.

curtain wall: The exterior defensive wall of a medieval castle.

cursus: A large prehistoric monument consisting of two parallel embankments.

Dissolution of the Monasteries: A set of administrative and legal processes between 1536 and 1541 by which Henry VIII disbanded Catholic monasteries, priories, convents and friaries in England, Wales and Ireland, and appropriated their income and estates.

dolmen: See portal tomb.

donjon: See keep.

gable: The pointed end wall of a building.

garderobe: A toilet (or latrine) usually built into the wall of a medieval castle or stone building.

glacial erratic: A large boulder carried by glacial ice and deposited at a distance from its point of origin.

Gothic: A twelfth- to thirteenth-century architectural style with features such as pointed arches, rib vaulting and flying buttresses.

high cross: A tall stone cross, often elaborately decorated with geometric designs or biblical depictions. Usually in association with early medieval Irish monastic sites.

henge: A large circular enclosure, usually comprised of earthen banks and ditches, and thought to have had a ceremonial function.

intramural: A passageway or feature within the walls of a building.

keep: The central tower of a castle, often houses domestic quarters.

kerbstones: A line of stones surrounding a megalithic tomb. Sometimes decorated, kerbstones helped to keep the mound or cairn in place, as well as marking the boundary of the tomb.

lavabo: A washing place for medieval monks or friars, usually located close to the refectory of medieval monasteries.

lintel: The stone immediately above a door or passageway.

longphort: An Irish term applied to the fortified encampments of Viking raiders in the ninth century.

machicolation: A defensive feature, appearing as a stone structure projecting from a wall, usually positioned over an entrance. It allowed defenders to drop stones, etc., onto an attacking force.

Martello tower: A circular tower usually positioned on the coastline or riverside. Constructed as a defence by the British army in the wars against Napoleonic France in the early nineteenth century.

megalithic: Derives from *mega*, meaning big, and *lithic*, meaning stone. A blanket term that refers to the many different types of large prehistoric stone tombs.

moat: A deep ditch filled with water. Usually associated with medieval fortifications.

motte: An early Norman fortification. Appears as a tall earthen mound that served as the foundation for a wooden or stone tower. Often accompanied by a bailey.

murder hole: Similar in purpose to a machicolation. A hole or aperture, usually positioned above a passageway or gateway, through which defenders can drop large stones, etc., onto the heads of the attackers.

nave: The main body of a church.

ogee-headed: A decorative window design dating to the medieval period.

Ogham: An early Irish script that usually dates to the early centuries ad. It consists of a series of horizontal or diagonal strokes crossing a vertical central line.

orthostat: An upright stone, usually in reference to the upright structural elements of a megalithic tomb.

Pale (the): The region under the effective control of the English Crown during the later medieval period. Contained parts of Louth, Meath, Dublin and Kildare.

palisade: A defensive structure consisting of a wooden fence.

passage tomb: The largest and most elaborate of the megalithic tomb types. Usually consists of a stone-lined passageway leading to a burial chamber. The passageway and chamber are then covered with an earthen or stone mound. Sometimes a mound may cover multiple passages and chambers. The most famous example in Ireland is Newgrange in County Meath.

Pattern day: An Irish Roman Catholic tradition that refers to the devotions that take place within a parish on the feast day of the patron saint of the parish, or on the nearest Sunday, called Pattern Sunday.

Penal Laws: A series of harsh and repressive laws that originated in the seventeenth century and were imposed in an attempt to force Irish Roman Catholics and Protestant dissenters (such as Presbyterians) to accept the reformed denomination as defined by the English state-established Anglican Church.

piscina: A stone basin in which clergy ceremonially washed their hands and communion vessels.

plantations: Land confiscated by the English Crown where the original inhabitants were replaced with English and Scottish Protestant settlers.

portal tomb: A megalithic tomb type typically consisting of a simple chamber formed of upright stones, with a large capstone. The monument was then possibly covered with a cairn of small stones or a mound of earth. Also known as a dolmen.

portcullis: A defensive gate in the entrance or gateway of a castle or fortification. Usually consisting of a large wood and metal grille that can be lowered into position in times of danger.

rag tree: A tree (usually positioned next to a holy well or church site) with strips of cloth or rags tied to its branches as part of a healing ritual. As the cloth unravels and rots so the disease or ailment is believed to fade away.

rath: See ringfort.

refectory: The dining hall of a medieval monastery.

ringfort: (Also known as rath). A roughly circular enclosure surrounded by one or more ditches with banks of earth or stone. Usually dating to the early medieval period, ringforts are one of the most numerous archaeological sites in the Irish landscape. The enclosures often defended houses and other ancillary structures. When the enclosure is constructed of stone it is often termed a cashel.

Romanesque: A style of architecture and art originating on the continent that became popular in Irish churches in the twelfth century. Architectural features include rounded arches, elaborate decoration and depictions of human heads, foliage and animals.

rood screen: A church feature, usually containing a crucifix, that separated the nave from the choir.

round tower: Iconic and uniquely Irish, round towers were tall, slender towers of stone primarily used as belfries.

sacristy: A building associated with a church or monastery, where vestments and communion vessels are kept.

sedile (plural sedilia): A seat within a medieval church for a priest, abbot or bishop.

Sheela-na-gig: Small sculptures of nude females (and occasionally males) exhibiting their genitalia. Their purpose is subject to debate: some believe they were a way of warding off evil spirits, others that they were a warning against the sins of the flesh.

solar: The private chamber of a medieval house or castle.

souterrain: A tunnel-like stone passageway, usually dating to the early medieval period. Mainly found in association with ringforts or monastic sites. Thought to have been used for storage or possibly refuge. May feature chambers and multiple passageways.

togher: A wooden or stone trackway across boggy or marshy ground.

transepts: The side arms of a church, running north and south from the main church building.

trefoil: A decorative feature typically dating to the thirteenth century.

Urnes: Elaborate artistic style usually consisting of stylised animals interwoven into tight patterns of Scandinavian origin.

wedge tomb: The most numerous of Ireland's megalithic tombs, and most commonly found in the western half of the country. The name refers to the simple wedge shape, as the height and width of the monument decreases from the front to the rear. Wedge tombs are the last of Ireland's megalithic tombs, and usually date to the Late Neolithic or Early Bronze Age periods.

USEFUL WEBSITES ON IRISH ARCHAEOLOGY, HISTORY, HERITAGE AND FOLKLORE

www.abartaheritage.ie

www.archaeology.ie

www.archaeologyireland.ie

www.buildingsofireland.ie

www.discoveryprogramme.ie

www.duchas.ie

www.excavations.ie

www.heritagecouncil.ie

www.heritageireland.ie

www.heritagemaps.ie

www.historicgraves.ie

www.irisharchaeology.ie

www.irishwalledtownsnetwork.ie

www.logainm.ie

www.megalithicireland.com

www.monastic.ie

www.museum.ie

www.nationalarchives.ie

www.nli.ie (National Library of Ireland)

www.pilgrimageinmedievalireland.com

www.timetravelireland.blogspot.ie

www.voicesfromthedawn.com

www.voxhiberionacum.wordpress.com

BIBLIOGRAPHY

Ashe FitzGerald, M. 2003. *The Aran Islands. A World of Stone*. Dublin: O'Brien Press.

Bhreathnach, E. 2014. *Ireland in the Medieval World AD 400–1000. Landscape, Kingship and Religion*. Dublin: Four Courts Press.

Bolton, J. 2008. *Antiquities of the Ring of Kerry*. Dublin: Wordwell.

Bourke, E. Hayden, A. and Lynch, A. 2011. *Skellig Michael, Co. Kerry. The Monastery and South Peak. Archaeological Stratigraphic Report: Excavations 1986–2010*. Dublin: Wordwell.

Bradley, R. 1997. *Rock Art and the Prehistory of Atlantic Europe*. London: Routledge.

Breen, C. 2007. *An Archaeology of Southwest Ireland 1570–1670*. Dublin: Four Courts Press.

Browne, C. R. 1893. 'The Ethnography of Inishbofin and Inishshark, County Galway.' *Proceedings of the Royal Irish Academy*, Vol. 3. JSTOR.

Bergh, S. 1995. *Landscape of the monuments A study of the passage tombs in the Cúil Irra region, Co Sligo, Ireland*. Stockholm: Riksantikvarieämbetet Arkeologiska Undersökningar.

Bergh, S. 2000. 'Transforming Knocknarea: The Archaeology of a Mountain.' *Archaeology Ireland Magazine*, Vol.14 (Summer, 2000). Dublin: Wordwell.

Carthy, H. 2011. *Burren Archaeology. A Tour Guide*. Cork: The Collins Press.

Chambers, A. 2009. *Granuaile: Grace O'Malley – Ireland's Pirate Queen*. Dublin: Gill & Macmillan

Cleary, K. 2005. 'Skeletons in the Closet: The Dead Among the Living on Irish Bronze Age Settlements' in *The Journal of Irish Archaeology*. Vol. 14. Dublin: Wordwell.

Cooke, T.L. 1842–3. *Autumnal Rambles about New Quay, County Clare*. Articles for the *Galway Vindicator*, published by Clare County Library through a Clare Local Studies Project.

Cotter, C. 2012. *The Western Stone Forts Project. Excavations at Dún Aonghasa and Dún Eoghanachta*. Vols. 1 & 2. Dublin: Wordwell.

Cotter, C. 2014. *Dún Aonghasa the Guidebook*. Dublin: Discovery Programme.

Corlett, C. 1998. 'The Prehistoric Ritual Landscape of Croagh Patrick, Co. Mayo' in *The Journal of Irish Archaeology*. Vol. 9. Institute of Archaeologists of Ireland.

Corlett, C. 2016. *Doe Castle Co. Donegal. Archaeology Ireland Heritage Guide No.74*. Dublin: Wordwell.

Croker, T. C. & Clifford, S. 1972. *Legends of Kerry*. Dublin: Anvil Press.

Crowley, J. and Sheehan, J. 2009. *The Iveragh Peninsula: A Cultural Atlas of the Ring of Kerry*. Cork: Cork University Press.

Crowley, J., Smyth, W.J., and Murphy, M. (eds). 2013. *Atlas of the Great Irish Famine*. Cork: Cork University Press.

Cuppage, J. 1986. *Corca Dhuibhne*. Dingle Peninsula Archaeological Survey. Oidhreacht Chorca Dhuibhne.

de Paor, L. 1955. 'A Survey of Sceilg Mhichíl.' *The Journal of the Royal Society of Antiquaries of Ireland*, Vol. 85, No. 2. JSTOR

de Valera, R. & Ó Nualláin, S. 1972. *Survey of the Megalithic Tombs of Ireland, Vol. III, Counties Galway, Roscommon, Leitrim, Longford, Westmeath, Laoighis, Offaly, Kildare, Cavan*. Dublin: Stationery Office.

Duffy, S. 2013. *Brian Boru and the Battle of Clontarf*. Dublin: Gill & Macmillan.

Ekin, D. 2008. *The Stolen Village: Baltimore and the Barbary Pirates*. Dublin: O'Brien Press

FitzPatrick, E. and Kelly, J. (eds) 2011. *Domestic Life in Ireland*. Dublin: Royal Irish Academy.

Gallagher, F. 2008. *The Streets of Sligo. Urban Evolution Over the Course of Seven Centuries*. Kilkenny: The Heritage Council.

Gosling, P. 1993. *Archaeological Inventory of County Galway Vol. I – West Galway*. Dublin: Stationery Office.

Hall, D. 2008. *Women and the Church in Medieval Ireland, c.1140–1540*. Dublin: Four Courts Press.

Halpin, A. and Newman, C. 2006. *Ireland, An Oxford Archaeological Guide*. Oxford: Oxford University Press.

Harbison, P. 1991. *Pilgrimage in Ireland. The Monuments and the People*. London: Barrie & Jenkins.

Harbison, P. 1992. *Guide to the National and Historic Monuments of Ireland*. Dublin: Gill & Macmillan.

Harbison, P. 1995. 'A Crucifixion Plaque in Stone?' in *Archaeology Ireland*, Vol. 9 Issue 2

Hayes-McCoy, F. and Judd, W. 2017. *Dingle and its Hinterland. People, Places and Heritage*. Cork: The Collins Press.

Heaney, S. 1969. *Door into the Dark*. London: Faber and Faber.

Hensey, R. 2015. *First Light. The Origins of Newgrange*. Oxford: Oxbow Books.

Hensey, R. and Bergh, S. 2013. 'The inns at Sligo are better than those at Auray … and the scenery far more beautiful': Carrowmore revisited. In M.A. Timoney (ed.), *Dedicated to Sligo: thirty-four essays on Sligo's past*. Publishing Sligo's Past, Keash.

Herity, M. Kelly, D and Mattenberger, U. 1997. 'List of Early Christian Cross Slabs in Seven North-Western Counties.' *The Journal of the Royal Society of Antiquaries of Ireland,* vol. 127. JSTOR.

Hjardar, K. and Vike, V. 2016. *Vikings at War*. Oxford: Casemate.

Jones, C. 2007. *Temples of Stone. Exploring the Megalithic Tombs of Ireland*. Cork: The Collins Press.

Kuijt, I. Lash, R. Donaruma, W. Shakour, K., Burke, T. 2015. *Island Places, Island Lives: Exploring Inishbofin and Inishark Heritage, County Galway, Ireland*. Dublin: Wordwell.

Lacy, B. 1983. *Archaeological Survey of County Donegal. A description of the field antiquities from the Mesolithic Period to the 17th century A.D.* Donegal County Council.

Lacy, B. 2012. *Lug's Forgotten Donegal Kingdom. The Archaeology, History and Folklore of the Sil Lugdach of Cloghaneely*. Dublin: Four Courts Press

Lacy, B. 2013. *Saint Columba. His Life and Legacy*. Dublin: The Columba Press.

Lafaye, A. 2013. *Reconstructing the Landscapes of the Mendicants in East Munster: The Franciscans*. Published on Academia.edu.

Lalor, B. 2016. *Ireland's Round Towers. Origins and Architecture Explored*. Cork: The Collins Press.

Leask, H.G. 1955. *Irish Churches and Monastic Buildings. Volume I: The First Phases and the Romanesque*. Dundalgan Press.

Leask, H.G. 1958. *Irish Churches and Monastic Buildings. Volume II: Gothic Architecture to AD 1400*. Dundalk: Dundalgan Press.

Leask, H.G. 1978. *Irish Churches and Monastic Buildings. Volume III: Medieval Gothic The Last Phases*. Dundalk: Dundalgan Press.

Mac Cárthaigh, C. and Whelan, K. (eds) 1999. *New Survey of Clare Island*. Volume I: History and Cultural Landscape. Royal Irish Academy.

Marshall, R. 2013. *Clare Folk Tales*. The History Press, Ireland.

Martin, C. and Parker, G. 1999. *The Spanish Armada*. Manchester: Manchester University Press

McDonald, T. 1997. *Achill Island – Archaeology, History and Folklore*. Dublin: Institute of Advanced Studies Publications.

McDonald, T. 2016. *A Guide to Archaeological and Historical Sites on Achill, Achillbeg and the Corraun Peninsula*. Tullamore: IAS Publications.

McGuinness, D. 2010. 'Druids Altars, Carrowmore and the Birth of Irish Archaeology.' *The Journal of Irish Archaeology*. Vol 19. Dublin: Wordwell.

Meehan, R. 2003. *The Story of Mayo*. Mayo County Library.

Mooney, C. 1958. 'The Franciscans in County Mayo.' *Journal of the Galway Archaeological and Historical Society*, Vol. 28.

Moore, F. 2007. *Ardfert Cathedral: summary of excavation results*. Dublin: Wordwell.

Morahan, L. 2001. *Croagh Patrick, Co. Mayo: Archaeology, Landscape and People*. Croagh Patrick Archaeological Committee.

Ní Ghabhláin, S. 1995. 'Church and Community in Medieval Ireland: The Diocese of Kilfenora.' *The Journal of the Royal Society of Antiquaries of Ireland*, Vol. 125.

O'Brien, W. and O'Driscoll, J. 2017. *Hillforts, Warfare and Society in Bronze Age Ireland*. Oxford: Archaeopress Archaeology.

Ó Carragáin, T. 2010. *Churches in Early Medieval Ireland. Architecture, Ritual and Memory*. London: Yale University Press.

Ó Cróinín, D. 1995. *Early Medieval Ireland: 400–1200*. London: Longman.

O'Dwyer, John G. 2017. *Pilgrim Paths in Ireland – A Guide*. Cork. The Collins Press

O'Hara, M. 1898. 'Rosserk and Moyne, Co. Mayo.' *The Journal of the Royal Society of Antiquaries of Ireland*, Vol. 8. No. 3.

O'Keeffe, T. 2015. *Medieval Irish Buildings 1100–1600*. Dublin: Four Courts Press.

Ó Nualláin, S. 1975. 'The Stone Circle Complex of Cork and Kerry', in *The Journal of the Royal Society of Antiquaries of Ireland*. Vol 105. Royal Society of Antiquaries of Ireland.

Ó Nualláin, S. 1978. 'Boulder Burials' in *Proceedings of the Royal Irish Academy. Section C: Archaeology, Celtic Studies, History, Linguistics, Literature*. Vol. 78. Royal Irish Academy.

Ó Nualláin, S. 1984. 'A Survey of Stone Circles in Cork and Kerry.' *Proceedings of the Royal Irish Academy. Section C: Archaeology, Celtic Studies, History, Linguistics, Literature*, vol. 84C, 1984, pp. 1–77. JSTOR.

Ó Riain, P. 2011. *A Dictionary of Irish Saints*. Dublin: Four Courts Press.

O'Sullivan, J. and Ó Carragáin, T. 2008. *Inishmurray. Monks and Pilgrims in an Atlantic Landscape*. Cork: The Collins Press.

Powell, E. 2007. *The High Crosses of Ireland. Inspirations in Stone*. Dublin: The Liffey Press.

Robinson, T. 1996. *Oileáin Árann*. Connemara: Folding Landscapes.

Rynne, C. 2006. *Industrial Ireland 1750–1930. An Archaeology*. Cork: The Collins Press.

Stalley, R. 1987. *The Cistercian Monasteries of Ireland*. London: Yale University Press.

Stalley, R. (ed). 2012. *Irish Gothic Architecture. Construction, Decay and Reinvention*. Dublin: Wordwell.

Sweetman, D. 1999. *The Medieval Castles of Ireland*. Cork: The Collins Press.

Timoney, M.A. (ed) 2002. *A Celebration of Sligo. First Essays for Sligo Field Club*. Sligo Field Club.

Toal, C. 1995. *North Kerry Archaeological Survey*. Kerry: Brandon Book Publishers.

Ua Cróinín, R. and Breen, M. 1998. 'Some Tower Houses in the Vicinity of Ennis' in *The Other Clare*, Vol. 22. Shannon Archaeological and Historical Society.

Walsh, P. 1990. 'Cromwell's Barracks: A Commonwealth Garrison Fort on Inishbofin, Co. Galway' in *Journal of the Galway Archaeological and Historical Society* Vol. 42. JSTOR.

Westropp, T. J. 1898. 'Notes on the Lesser Castles or "Peel Towers" of the County Clare.' *Proceedings of the Royal Irish Academy (1889–1901)*, Vol. 5. JSTOR

Westropp. T.J. 1917. 'Fortified Headlands and Castles in Western County Cork. Part I. From Cape Clear to Dunmanus Bay' in *Proceedings of the Royal Irish Academy (1914–1916)*. Vol. 32. JSTOR

Woodman, P.C. Anderson, E. and Finlay, N. 1999. *Excavations at Ferriter's Cove 1983–95: Last Foragers, First Farmers in the Dingle Peninsula*. Dublin: Wordwell.

Wood-Martin, W.G. 1888. *The Rude Stone Monuments of Ireland (Co. Sligo and the Island of Achill)*. Dublin: Hodges, Figgis & Co.